Steven M

Doctor ....

2014-2015

The Critical Fan's Guide to Peter Capaldi's Doctor (Unauthorized)

Steven Cooper

Punked Books

Published in 2016 by Punked Books
An Authortrek imprint

(www.authortrek.com/punked-books)

Cover image ©istockphoto.com/agsandrew

First Edition

ISBN 978-1-908375-31-5

Contents

Foreword

After three successful seasons at the helm of *Doctor Who*, masterminding the adventures of Matt Smith's Doctor, and culminating with the show's Fiftieth Anniversary celebrations at the end of 2013, Steven Moffat was faced with the need to establish a whole new direction for the show with the introduction of a new Doctor, Peter Capaldi. This book covers all 26 episodes broadcast in 2014 and 2015, from the start of the Capaldi era with *Deep Breath* to the latest Christmas special, *The Husbands of River Song*.

With two full seasons' worth of episodes to cover, the book follows a slightly different format to the three previous volumes in this series, each of which dealt with one season of the Matt Smith era. Each chapter contains an extensive review and analysis discussing its particular episode in depth; these pieces are based on the reviews I wrote for *Slant Magazine* (published online in their *House Next Door* blog) as the episodes were first being shown, but have been completely rewritten and expanded (by a factor of three to five times in each case). Following each review is a short section entitled "Reflections," in which I look back on the episode from the perspective of having seen the two completed seasons. In this section, I will note links and foreshadowings for future episodes (the inclusion of which is a favourite device of Moffat), point out cases where related interviews or DVD extras are of interest, and discuss external factors such as the reaction to the episode by fans and/or the general public.

I wish to thank Kevin Mahoney, owner of Punked Books and co-author of the previous volumes in this series, for giving me the opportunity to expound upon my appreciation for *Doctor Who* in general and the work of Steven Moffat in particular. For me, these two years contain some of the best work of Moffat's time on the show – along with some elements that fail to hit the mark for a variety of reasons. But it was ever thus with *Who*, which should always be striving to do new things. If ever a season came along whose reach did not exceed its grasp, it would no longer be the same show I fell in love with nearly forty years ago.

Steven Cooper
July 2016

1: Deep Breath

Writer: Steven Moffat
Director: Ben Wheatley
Originally Broadcast: 23 August 2014

Cast

The Doctor: Peter Capaldi
Clara: Jenna Coleman
Madame Vastra: Neve McIntosh
Jenny: Catrin Stewart
Strax: Dan Starkey
Half-Face Man: Peter Ferdinando
Inspector Gregson: Paul Hickey
Alf: Tony Way
Elsie: Maggie Service
Cabbie: Mark Kempner
Barney: Brian Miller
Waiter: Graham Duff
Courtney Woods: Ellis George
Policeman: Peter Hannah
Footman: Paul Kasey
The Eleventh Doctor: Matt Smith
Missy: Michelle Gomez

When it was announced in August 2013 that Peter Capaldi would be taking over the role of the Doctor for the following year's series, *Doctor Who*'s public profile was bigger than ever before. The show was riding the huge wave of media interest building up to its Fiftieth Anniversary celebrations and the departure of Matt Smith which would follow shortly afterwards at Christmas, and the reveal of the new Doctor became a glitzy live, prime-time TV event in its own right. In 2014, Capaldi and co-star Jenna Coleman would embark on a whistle-stop tour taking in half a dozen cities around the world to promote the new season – a sign that the growing global recognition for the revived *Doctor Who* series over the past decade had now reached unprecedented levels.

Unlike the mixed reaction to the virtually unknown 26-year-old Matt Smith becoming the Doctor, Capaldi's casting was met with almost universal approval. The highly respected actor's long list of film and TV roles included two previous appearances in the *Doctor Who* universe – as Caecilius alongside David Tennant's Doctor in 2008's *The Fires of Pompeii*, and his powerful performance as the doomed civil servant John Frobisher at the centre of the *Torchwood* mini-series, *Children of Earth* (2009). At fifty-five (the same age as the original Doctor William Hartnell was when he began in the show, although Hartnell both looked and played older than Capaldi) he would clearly provide a huge contrast to the previous Doctor and an opportunity for the show to change direction. Writer and showrunner Steven Moffat spoke of how the new Doctor would be more in the patrician mould of the classic series than the "youthful boyfriend" exterior projected by both Smith and Tennant (though both of them could show plenty of power when needed, of course). It's ironic, then, that by the end of *Deep Breath*, the viewer is left decidedly equivocal about the new Doctor. This is quite deliberate on Moffat's part: the Doctor's new prickly attitude, towards both humans in general and his companion Clara in particular, is meant to be uncomfortable and challenging. With Matt Smith's entrance in 2010 (*The Eleventh Hour*), it was essential to immediately win over the audience and quash any doubts about the new lead actor, a task which that episode accomplished excellently. Here, with Capaldi's quality as an actor already known and highly anticipated, Moffat was able to take a different tack, instead crafting a very similar transition from a youthful Doctor to an older, spikier personality as the classic series tried in 1984 when Peter Davison gave way to Colin Baker.

It's an approach that carries considerable risk, as that earlier attempt proved; Colin Baker's first story was a shambolic failure (although the performance of Baker himself is by far the best thing in it) which heralded the classic series entering its final years of terminal decline. *Deep Breath* does very much better, providing a solid launch for the new Doctor; however, the episode could have been much more effective, had it not been for one unfortunate marketing decision. In an effort to keep the publicity juggernaut rumbling along, Moffat and/or his superiors at the BBC decided that this episode, like the previous year's Fiftieth Anniversary special, should receive a cinematic release alongside its television broadcast. This required the running time to be extended to 75 minutes, a length which is simply unnecessary for the telling of this particular story. The result is that the episode is full of meandering and padding, with momentum continually being built up

7

and then dissipated by slackness that would have been tightened and removed had Capaldi been given the same 60-minute debut that the two previous Doctors had.

The teaser, featuring the returning Paternoster Gang of Vastra, Jenny and Strax, opens the episode with the same rather whimsical feel as their previous appearances such as 2013's *The Crimson Horror*. The presence of the lizard woman, her ninja-skilled maid/wife, and their dim Sontaran butler does mean that realism takes a back seat to heightened, steampunk-style storytelling. However, that's no bad thing as Moffat has the TARDIS being vomited onto the banks of the Thames in Victorian London by a time-displaced dinosaur that had accidentally swallowed it (cheerfully ignoring the fact that the *Tyrannosaurus rex* shown is far too large; while *T. rex* was a huge animal, the idea of one being big enough to choke on a police box is ridiculous). The dazed Doctor and Clara stumble out, and Capaldi gets to have fun with the Doctor's traditional post-regeneration loopiness (and some of his funny moments resonate strongly with those in Tom Baker's first episode nearly forty years earlier – no doubt a deliberate homage by Moffat and Capaldi, who are both lifelong fans of the show). As the Doctor falls unconscious into the mud, Vastra's wry comment "Well, here we go again" (itself a callback to a similar comment at the Jon Pertwee/Tom Baker changeover) leads into a striking new title sequence. Full of spinning gears and spiralling clock faces, it's based on a fan-created sequence published on YouTube in 2013 shortly after Capaldi was announced (the fan in question, Billy Hanshaw, receives a "Title concept" credit). The visuals are great, but the theme music's main melody, presented in a new high-pitched wailing vibrato, will take some getting used to.

The longueurs mentioned above are particularly evident in the Vastra/Jenny/Strax material in the first half of the episode. All that really happens is that Vastra calms the Doctor down and gets him to sleep, and then helps Clara work through her reactions to his change of appearance. However, while there are good moments (the Doctor's exclamation of "Don't look in that mirror! It's absolutely furious!" is perfectly played), these scenes are excessively long-winded, with the Doctor blathering on about Clara's accent having changed (an admittedly clever exploitation of the incidental fact that Capaldi and Neve McIntosh are both Scottish) and how he never needs sleep being a joke that takes a very long time to get to the punchline. There are also troubling inconsistencies of character. In the teaser, Jenny is made to disbelieve that this is the Doctor, simply in order to duplicate the "I don't understand... who is he? Where's the Doctor?" / "Right here... *he's* the Doctor" moment from 2005's *The Christmas Invasion* – and yet, immediately afterwards she's the one providing reassurance to Clara that the Doctor is still the same underneath. Meanwhile, after her experiences in the previous two episodes (to say nothing of any lingering memories from her "Impossible Girl" storyline, which saw her encounter all the previous Doctors), Clara should hardly be so disconcerted by the Doctor changing his face and becoming older. Vastra challenges her (in a scene reminiscent of her similar confrontation with the Victorian version of Clara in 2012's *The Snowmen*), apparently taking offence at Clara's reaction to losing her "boyfriend." While some interesting ideas are expressed here (notably, that the Doctor was showing a special trust in Clara by regenerating into a form without the youthful veneer and closer to his 'true' nature), the scene seems over-anxious to push the audience into accepting the new Doctor, with Clara being considered foolishly wrong-headed for her reluctance. The characters stop being real people and are temporarily reduced to pawns being moved around by the writer. It's difficult to decide which is the sillier moment, between Clara's passionate declaration that Roman emperor Marcus Aurelius was "the only pin-up I ever had on my wall when I was fifteen," or Jenny breaking into applause and excited whooping when Clara finally loses her temper and snaps back at Vastra. In a tighter edit, most of this sequence would have been deservedly left on the cutting-room floor.

The actual story starts to move with the appearance of a new macabre Moffat creation, the Half-Face Man. This creature, first seen as he kills a luckless passer-by to steal his eyeballs, is later revealed to be the leader of a group of robots stranded on Earth that are harvesting skin and organs to both disguise themselves and repair their ship in order to return to their "promised land." Moffat here reuses the dim but single-minded clockwork droids he invented for his memorable 2006 episode, *The Girl in the Fireplace*, and acknowledges the debt by having the Doctor several times *almost* manage to remember that he's encountered a situation like this before. (Unfortunately, he ends up doing this once too often, with the Doctor eventually finding a component in the robots' ship implausibly labelled "Sister ship of *Madame de Pompadour*" – and still the penny doesn't drop.) The effects for the chief robot – with half of his head an open mesh of metal, revealing the clockwork within – are spectacular, but it's the physical performance of actor Peter Ferdinando that really sells the creature. His jerky, mechanistic movements are never overdone, but perfectly convey the impression of this clockwork mechanism processing information and deciding on a course of action. In fact, the whole visual realisation of the episode (with the exception of a couple of obviously green-screened shots of the Doctor on horseback) is beautifully achieved by director Ben Wheatley.

The aforementioned horseback sequence sees the Doctor spring into action as he witnesses the unfortunate dinosaur suddenly bursting into flames. His friends catch up with him at the scene of the crime, and Capaldi has his first chance to show compassion ("She was scared and alone") and intellect (immediately asking the question, "Have there been any similar murders?"), along with abrasiveness towards anyone less intelligent than himself, dismissing all humans as "pudding-brains." However, the Doctor soon disappears off on his own again, leaving Vastra to carry on the investigation. Next morning, we have more blatant padding with Strax and Clara (although his "sending up" of *The Times* by throwing the paper at her so hard it knocks her over is a wonderful laugh-out-loud moment). The sequence where Strax uses a lorgnette-like device to give Clara a "medical examination" has only one reason to exist: the lorgnette, along with similar gadgets employed by Jenny and Vastra (the scanning gauntlet used in the teaser, and the hatpin that functions like a remote key-lock for Vastra's carriage) were created by the winners of a competition held by the children's magazine programme *Blue Peter*. Moffat no doubt felt obliged to include them, even though the lorgnette scene in particular connects to nothing and goes nowhere. Later, Jenny poses like an artist's model while Vastra is apparently painting her portrait; the laboured punchline is reached when Vastra turns the easel around to reveal not a canvas but a map of London plotting the recent incidents of "spontaneous combustion." The episode mostly misses the opportunity to explore more deeply the relationship between Vastra and Jenny (for example, the question of why Jenny pretends to be Vastra's maid even in private is raised only to be immediately ignored), instead opting for rather superficial bantering that veers wildly between being playful and irritating. (And the way the climax of the story allows them to be shown kissing, but only after contriving a ridiculous 'explanation' for them to do so, was entirely irritating.) Fortunately, the plot starts moving again as Clara bursts in brandishing a newspaper advertisement referring to "the Impossible Girl" – apparently placed by the Doctor – which leads her to a certain restaurant in the city.

In the interim, the still disoriented Doctor has been wandering the streets ("By now, he's almost certainly had his throat cut by the violent poor," Strax cheerily informs Clara), where we find him examining his face in a mirror, watched by a bewildered beggar (a lovely cameo from Brian Miller, husband of the late Elisabeth Sladen). The fact that Capaldi has previously appeared in *Doctor Who* is cheekily alluded to as the Doctor finds his new appearance strangely familiar, but can't work out where he's seen it before ("Who frowned me this face? ... It's like I'm trying to tell myself something. Like I'm trying to make a point"). Exactly what the Doctor will make of this coincidence remains a matter for future episodes; he is suddenly distracted into an extended riff about his prominent eyebrows – a facial feature which had drawn comment from the moment of Capaldi's casting (rather like Matt Smith's chin) to such an extent that he was able to make a memorable split-second appearance in *The Day of the Doctor* (before any work had been done on designing his Doctor's costume) in a shot showing no more than the upper half of his face. The Doctor then fixates on his new accent, leading to more parochial humour ("I am Scottish! Oh, that's good... I can really complain about things now!"); his earlier joke about his eyebrows being "independently cross" and wanting to secede from the rest of his face is a sneaky reference to the then upcoming referendum on Scottish independence, very much in the news as this episode was broadcast. Capaldi is compelling as he seizes the chance to show the Doctor's mercurial changes of mood; with unexpected menace, he advances on the beggar, demanding the man's coat because of the cold, before being distracted again by a discarded newspaper showing a reference to spontaneous combustion. (It becomes apparent that this is the method being used by the robots to destroy the bodies of their victims and conceal the evidence of their organ harvesting; it's a phenomenon peculiarly suited to a Victorian-era story, thanks to its famous use in Dickens' *Bleak House*.)

A long sequence in the restaurant reunites the two leads, and helps to bring the new Doctor's character into focus. He is now wearing the beggar's coat, and claims to have given his watch in exchange for it, but neither Clara nor the audience can be totally confident that he is telling the truth. Capaldi and Coleman both shine, as Clara, having enjoyed a relationship with a youthful Doctor that consisted largely of playful bantering, now finds herself confronted with a much older, more remote man who seems to be a lot less concerned about the feelings of others. What finally forms a connection between them is the realisation that they both assumed the other had placed the advertisement, and both were wrong – they have walked into a trap. It's a superbly creepy moment as they recognise that the patrons at the other tables are not actually eating – or breathing – and get up to leave, only for the robots to block them with a smooth, synchronized movement. They are starting to work together again as they are confronted by another robot disguised as a waiter, although the Doctor is certainly no respecter of personal space now either, pulling a hair from Clara in order to test the air flow in the room and, to her revulsion, ripping off the waiter robot's face and placing it against her own.

They are captured and dropped down into the robots' damaged ship under the restaurant. There's a fun sequence with them using the sonic screwdriver to escape, showing the two of them functioning as a team again as Clara begins to look past the change ("You should make that thing voice-activated... Oh, for God's sake, it is, isn't it?"). Their exploration of the area, past a number of inactive robots (including a recharging Half-Face Man), is just as slowly paced as the rest of the episode; here, however, the measured tempo works to raise the tension. Then, the work Moffat has put into keeping us uncertain about the new Doctor's character is paid off, as all the robots come to life and Clara is trapped by a closing door – and the Doctor deliberately makes no attempt to rescue her. It's a truly shocking moment as he runs off, leaving her alone and defenceless.

Given a whole centre-stage sequence to herself, Coleman excels at showing both Clara's fear and her resourcefulness. Remembering the Doctor's earlier discovery of the unbreathing robots, she tries to hold her breath to fool her captors and slowly walk free of their clutches, in a nail-biting sequence that only ends when she can't stop herself from taking a gasping breath, passes out and is captured. As she is interrogated by the Half-Face Man, interpolated flashbacks to her first day of teaching at Coal Hill School cleverly parallel her current situation and show us how Clara manages to hold down her alarm and use the robot's desire for information about "the other one" to retain the upper hand in the exchange. But ultimately, she still believes the Doctor, no matter how changed, "will have my back" – and her faith is rewarded as he returns and immediately takes control of the situation, having listened in to all the information she extracted from the robot. One mystery remains, though, as they realise that the advertisement that drew them to the restaurant was not placed by the robots either. However, there's no time to investigate further: a cry of "Geronimo!" (the previous Doctor's catchphrase) signals the arrival of Vastra, Jenny and Strax, and the Doctor somewhat recklessly follows the Half-Face Man back up to the restaurant. It emerges that the chief robot intends to flee in the ship's "escape capsule," which is in fact the restaurant itself – leading to the bizarre, ghoulish sight of a balloon made from human skin, flying over London and carrying the restaurant chamber.

The climax attempts to create tension by intercutting between an action sequence below and the Doctor's face-off with the Half-Face Man in the restaurant. Unfortunately, the fight between Clara's group and the robots is very static and poorly choreographed. The repetitive cutaways do nothing but distract from the fascinating confrontation between the Doctor and his opponent. With only words to work with, the Doctor tries to convince the robot that there is no point to continuing his prolonged existence – that his quest to find the "promised land" is nothing but a chimera, a quirk of "all the humanity you've stuffed inside you." He points out that the robot is like a broom that has had its handle and brush replaced many times over the years: "You have replaced every piece of yourself... time and time again. There's not a trace of the original you left. You probably can't even remember where you got that face from!" Capaldi beautifully shows the Doctor realising how this description can apply to both of them. A clever piece of direction reinforces the moment, as the Doctor holds up a metal tea tray to show the robot his reflection – only to see his own reflection in the back of the tray.

Half-Face Man: "It cannot end."
The Doctor: "It has to. You know that. There's only one way out."
Half-Face Man: "Self-destruction is against my basic programming."
The Doctor: "Murder is against mine!"

With consummate skill, Moffat crafts a climactic moment that makes use of the uncertainty regarding the new Doctor's limits that he has carefully maintained throughout the episode. As the two grapple in the doorway of the restaurant high above London, the Doctor warns the robot not to underestimate the lengths he will go to in order to protect the humans below. Then the robot stops struggling – has the Doctor got through to him? The Doctor says, "You realise, of course, that one of us is lying about our basic programming." We cut away to the battle below, and all the droids deactivate as their chief dies. When we cut back, the Half-Face Man is impaled on the tip of Big Ben's tower – did he commit suicide, or did the Doctor push him? Capaldi's brooding look into the camera challenges the viewers to think the worst of him. We are left to contemplate how much we still don't know about the Doctor's new persona as the scene dissolves into an epilogue.

The Doctor has already departed; Clara has been left behind, and starts thinking about joining Vastra's group, until the Doctor suddenly comes back for her. Entering the TARDIS, she finds its interior slightly remodelled, with bookshelves around the upper level (to which she reacts with the now traditional "You've redecorated... I don't like it" joke first used in 1973's *The Three Doctors*). More importantly, the Twelfth Doctor is revealed in his new, rather severe outfit, strongly reminiscent of the formalwear worn by Jon Pertwee's Doctor at the outset of his era in 1970. The Doctor hints that his preoccupations will now be more inwardly focused:

The Doctor: "I've lived for over two thousand years, and not all of them were good. I've made many mistakes, and it's about time that I did something about that. Clara, I'm not your boyfriend."
Clara: "I never thought you were."
The Doctor: "I never said it was your mistake."

Faced with this confirmation that her relationship with the Doctor has altered permanently, Clara is only convinced to continue travelling with him thanks to a totally unexpected twist – a phone call from his past self. Matt Smith makes a lovely, bittersweet cameo as Moffat ingeniously ties up the moment at the end of *The Time of the Doctor* when Clara found the TARDIS phone hanging off its hook, just before she witnessed the regeneration. He helps her to understand that, however changed, the Doctor still needs her, and they walk off with a reference to chips just like the Doctor and Rose in 2005's *The End of the World*, having finally achieved an understanding.

But instead of leaving everything resolved, Moffat ends with an unexpected revelation. In an unexplained ending scene, the Half-Face Man somehow arrives in his "promised land" after all, as he wakes up in a strange garden and a woman calling herself Missy welcomes him to "Heaven." Clearly she was behind the mysterious advertisement, and a connection is also made with an unresolved plot thread from

Clara's first episode, *The Bells of Saint John*, where we never found out the identity of the woman who gave her the Doctor's phone number, resulting in their initial meeting. As the Doctor says, "There's a woman out there who's very keen that we stay together." I look forward to finding out where we're going from here.

Classic Who DVD Recommendation: As mentioned above, the Doctor's latest personality change strongly resonates with 1984's *The Twin Dilemma*, which introduced the sixth Doctor, Colin Baker. Also starring is Nicola Bryant as Peri, who has even more trouble with her new Doctor than Clara does in *Deep Breath*. It's not as bad as its reputation (in favourite story polls covering the entire series it routinely ends up at the very bottom of the list), but it's weak enough in both script and production that it can really only be recommended as an example of how *not* to go about changing your leading man.

Reflections: Looking back at *Deep Breath* from the vantage point of early 2016, after two years of Peter Capaldi's Doctor, the episode feels even more than it did at the time like Tom Baker's debut story *Robot* (1975) – a stylistic hangover from the previous era. The Twelfth Doctor's character is consistent enough with what followed, particularly the aloofness and inwardness that would dominate his first season, although his remark about needing to correct past mistakes turned out to be a bit of a red herring, unless he was simply referring to his deliberate stepping back from forming warm relationships with humans. However, the characters of Vastra, Jenny and Strax seem quite out of place after the Capaldi era's turning away from the more fantastical atmosphere of the Matt Smith period. It's notable that after the opening scenes, the Doctor barely interacts with them again at all, and definitely not with any amiability. He has moved on, and the Paternoster Gang have receded into his past in the same way that Tom Baker's arrival signalled the end of the Doctor's close ties to the UNIT characters who had been such close associates of the Jon Pertwee incarnation. Certainly the notion of a spinoff series starring the trio, which seemed a real possibility a couple of years ago, appears to have faded away; the actual spinoff being produced for 2016 (*Class*) is based around a setting more connected to the Capaldi era: present-day Coal Hill School.

As far as planting seeds for the future is concerned, we see flashes of Clara's pupil Courtney Woods, who would later appear multiple times, most prominently in *The Caretaker* and *Kill the Moon*. The Doctor's pondering about where his new face came from would be paid off rather wonderfully next season in *The Girl Who Died*. There are also a couple of lines that resonate unexpectedly with later episodes: Vastra's exclamation to Clara that "You might as well flirt with a mountain range" has an unexpected poignancy after *The Husbands of River Song*. And the Doctor's description of the robots "trying to get home the long way round" looks both backwards to *The Day of the Doctor* and forwards to *Heaven Sent*.

Most obviously, of course, *Deep Breath* introduced the mystery of Missy, which would be teased throughout the season before being paid off in the final two-parter. Michelle Gomez's performance made the character immediately compelling, although with the benefit of hindsight the final scene doesn't make a tremendous amount of sense: the Half-Face Man is not human, so for what possible reason would he be among those brought into Missy's Nethersphere? When rewatching the episode with full awareness of Missy's identity, the scene loses most of its impact and simply undermines the closure created by the prior Doctor/Clara street scene. Perhaps it would have been better placed directly after the sight of the Half-Face Man's dead body and before the epilogue; that would have allowed the episode to end on a strong note of accomplishment as Clara and the Doctor are finally at ease with each other again.

2: Into the Dalek

Writers: Phil Ford & Steven Moffat
Director: Ben Wheatley
Originally Broadcast: 30 August 2014

Cast

The Doctor: Peter Capaldi
Clara: Jenna Coleman
Journey Blue: Zawe Ashton
Colonel Morgan Blue: Michael Smiley
Danny Pink: Samuel Anderson
Gretchen: Lauren Dos Santos
Ross: Ben Crompton
Fleming: Bradley Ford
School Secretary: Michelle Morris
Mr Armitage: Nigel Betts
Courtney Woods: Ellis George
Dalek: Barnaby Edwards
Voice of the Daleks: Nicholas Briggs

After last week's season opener, which cushioned the shock of the new Doctor by surrounding him with the characters and trappings of his predecessor's time, the real Peter Capaldi era starts with *Into the Dalek*. Writer Phil Ford, who took David Tennant's Doctor into unfamiliar and uncomfortable psychological places in 2009's *The Waters of Mars*, provides a tale that gives Capaldi the opportunity to show how different his Doctor is from Matt Smith's. It's a thematically rich episode that delves deep into the Doctor's psyche as he explicitly questions his own nature and motivations. It's also disconcerting to watch, with the Doctor being shown as possibly the most detached and downright unfriendly he has ever been – an imperious, distant figure who seems to have little interest in relating to the humans he meets.

Clara is definitely left in no doubt that the Doctor's life no longer revolves around her to the extent she enjoyed with his previous incarnation. After being sent off to fetch coffee at the end of the last episode, he doesn't rejoin her for three weeks, during which time she has made her way back to Coal Hill School and resumed her teaching

17

duties. He's been distracted by something of more immediate interest, as he uses the TARDIS to save Journey Blue, a member of a far-future group of human soldiers fighting a losing battle against a superior Dalek force. He seems a little surprised himself at his impulsive action to materialise the TARDIS around her, rescuing her from her small ship that had been hit by Dalek fire and was about to explode. His manner towards her is hardly reassuring, looming over her as she lies on the floor, disoriented and tearful; her cry of "My brother just died!" is met briskly with "His sister didn't, you're very welcome." He brushes off her attempts to take control of the situation, refusing to be intimidated by her gun and making her say 'please' before returning her to her uncle Morgan Blue, commander of the hospital ship *Aristotle*, which is hiding from the Daleks in an asteroid belt.

Indeed, he only returns to fetch Clara because he wants something from her – her answer to the question, "Am I a good man?" The series (particularly since the revival in 2005) has made great play out of the idea that the Doctor's human companions are there to provide his moral compass; when travelling on his own, this new Doctor is presented as showing no empathy whatever. As he and Journey emerge onto the *Aristotle*, he tells her, "Dry your eyes, Journey Blue – crying is for civilians. It's how we communicate with you lot." It seems that one of his personality traits is going to be an antipathy to soldiers even more blunt than that shown by David Tennant's Doctor in the 2008 two-parter, *The Sontaran Stratagem* and *The Poison Sky*.

Journey: "Don't like soldiers much, do you?"
The Doctor: "You don't need to be liked. You have all the guns."

This is something the show has often been somewhat hypocritical about. The Doctor might be reluctant to wield a weapon himself, and tends to disparage those who use them, but he is no pacifist, and is quite willing to take advantage of military help (notably in the 1970's, when Jon Pertwee's Doctor had a close association with UNIT). Not to mention the enormous significance of the Time War and his role in it, running right through the revived series from its outset in 2005 to the revelation in 2013 that a whole secret incarnation of the Doctor played a central role in both fighting it and ending it. That traumatic experience, although finally now completely in his past after the events of *The Day of the Doctor*, has perhaps caused a certain amount of self-loathing and self-doubt to bubble to the surface of his

18

personality during his latest regeneration. When he brings Clara aboard the *Aristotle* and introduces her to the others, he is openly scornful: Journey is just "gun girl – she's got a gun, and she's a girl." Morgan is "a sort of boss one... probably her uncle but I may have made that up to pass the time while they were talking," and he describes Clara as his "carer" ("She cares, so I don't have to"). Capaldi imbues the scene (and in fact, the whole episode) with a powerful sense of cold disdain; even that witty last line, which other Doctors might have softened with a twinkle in the eye, is played as a completely honest statement of feeling.

In some ways, this removal of cosiness is taking the Doctor right back to his roots: when *Doctor Who* began in 1963, William Hartnell's version of the title character was very much not the hero of the show, instead being self-centred and hostile towards the human interlopers who found themselves on board his TARDIS. Similarly, Tom Baker's Doctor can be found in a brooding, remote mood at the beginning of 1975's *Pyramids of Mars*, displeased with his previous self's involvement with UNIT and looking to break away. But Hartnell's Doctor soon softened and warmed to his companions, and Baker was never far away from a big grin and the enjoyment of adventure. It seems that Clara's task of "humanising" this new Doctor will be a more long-term project; he remains grumpy and sour all through this episode, even as she helps him deal with the "patient" that the humans have secreted aboard the *Aristotle*: a damaged Dalek which has developed a strange malfunction – it proclaims that all Daleks must be destroyed. Clara immediately notes the Doctor's refusal to accept the idea of a 'good' Dalek ("That's a bit inflexible, not like you. I'd almost say prejudiced"), but his reluctance is understandable, given the Daleks' implacable hatred of all other life forms. The cleverest feature of the episode is how it finds a way to show a Dalek behaving as no Dalek ever has before without undermining the core of the creatures' character that has remained remarkably constant for over fifty years.

It was showrunner Steven Moffat (who also gets a co-writer credit) who contributed the idea that the title of the episode should be literally true, with the Doctor, Clara, Journey, and a couple of other soldiers being miniaturised and sent inside the Dalek to find the cause of the malfunction. (Moffat's touch is also visible in the clever use of little flashbacks and flashforwards in the first few scenes, both on Earth and aboard the *Aristotle*, to set up the plotlines and get the exposition across in the most arresting way possible.) The "nano-scaler" technology that enables them to do this is an obvious homage to *Fantastic Voyage* (1966). However, director Ben Wheatley eschews anything like the psychedelic visuals of that movie, except for the actual moment of entry through the Dalek's eyestalk, presented surrealistically with striking slow-motion, distorted images. After that, apart from a few CGI long-shots to establish a sense of scale, the inside of the Dalek is disappointingly mundane, appearing very like the sort of grimy industrial environments often used in *Doctor Who* to depict old spaceships or underground bases, with a few miscellaneous tubes and cables strewn about. It's no wonder the Doctor comes up with "Rusty" as a nickname for the stricken Dalek.

The Doctor gets another chance to show off his new hard-nosed attitude, allied to a ruthless pragmatism, when one of the soldiers rather foolishly triggers an attack of "antibodies" – floating, zapping spheres that act as an automatic internal defence mechanism for the Dalek. Rather than futilely try to save him, the Doctor takes advantage of his death to locate a way past the antibodies into the inner chambers. In an amusing coincidence, Capaldi's second story, just like Matt Smith's before him (2010's *The Beast Below*), sees him and his companions tumbling into a pool of slimy goo representing the innards of a giant creature they are inside. But this time, there is very little humour about the situation. Journey is furious at the loss of her fellow soldier (to which the Doctor simply fires back, "He was dead already – I was saving *us*!"), and justifiably explodes at him when he callously points out that the dead man is still with them in the pool of sludge ("Top layer, if you want to say a few words"). As he leads them further into the interior of the Dalek, with a completely unnecessary jab at Clara's appearance thrown in for good measure, the Doctor's new characterisation is in real danger of veering from abrasive to outright unpleasant, to the detriment of the show.

Fortunately, after this low point, the Doctor's character recovers somewhat as he begins to get to grips with the problem of what happened to "Rusty" to change its behaviour. They discover that an internal radiation leak has somehow interfered with the Dalek's systems that automatically suppress all memories and experiences that would corrupt its fundamental purpose. This is a new development, invented by Ford for this episode, but one that has been logically extrapolated from the Daleks' previous appearances. Like the Cybermen, they are biologically capable of feeling a wide range of emotions, but their mechanical support systems deliberately cripple that range, inhibiting any aspects of their experience that would get in the way of a single-minded goal: in the Cybermen's case, converting other humanoids into Cybermen, and in the Daleks' case, exterminating all non-Dalek life. Unable to deal with the endless renewing of non-Dalek life in the universe as it witnesses stars being born and new species evolving, "Rusty" has effectively fallen prey to despair. (I particularly liked the way the story introduced a new meaning for the creatures' frequent catchphrase, "Resistance is futile.") Nicholas Briggs, who has provided all of the voices for both Daleks and Cybermen since 2005, effectively conveys the Dalek's bewilderment as it tries to cope with its expanded universe of emotions, giving the Doctor a momentary wild hope that just maybe, a Dalek can *learn* to be non-hostile.

Fixing the radiation leak proves to be no problem at all; the Doctor easily seals it up with a wave of his sonic screwdriver ("An anticlimax once in a while is good for my hearts"). However, he then finds himself with a much bigger problem as "Rusty" immediately comes back to its true Dalek nature. It's a clever counterpoint to the seminal 2005 episode *Dalek* – again, an isolated, injured Dalek is restored by a misguided act of compassion, breaks free and begins an unstoppable killing spree. The Dalek transmits a message to its fellows, giving away the *Aristotle*'s position. Morgan and his soldiers try to hold off a force of Daleks attacking the ship in a standard "doomed last stand" action sequence that propels the rest of the episode, as the Doctor and company inside the Dalek must quickly find a way to reverse what they have done before all the humans are wiped out.

Journey: "Let me get this straight. We had a good Dalek, and we made it bad again? That's all we've done?"
The Doctor: "There was never a good Dalek. There was a broken Dalek, and we repaired it."
Journey: "You were supposed to be helping us!"
The Doctor: "I gave it a shot, it didn't work out. It's a Dalek, what did you expect?"

The angry confrontation between Journey, Clara and the Doctor is compelling, due to the intense performances of all three actors (although thanks to an overenthusiastic foley artist, Clara slapping the Doctor's face becomes a ridiculously over the top moment, briefly jolting the viewer out of the scene). Clara sharply upbraids the Doctor for taking a grim satisfaction in having "proven" his contention that a good Dalek is an impossibility ("We're going to die in here, and there's a tiny piece of you that's *pleased*. The Daleks are evil after all, everything makes sense, the Doctor is right!"). It's here that the episode is most successful in making use of the Doctor's new characterisation, placing him and Clara believably at odds with each other, in the same way that the Doctor and Rose clashed in the earlier *Dalek* episode. There's also another parallel with *The Beast Below*, where the companion is able to provide the solution to the problem when the Doctor can't. Clara shows that he was right to bring her along, as she prompts him to realise that if they can undo the Dalek's memory suppression, he can get into its mind and attempt direct communication with it.

There's no way for Clara to get back to the Dalek's memory vaults without triggering another antibody attack, so Journey's fellow soldier Gretchen sacrifices herself to provide a distraction. Regrettably, what should be an intense moment feels forced and unearned; a woman who has known him for all of half an hour is somehow persuaded to give up her life simply by the Doctor's promise that he will do something "amazing." The actors do their best to convince us that no other course of action is possible, but the emotional effect that the scene should generate just isn't there. And so Gretchen dies – only to find herself suddenly facing the mysterious "Missy" from the end of last week's episode. Is this some kind of afterlife, or has she actually been transported elsewhere? (Interestingly, the whiteout effect, together with the fading out of all sound but Gretchen's scream, is very like the start of the episode when Journey was taken aboard the TARDIS.) There are only questions without answers at this point, and the weirdness of this unexplained intrusion is only heightened by the jarring cut straight back to the action on the *Aristotle*.

Unfortunately, the science of the resolution doesn't stand even the slightest examination, being more on the level of the children's spinoff series, *The Sarah Jane Adventures* (for which Ford was the main writer). The freeing of the Dalek's suppressed memories is depicted by showing Clara crawling through some tubing to switch on a few random lights; Journey's lampshade-hanging "Seriously?" is the only concession made to the thorough implausibility of the plotting here. But it's almost worth it for the intensity of the Doctor's speech to the Dalek as he establishes mental contact with it. Unlike the earlier moment with Gretchen, this scene successfully makes its points about the Doctor's nature, with its thought-provoking suggestion that he views himself as not really becoming "the Doctor" until he encountered the Daleks (in only his second adventure, back in 1963). Even better is what happens next – the Dalek fixates on the Doctor's hatred of its kind and absorbs it into itself. Capaldi shows the Doctor's horror and disgust as perhaps the most memorable line from the 2005 episode ("You would make a good Dalek") is now shown to be true – infused with the hatred learned from the Doctor, "Rusty" remains an implacable killing machine, but now focused wholly on killing other Daleks. It quickly destroys the attacking Daleks and saves the *Aristotle*. But any sense of triumph is muted as the Dalek expresses its fellow feeling for the Doctor ("I am not a good Dalek. *You* are a good Dalek"), and leaves to continue its crusade against its own kind. (In fact, this ending was originally much less open; dubbing scripts for the first five episodes were leaked onto the internet before the season premiered, and the one for this episode revealed that a brief scene after this was cut, where "Rusty" self-destructs in order to destroy the Dalek command ship.) It's no wonder that when Clara finally answers the Doctor's question "Am I a good man?" it can only be with a less than ringing endorsement: "I don't know... but I think you try to be."

In an unsubtle but effective directorial touch, after "Rusty" destroys the other Daleks aboard the *Aristotle*, it pauses under a stream of water, which flows down its dome like tears – an echo of Journey's tears at the opening of the story. The crying soldier motif also appears in a secondary strand, in which the Doctor (as yet) has no involvement: unknown to him, Clara has met Danny Pink, a fellow teacher at her school who is an ex-soldier with evidently something traumatic in his past. Their initial encounter is played for comedy, but a spark is kindled and they are obviously on course to develop a deeper relationship. In the final scene, Clara is brought up short when Danny wonders if she has "a rule against soldiers" – an implied criticism of the Doctor, who rejected Journey's desire to join him as a companion on no better grounds. Throughout the episode, Zawe Ashton's warm-hearted portrayal of Journey has clearly been intended to rebuke the Doctor's anti-soldier prejudice, and the culminating scene where her offer is coldly rejected is uncomfortable to watch. As Danny and Clara agree to go for a drink to get to know each other better, it seems he is destined to cause the Doctor a certain amount of disquiet when they finally meet; judging by this episode, the Doctor will thoroughly deserve it.

Classic Who DVD Recommendation: A previous homage to *Fantastic Voyage* can be found in the 1977 story that introduced K9, the Doctor's fondly remembered robotic dog: *The Invisible Enemy*, starring Tom Baker and Louise Jameson.

Reflections: Danny Pink certainly did end up getting under the Doctor's skin, even though their actual encounter was delayed until halfway through the season. Before then, Clara successfully managed to keep the two strands of her life separate. She had been doing this with the previous Doctor as well, but there was never a sense that we needed to see any more than brief glimpses of her mundane life – just enough to show that she *had* a life on Earth, devoted to either child care or teaching. Now, for the first time, the companion is given a developing story that takes place apart from the Doctor – in fact, one in which he is the cause of increasing difficulties, until he finally intrudes into it irrevocably in *The Caretaker*. With the Doctor's new personality moving him away from his previous carefree friendship with Clara, this was a good way to create interesting conflict between them (both here and in later episodes, the Doctor is simply oblivious to the idea that she might have other things to do than go on an adventure with him). Unfortunately, Clara's relationship with Danny was never quite as successful as it should have been thanks to the rather tepid chemistry between the actors (not so much here, but definitely in later episodes when they are supposed to be deeply in love).

As I alluded to in the previous chapter, the Twelfth Doctor's introduction was not unlike that of Colin Baker's sixth incarnation in 1984. Once again, a decision was taken to knock the audience off balance by making the new Doctor frankly unlikeable. Back then, the thin justification of the Doctor being "alien" was all that was provided to account for his new manner. But while more thought was clearly put into the writing of the Doctor's character in the modern episodes than was the case thirty years ago, after two seasons it is undeniable that Capaldi's Doctor has not been embraced by the viewers to the same extent as Matt Smith (and before him, David Tennant). In the UK, after the audiences in 2014 were at more or less the same level as the previous few years, the 2015 season saw a significant drop right from the first episode. This implies that any cause *within* the show for the decline must come from the stories of Capaldi's first year.

Looking at the 2014 stories as a whole, it's not hard to see why some viewers were put off, as the aloof, even disagreeable Doctor of *Into the Dalek* proves to be a harbinger of the whole season. He unbends a little in the next few episodes, but it's not until right at the end of his fifth story, *Time Heist*, that we have a scene showing the Doctor relaxed and having fun in the TARDIS, making jokes with friends as his previous selves would have done. But then, the next four or five episodes bring the conflict between the Doctor, Clara and Danny to the forefront, with the Doctor/Clara relationship increasingly viewed as less than healthy (an idea which would culminate in the "hybrid" arc of the next season). Finally, the season climaxes with an exceptionally grim finale that seems to bring the Doctor and Clara's story to the bleakest of conclusions. It all made for some powerful drama, and both Capaldi and Coleman delivered several knockout performances. However, anyone watching primarily for straightforward action adventure, with a hero and companion to identify with (or imagine joining on their escapades), would have been left out in the cold.

There were other issues, too: as will be discussed, the scheduling and promotion of the 2015 series was notably poorly handled in comparison to previous years. Also, while it's still common in some circles to see 21st-century *Who* referred to as the "new series," that label is increasingly inappropriate for a show that is now over a decade old in its own right (as well as being part of a continuity stretching back over fifty years). For the first time since the 1980's, a substantial part of the audience has never known a time when *Doctor Who* was not running – and as the saying goes, familiarity breeds contempt (or, at least, a drifting away). But these headwinds that Moffat and Capaldi had to contend with as they laboured to establish this very different Doctor should not obscure the string of powerful performances Capaldi provided almost from the start. His ability to create compelling viewing even without the presence of any other actors – often with speeches delivered directly to the audience – was first seen in this episode, but would return in *Listen* and be taken to an extreme in next year's *Heaven Sent*. In his second year, some significant retooling of the Twelfth Doctor would take place to bring him back towards what we might call the mainstream of the Doctor's character, with a greater emphasis on comedy in particular. But by then, it would appear, quite a few viewers had already tuned out.

3: Robot of Sherwood

Writer: Mark Gatiss
Director: Paul Murphy
Originally Broadcast: 6 September 2014

Cast

The Doctor: Peter Capaldi
Clara: Jenna Coleman
Robin Hood: Tom Riley
Quayle: Roger Ashton-Griffiths
Quayle's Ward: Sabrina Bartlett
The Sheriff of Nottingham: Ben Miller
Alan-a-Dale: Ian Hallard
Friar Tuck: Trevor Cooper
Little John: Rusty Goffe
Will Scarlett: Joseph Kennedy
Walter: Adam Jones
Herald: David Benson
Guard: David Langham
Knight: Tim Baggaley
Voice of the Knights: Richard Elfyn

For the third time since *Doctor Who* returned in 2005, Mark Gatiss gets the opportunity to provide a new Doctor's third adventure, and his first historical story. In *The Unquiet Dead* the Doctor accidentally encountered Charles Dickens, while in 2010's *Victory of the Daleks* the Doctor was invited to pay a visit to Winston Churchill. Here, at the urging of Clara, he takes a trip back to 12th-century Nottingham, the time and place of someone she's always wanted to meet. The result is a light-hearted episode that allows Peter Capaldi to introduce both verbal and physical comedy into the hitherto rather sombre portrayal of the Twelfth Doctor, but also incorporates some deeper moments that continue the work of exploring the new Doctor's character.

Clara's sudden admission of having a passion for the tale of Robin Hood since childhood is obviously just a convenience to get things started (although, given that we were told two episodes ago that as a teenager she had a pin-up of Marcus Aurelius, I suppose it's not totally out of character either). The Doctor tries to talk her out of it, telling her she'll be disappointed to learn that Robin Hood is just a story – he doesn't believe in "old-fashioned heroes," and rejects Clara's implication that he himself belongs in that category. Naturally, as soon as he steps out of the TARDIS the bemused Doctor comes face to face with the legendary brigand, large as life – a handsome archer in the classic Lincoln green outfit, right down to the hat with a feather in it, who shoots an arrow at the police box and follows up with a sly wink to the camera. While Clara is beside herself with fangirl-ish glee, the Doctor finds himself quickly swept up into a swashbuckling fight against Robin, who cheerfully intends to relieve this "bony rascal" of his magic box.

First and foremost, this episode is a "romp" – and a very broadly written and played one, at that. Reaction to comedy is always subjective, of course, but I found a lot to enjoy here. The Doctor seems to have fallen straight into the classic Robin Hood tale, and several tropes from that tale are subverted for comic purposes. The fight at the river crossing becomes the Doctor facing off against Robin armed only with a spoon, which results in both of them getting a dunking in the river. The next day, the archery tournament for the golden arrow devolves into a hilarious game of one-upmanship, with the Doctor and Robin repeatedly splitting arrows in turn until finally the Doctor loses patience and blows up the target with his sonic screwdriver. Not all of the gags work: in particular, the *Austin Powers*-style innuendo about Errol Flynn ("He had a big… ego") lands with a thud. (However, the later eyebrow-raising "I'm going to need a sample" as the Doctor marches purposefully towards Robin carrying a goblet did induce a chuckle, especially after Robin's wary reply, "Of what?") But it's only the introduction of the Merry Men that falls completely flat. As with all the other elements of the Robin Hood legend, Will Scarlet, Friar Tuck, and the rest are all present and correct, but the script has no interest in doing anything with them at all. They come across as so one-dimensional as to inadvertently give credibility to the Doctor's idea that he has accidentally landed in some kind of "theme park from the future." It's a great pity that a very capable actor like Trevor Cooper, who can been seen in a much more substantial role in 1985's *Revelation of the Daleks*, is saddled with just a handful of bland, functional lines and no chance to make any kind of impression.

The episode is very linear, employing none of the Moffat-style tricks with narrative sequence that Gatiss experimented with in his last episode, *The Crimson Horror* in 2013. The initial comic scenes with the Doctor and Robin are intercut with dramatic moments showing our villain, the Sheriff of Nottingham, burning a peasant village after stealing their valuables – and, just to drive home his total lack of redeeming features, casually killing an old man named Quayle who offers a token resistance. With the basic premise set up, it's back to comedy as the Doctor and Clara meet the Merry Men, and the Doctor tries and fails to prove they're not real (for a moment he wonders if they have landed inside a Miniscope – a nice callback to a piece of futuristic technology featured in 1973's *Carnival of Monsters*). This leads naturally to the archery contest, where the Doctor's display gets the attention of the Sheriff and leads to the capture of him, Clara and Robin – but only after Robin has lopped an arm off one of the Sheriff's knights, revealing them to be well-disguised robots able to fire laser bolts from their faces. In the Sheriff's castle, Clara confronts the villain while the Doctor and Robin investigate and discover the damaged spaceship that brought the robots to Earth. The straightforward plot development is redolent of many classic series stories, particularly with elements like the workforce of conscripted peasants melting down the stolen gold and constructing some kind of circuit for the ship, and whom the Doctor has to rouse into rebelling against the robots. Among these peasants he encounters a young woman, coyly credited only as "Quayle's ward," who turns out to be Robin's lost love, Marian.

Tom Riley's portrayal of Robin dances dangerously close to pantomime at times, particularly in the first half, as he constantly irritates the Doctor by laughing at anything and everything. But he and Peter Capaldi put together some excellent comic sequences, my favourite being the scene in the dungeon cell when they are chained up and successfully employ the old "distract the guard, knock him out and steal his keys" trick – only for their squabbling to result in the keys disappearing through a grate in the floor ("Well, there is a bright side... Clara didn't see that"). He also handles the swordfighting and other physical derring-do with appropriate panache, and as the episode progresses he gradually shows more depth in Robin's character as he begins to fully understand the situation. The first hint of something more than the laughing rogue comes in an early scene with Clara when Robin lays out his background as an exiled nobleman and his life with Marian (helpful exposition for those in the audience not familiar with the Robin Hood folklore), where Riley allows some seriousness to come through, showing Robin's pain at having to live as an outlaw.

Even better is the scene back at his camp after he has rescued Clara from the castle; confused and angry after the Doctor's accusation that he is just another robot, and not real at all, Robin shows some genuine menace as he demands that she tell him what she knows, determined not to be anyone's tool.

The production of the episode, under new director Paul Murphy, lives up to the BBC's usual standard of excellence with period pieces. The dissolve from the TARDIS interior to the materialisation in Sherwood Forest is a magical moment, the sunlit exteriors of the forest and the castle courtyard provide an excellent change from the dark palettes of the previous two episodes, and the robot knights are a very sleek and impressive design. When the Doctor finally discovers the camouflaged spaceship (with, amusingly, almost a sense of relief – "At last, something real… no more fairytales"), it's a striking, minimalist set with flat grey walls and unfussy open spaces that contrast nicely with the castle interiors. It's also at this point that the Doctor finally becomes aware of the season arc plot that's been bubbling away without his knowledge – there's no appearance of the mysterious "Missy" this week, but he does find a mention of "the Promised Land" (as in *Deep Breath*) as the ship's destination. The databanks also apparently contain records of all the dramatizations of the Robin Hood legend over the centuries, reinforcing the Doctor's belief that Robin cannot be real. A droll touch in the torrent of rapid-fire images is a still of Patrick Troughton as Robin from a TV adaptation made in 1953, more than a decade before his own stint in the role of the Doctor.

It's a great episode for Jenna Coleman, and not only because she gets to show again how well period costume suits her. With the Doctor distracted by his bickering with Robin, Clara takes charge of the situation, and it's no surprise that in the prison cell, she gets picked out as the leader of the trio. Coleman also does very well with Clara's scenes opposite the Sheriff, playing along with the man and extracting the story of his encounters with the robots and their ship. Ben Miller too gives a fine performance, playing it straight and presenting the Sheriff as an intelligent, powerful opponent, rather than an exaggerated, moustache-twirling villain. His ambitions may be comically small-scale compared to the normal run of *Doctor Who* adversaries ("For Nottingham is not enough… After this, Derby! … Then, Lincoln!"), but Miller judges very well when to let a sudden outburst of anger break through the smooth, urbane surface, reminding both Clara and the audience that this man is indeed dangerous.

Regrettably, the broadcast of this episode was affected by recent murders in the Middle East and in London, which induced the production team to cut out a sizeable section from the climactic fight in which Robin would have chopped the Sheriff's head off – only for the man to reveal that he has been turned into a cyborg himself by the robots, nonchalantly reattach his head and continue the fight. In the circumstances, the reluctance to show a comic beheading is understandable, but it's unfortunate that the crux of the plot – that it's the Sheriff, not Robin, who is the real "robot of Sherwood" – is obscured in the edited version. Nevertheless, the excision was deft enough that it's difficult to tell there is anything missing; in fact, it could even be argued that the climax benefits from being tightened up in this way.

Gatiss uses the presence of Robin to continue the work of the previous two episodes in exploring facets of the new Doctor's character. He no longer has any patience with the sort of banter that his previous self would have enjoyed, and finds himself most uncomfortable with the idea that someone like Robin could actually exist:

Clara: "When did you stop believing in anything?"
The Doctor: "When did you start believing in impossible heroes?"
Clara: "Don't you know?"

In all three episodes so far, this Doctor has faced a character that reflects some aspect of himself, and here his first response is to reject the likeness that Clara sees between him and Robin. He automatically assumes that Robin and his men represent some kind of disruption in history that he must correct, and yet he can't find anything to back up his instinctive reaction. I enjoyed the way the story keeps the Doctor off balance; it's been quite a while since we've seen him so completely in the dark as he is here. The modern *Who* series, with its focus on telling most of its stories in 45 minutes, is simply not able to devote as much time as the classic series did to showing the Doctor in scientist or explorer mode – investigating a strange situation, forming theories and testing them. It's all the more pleasing, then, when such an instance does come along, even though in this case he is not successful at solving the mystery of Robin. Because the big twist is that there is no twist: in spite of the pun in the episode's title, Robin turns out to be exactly what he claims to be. The Doctor (like us) has no choice but to accept the fact that, just this once, reality is living up to the folktale – even as his baffled frustration ("He's a legend!") signals the perfectly timed arrival of the hero, with Clara at his side, for his final battle with the villain.

The climactic action is not the strongest part of the story. The Doctor leads the peasants to easily defeat the robots by reflecting their lasers back at them – a resolution that trivialises the previously powerful creatures and makes them look ridiculous. Then he and Clara have nothing to do but look on as Robin and the Sheriff duel, although the way in which Robin's final defeat of the Sheriff refers back to his fight with the Doctor at the river crossing is clever. Once the foe is dispatched, the only remaining problem is the ship itself, which takes off but is too damaged to reach orbit, meaning its imminent explosion will cause devastation. The plotting descends to the same children's TV level that marred the conclusion of the previous episode as, given that the ship is powered by the golden circuitry, somehow shooting the golden arrow into the side of the ship enables it to fly high enough to self-destruct safely. The cuteness of this ending, successfully weaving together all the elements of the story, is in inverse proportion to its believability, although Gatiss deserves some points for constructing a climax that requires the combined efforts of the Doctor, Clara and Robin – thanks to Robin's arm being injured in his duel with the Sheriff, they have to help him draw back his bowstring to fire the arrow.

Fortunately, the reflective final scene is much more satisfying. Even though he might not want to admit it, a streak of Robin Hood-style uncynical heroism has always been an essential part of the Doctor's character. The heart of the story is the Doctor's journey from dismissing Robin as a "silly story" to finally accepting him, and thereby getting back in touch with a part of himself that seemed to have gone missing after his regeneration. Their final talk certainly wins no awards for subtlety, with Robin (having been told the truth about the Doctor by Clara) making the parallel between the nobleman and the Time Lord in an extremely on-the-nose fashion. Nevertheless, it ensures that they part on good terms, and the Doctor's farewell gift of reuniting Robin with Marian (although it's probably best not to wonder just how long she was standing there behind the TARDIS in silence, waiting for it to disappear) signals that he too is ready to be a hero again.

31

Classic Who DVD Recommendation: 1983's *The King's Demons*, starring Peter Davison, with Janet Fielding and Mark Strickson, is set just a few years later, in the time of King John, and also features a humanoid robot at the centre of the plot. What's more, the Master as played by Anthony Ainley bears more than a passing resemblance to Ben Miller's Sheriff here.

Reflections: This fun and frothy episode is clearly the most deliberately comedic of Peter Capaldi's first season. It was well positioned between the severe *Into the Dalek* and the creepiness of *Listen*, providing some much needed lightening of tone. However, Capaldi's Doctor remains rather strait-laced, entering into the humour only reluctantly and confining himself mainly to sarcastic ripostes to Clara and Robin. This snarkiness would continue throughout the season; rather like Jon Pertwee's Doctor (which his appearance harks back to), it's really only in his second year that his initially grumpy persona would loosen up and become amenable to more relaxed comic repartee.

As mentioned above, it's a very traditional-feeling story, even down to a quasi-romantic bond between the companion and the principal guest character – a frequently occurring element in the classic series, which even had several cases of companions departing as a result of a whirlwind infatuation with a man they had only just met. The rise in the 1990's, after the classic series had ended, of serialised storytelling in long-running science fiction shows (major examples being *Star Trek: Deep Space Nine*, *Babylon 5*, and *The X-Files*) made it increasingly untenable for a modern series to expect its audience to believe in a deeply felt relationship that lasted only one episode and was forgotten the next week. This created a particular problem for *Doctor Who* when it returned in 2005, since the essence of the show is constantly varying its stories' locales and secondary characters. It was inevitable, therefore, that modern *Who* would concentrate on making full use of its only continuing elements – exploring the relationship between the companion and the Doctor, and giving the companion a properly developed home life which changed as a result of their experiences. So an episode like this feels very much like a throwback, even though Clara's regard for Robin (possibly transferring some of her feelings towards the previous Doctor), which might have turned into a full-on romance had this episode been made for the classic series, is restricted to the schoolgirl crush level. And, of course, it would not have worked at all had the episode been placed any later in the season, after Clara had become fully involved with Danny Pink.

The historical episodes of 21st-century *Doctor Who* have tended to construct their depictions of their subjects on the theory that an accurate and complete portrait is not the primary aim; the preference is to show a famous person from history in accordance with the pre-existing impression of them in the general popular consciousness (see, for example, the caricatured Churchill in *Victory of the Daleks*). That tendency is taken to an extreme here: it is quite certain that Robin Hood, even assuming he existed at all, would have had very little in common with this Hollywood version. The Doctor exasperatedly says, "Perfect eyes, perfect teeth... nobody has a jawline like that!" – and yet the episode confounds him by brazenly insisting that no, this is how it *really* was. Robin's fourth-wall-breaking wink at the audience in the final scene ("And remember, Doctor, I'm just as real as you are") shows how Gatiss is deliberately making use of the contradiction, daring the viewers not to suspend their disbelief by reminding them that everything they have seen is, after all, a constructed story. (In next season's *Sleep No More*, he would go on to play more games with the audience, in an even more extreme fashion.) In this way, *Robot of Sherwood* could be considered the ultimate development of the modern *Who* "celebrity historical" – as Robin says, "History is a burden... Stories can make us fly."

4: Listen

Writer: Steven Moffat
Director: Douglas Mackinnon
Originally Broadcast: 13 September 2014

Cast

The Doctor: Peter Capaldi
Clara: Jenna Coleman
Danny Pink/Orson Pink: Samuel Anderson
Rupert Pink: Remi Gooding
Reg: Robert Goodman
Figure: Kiran Shah

Since taking over *Doctor Who* in 2010, Steven Moffat has been preoccupied with writing the big, blockbusting episodes – season openers, finales, Christmas specials, and so on – often centred around major turning points in the Doctor's life. For the 2014 season, he deliberately reserved a slot in the schedule where he could tell a small-scale story focusing on the kind of creepiness he displayed during the Russell T Davies era, with acclaimed episodes like *The Empty Child* (2005) and *Blink* (2007). Rather than simply duplicate his past successes, though, *Listen* brilliantly combines the two approaches with a highly innovative story structure, mixing unnerving ideas and a slowly developing mystery that reveals a part of the Doctor's life we have never seen before, to produce the best episode of the season so far.

Right from the start it is apparent that this is going to be an unusual episode, as the opening shot shows the Doctor sitting cross-legged and meditating on the roof of the TARDIS as it floats in space, before he suddenly opens his eyes, looks straight at us and fiercely whispers, "Listen!" The single-word story title will recur at a number of important moments throughout, the first one being at the end of the pre-titles teaser that consists entirely of the Doctor talking to himself, making notes on his blackboard and setting out the premise of the story. His informal appearance, with a simple pullover and jacket replacing his more tailored costume of previous episodes, tells us this is a day off for him – for once he is pursuing his own interests, rather than randomly arriving somewhere and getting swept up in other peoples' concerns. He is mulling over the concept of a race of creatures capable of "perfect hiding" – creatures that are constantly near us but never leave any real evidence of their presence. If such a creature existed, how could it be detected? Capaldi spins a compelling soliloquy as he shows the Doctor intrigued by the idea of a creature that cannot even be sensed ("except in those moments when, for no clear reason, you choose to speak aloud…") and wonders what it would do. He is answered when he notices a message has been chalked on his blackboard: the single word, *LISTEN* – the first of many delicious moments where this episode conjures an unsettling atmosphere from the simplest of means.

As usual, he decides he needs Clara with him while he explores this intriguing idea. Since her "impossible girl" mystery was resolved last season, Clara has really blossomed as a character, and Jenna Coleman has been given a much greater range of material to play. Clara is still striving to keep the two strands of her life separate, and part of the enjoyment of this episode is the way the weirdness of her adventure with the Doctor becomes intimately interwoven with her disastrous first date with Danny Pink. Coleman and Samuel Anderson have fun portraying these two people who are obviously attracted to each other, as shown in an unguarded moment when they are relaxed and laughing at their shared experiences at work, but who keep tripping themselves up thanks to mutual edginess. In Clara's case, as she will later admit, "I mouth off when I'm nervous… Seriously, it's got a mind of its own." Danny is extremely touchy about his soldiering past, which evidently contains some painful memories we haven't yet seen, and a passing joke from Clara implying he might be quick to kill provokes an angry flare-up about the work he has done providing humanitarian aid. In turn, she is offended by his dismissive reference to "people like you" making assumptions about him, and storms off. The date and its aftermath are told in Moffat's characteristic quick-fire mix of flashback and real-time scenes, which helps to make a fairly standard dramatic situation (albeit one new for *Doctor Who*) fresh and interesting.

Back home, Clara is surprised to find the TARDIS parked in her bedroom. The last time the Doctor landed in his companion's bedroom was back in 2010's *Flesh and Stone*, when Matt Smith's incarnation found himself hastily fending off Amy's confident advances. Here, there's absolutely no sexual suggestion in the atmosphere at all; the Doctor impatiently dismisses Clara's dating woes as he bustles her into the TARDIS. "I haven't actually said yes," she says, mostly to herself – but by then she's already inside, and soon caught up as usual in pursuit of a new adventure with the Doctor. I could do without the repeated jabs at Clara's weight and appearance, though; almost from the beginning Capaldi's Doctor was tossing disparaging comments at Clara, but in *Deep Breath* they could be considered part of the usual disorientation that follows a regeneration. Their continued use, however, both in *Into the Dalek* and here, indicates a more permanent change in the Doctor. Derogatory remarks about her makeup, or the shape of her face or eyes, are obviously intended as humour (and sometimes even work in that regard), but they would be very unpalatable if they were not so patently ridiculous (due only to Clara being played by the obviously attractive Coleman) – and if Clara didn't let them just wash over her without any reaction, or occasionally respond in kind. The goal is clearly to establish a contrast with the previous Doctor's relationship to her, but I think the point has now been quite sufficiently underlined.

The Doctor being in full-on investigation mode, driving the story from the start, provides a showcase for Peter Capaldi. He is full of energy as he shows Clara how he has been looking through records of dreams (or *are* they dreams?) recurring throughout history in search of his "perfect hiding" creatures. The startling image of a hand reaching out from under a bed to grab an unwary ankle is a wonderfully spine-tingling idea that anyone in the audience can relate to – and an excellent new twist on the "monster under the bed" concept Moffat previously employed to great effect in 2006's *The Girl in the Fireplace*. When Clara admits that she had that dream when she was a child, he links her to the TARDIS's telepathic interface in order to navigate to that time and place, and is grinning with almost disturbing intensity at the prospect of finding out "what's under your bed." Moffat's virtuosity is on full show, as he constructs a plot that will jump through an assortment of wildly contrasting settings, and yet manages to link them together with clockwork precision. A post-date phone call from Danny distracts Clara at a crucial moment, causing the TARDIS to land in his childhood rather than hers, at a gloomy children's home in the 1990's where a lonely boy called Rupert ("It's a stupid name... I'm going to change it") has been scared by a dream.

Clara's experience working with children enables her to quickly establish a rapport with Rupert (an excellent, believable performance by first-time child actor Remi Gooding), and soon they are both scrambling under his bed, as she demonstrates to him that there's nothing to fear. Except that there is: without warning, the bed above them creaks as something climbs onto it. It's an unnervingly still figure hiding under the bedspread, which could be simply one of the other children in the home trying to scare Rupert as a prank – or, just possibly, an alien creature of unknown power that should never be seen, now accidentally cornered. When the Doctor turns up, he too treats the thing on the bed seriously, even as he indulges in antics like pretended disappointment at learning that not every book is a *Where's Wally* book ("Really? Well, that's a few years of my life I'll be needing back"), and delivers an earnest speech reassuring Rupert that being scared is good ("scared is a super power. It's *your* super power") in an engagingly silly manner calculated to gain the boy's trust, so that he will be willing to turn his back on the unknown figure, and let it go in peace.

The central uncertainty about the nature of what the Doctor is pursuing is at the heart of the story. Does the "perfect hiding" creature he postulates actually exist, or is the whole thing a chimera, based ultimately on fear of the unknown? The marvellously original idea of having a "monster" that cannot be shown or heard presents a tough challenge for director Douglas Mackinnon. Every strange manifestation the Doctor and Clara encounter has to support both possible interpretations. Mackinnon mostly succeeds at this careful balancing act, although he does add an unjustified flash of light when the figure disappears from Rupert's bedroom, which interferes with the ambiguity the script is trying to achieve. There are also a few odd, non-naturalistic touches in the storytelling. Some are just harmless quirks, like the Doctor's ability to silently vanish in an instant while Reg the caretaker has his back turned, or his appearing in Rupert's room just as suddenly. But the disappearing coffee ring on Reg's desk, which simply fades away in plain sight while the man looks on, is a bit of unnecessary weirdness for its own sake. Nevertheless, the whole sequence in the spooky old building is well told, with the tension relaxing after the crisis is over as Clara helps the boy place a ring of plastic toy soldiers protectively around his bed. Given who Rupert will grow up to become, it's not surprising that he says "Dan" when she asks what they should call the chief soldier, to Clara's consternation. Fortunately for her, the Doctor brings the scene to an end by putting Rupert to sleep with the touch of one finger to the boy's forehead, recalling an ability displayed by Sylvester McCoy's Doctor in *Survival*

(1989). His passing it off as "Dad skills" is both a funny punchline and a useful reminder of how much of his background remains a mystery – hidden preparation for the ending of the episode.

Clara's expression when she realises that, thanks to her and the Doctor's visit, Rupert will grow up to become "Dan the soldier man" is hilarious. She asks the Doctor for a favour… and so a (slightly) older and wiser Clara returns to the restaurant and tries to patch things up with Danny from the point where her earlier self had left off. But the date is destined to remain a disaster; after accidentally dropping Rupert's name into the conversation, she is unable to recover – and is certainly not helped by the surreal appearance of a spacesuited figure in a corner of the restaurant beckoning to her. This time, it's Danny who gets upset ("I don't do weird") and walks out. An angry Clara stalks back into the TARDIS in pursuit of the spacesuited man, only to find herself confronting a characteristic Moffat surprise. While she was with Danny, the Doctor (using her telepathic connection with the TARDIS) extrapolated her timeline into the future, and has brought back her and Danny's descendant, Colonel Orson Pink – a pioneer time traveller from the 22nd century whose experimental ship malfunctioned (an echo of a plot strand in 2013's *Hide*) and left him marooned at the end of the universe. I'm in two minds about having Samuel Anderson play Orson as well as Danny. On the one hand it provides a moment of instant recognition (and confusion) as he takes off the spacesuit helmet. On the other, it's a serious challenge to believability; as Anderson plays them, they are so similar that the unavoidable impression is of Danny dressed up in a rather unconvincing wig.

The canvas of the story widens hugely, even while it remains focused on just three characters, as the Doctor takes them back to the farthest future, to Orson's crashed time-ship (which, in a clever piece of set design, has its walls studded with round lighting features that echo those in the TARDIS). This location is essential to continuing the Doctor's quest; he wonders if after all other life has ended, the shadowy creatures he is pursuing might finally show themselves. The script exhibits a weakness here, though, by not bothering to provide any kind of justification for Orson's ship, which had only been intended to make a short, exploratory journey, ending up somewhere even the TARDIS would normally have difficulty reaching. (To play armchair script editor for a moment, perhaps a line could have been included explaining how the ship – built by humans unfamiliar with the hazards of time travel – became trapped in some kind of self-perpetuating instability, a cycle that kept repeatedly kicking it forwards in time, until it could literally go no further. A small amount of hand-waving like that would have been enough to paper over the plot hole.) Nevertheless, this sequence is even more successfully creepy than the earlier scenes in the children's home. The Doctor again exclaims "Listen!" – drawing attention to the complete silence at the end of everything. He tells a transparent lie about the TARDIS needing to recharge so they have to spend a night here, to Orson's dismay. Despite a show of bravery, the man is just as jittery about the dark and the unknown as the boy, Rupert. When Clara leads him into the TARDIS to wait in safety, she discovers that Orson carries with him the little plastic chief toy soldier – now a family heirloom. She tries to lighten the mood with a joke ("Take my advice... when you get home, stay away from time travel"), but as he gives her the toy, they both recognise the connection between them.

Appropriately for an episode called *Listen*, sound design has a crucial part to play. As in the children's home, the sequence of the Doctor and Clara waiting in the darkened time-ship foregoes the show's usual lavish incidental music in favour of long stretches of silence or spooky ambient noises, to excellent effect. The essential uncertainty about the existence of the Doctor's hypothesised creatures is carefully maintained amid various scratching and hissing noises that might or might not be mechanical in nature. A loud, repetitive knocking starts – but, as the Doctor points out, it could just be an effect of the hull cooling in the night. The tension is as extreme as in 2008's *Midnight*, except that in that episode there was no doubt that *something* was outside, trying to get in. Here, though, they are not trapped – at any point, they can simply get in the TARDIS and leave. But the Doctor refuses to go; his need for information and knowledge has always been a central characteristic, and the prospect of finally getting a definitive answer to the mystery holds him there, even after Clara cracks and he angrily orders her back into the TARDIS. Thanks to a highly convenient (for the writer) failure of the scanner screen, she and Orson are unable to see what happens at the crisis, when the Doctor faces the opening airlock of the ship. He is found unconscious – either from an attack, or from flying debris. Clara quickly takes the TARDIS away from there, meaning the truth of what happened will never be revealed; it seems like the story can go no further, with fear of the unknown having triumphed.

But now comes the totally unexpected twist as, thanks again to Clara's link with the TARDIS (it's not spelled out, but we must presume that, as with Danny's phone call, the Doctor's sudden lurch and gasp while Clara is connected to the console provides the distraction that diverts them here), they arrive in a dimly lit, nondescript barn where another young boy is quietly sobbing, afraid of the dark. This is not somewhere the TARDIS is ever supposed to be, but as the Doctor confessed earlier, they only got to the end of the universe because "some idiot turned the safeguards off." Hiding under the boy's bed as a couple of adults enter, Clara overhears a comment about how he'll "never make a Time Lord" – and her horrified realisation that she is in the Doctor's own childhood is superbly played. No doubt some will be aghast at Moffat pulling back the curtain on a part of the Doctor's past that has always been (and, for the most part, should remain) shrouded in mystery, but for me it was worth it for the jaw-dropping revelation of the significance of that random barn that John Hurt's Doctor found in 2013's Fiftieth Anniversary special, *The Day of the Doctor*. As the Doctor in the TARDIS starts awake (with a fan-pleasing cry of "Sontarans, perverting the course of human history!" – Tom Baker's first line as the Doctor nearly forty years earlier), Clara knows she has to do something to stop him from interfering with his own past. Instinctively, she reaches out from under the bed to grab the boy's ankle as he stands up – and her quick thinking, persuading him that this is all just a dream, and that he should go back to bed, turns the whole story into one of Moffat's patented loops of cause and effect.

As usual with Moffat's best scripts, many lines or scenes echo or mirror each other to bind a deliberately disjointed collection of story pieces into a cohesive whole. Both Rupert and the Doctor must make a promise *not* to investigate something. The Doctor's "Do as you're told" to Clara in the time-ship is reflected back at him when she has to convince him, without telling him why, to take off from the barn without looking at where they've been. Fear, and how to react to it, has run through the whole story, from the Doctor's universe-spanning quest to the mundanity of Clara and Danny's first date. And everything comes together in a final monologue from Clara, which begins (how else?) with the word, "Listen…" Having successfully kept the Doctor's timeline intact, Clara goes to leave – but cannot help being drawn back by the boy's continued crying. She comforts him with words inspired by those she had earlier heard the Doctor himself telling Rupert. Murray Gold's music comes to the fore in this ending sequence; a steadily unfolding string melody underpins Clara's words, with gentle harmony changes marking each stage of the final montage. "Fear is like... a constant companion, always there," she says, and all the characters are rewarded for coming to terms with their fears: Orson gets to return home, Clara and Danny finally share a kiss, and the Doctor, with satisfaction, underlines *LISTEN* on his blackboard, giving a sense of "mission accomplished." Whether or not he ever realises that his "monster under the bed" all those years ago was Clara herself – fittingly, the ending remains ambiguous on this point – the important message that it's OK to be scared strikes home. As the little toy soldier completes its journey – from Rupert, to Orson, to Clara, to be left with the young Doctor – what threatened to be just a shaggy dog story turns into something truly exceptional.

Classic Who DVD Recommendation: A difficult decision, since there really isn't a story like this anywhere in the classic series, but I've decided to go with the first *Doctor Who* story ever shown, 1963's *An Unearthly Child*. The introductory episode is justly famous, but the following three, where William Hartnell's original Doctor and his companions are stuck in the Stone Age and desperately trying to escape, are often unfairly dismissed. They do, however, feature the very first occasion when the Doctor shows empathy towards his human fellow travellers, a moment which also provides *Listen* with its evocative final line: "Fear makes companions of us all."

Reflections: As can be gathered from the above review, for me *Listen* is Moffat on top form, packed with original ideas and intricate technique, but also with a very satisfying emotional core underneath all the surface fizz. It looks forward to his episodes at the climax of the next season: *Heaven Sent* will take the idea of the Doctor monologuing and investigating on his own to the limit, not to mention drawing central plot elements from the Doctor's past and letting the music carry the story during critical sequences. Then, *Hell Bent* will revisit both the barn and the end of the universe, and will also restrict the greater part of its storytelling to just the regular characters. It's not perfect, of course; I've already mentioned the plot hole of Orson Pink's over-contrived arrival at the end of the universe. Another such issue is that while the story thoroughly explains where the Doctor's dream came from, it offers no hint as to how other people all through history have come to have the same dream. (Interestingly, the leaked dubbing script of this episode reveals that the intention was to have voiceover lines from Clara – copies of her "This is just a dream" from the final sequence – during the earlier montage, implying that their dreams did originate from the Doctor somehow. Dropping this must have been a late decision, but a good one; it doesn't really address the objection and would just have been confusing.)

As for Orson himself, after one fleeting reference in *The Caretaker* he is never mentioned again, and his very existence becomes problematic in the light of Danny's fate at the end of this season. But Moffat always places more importance on making each of his episodes as effective as possible in its own right. In *Listen*, the story requires Danny and Clara to have descendants; in *Dark Water* and *Death in Heaven*, the story requires Danny to die and stay dead. The inconsistency that emerges when the season is considered as a larger whole is of less concern to him (as is apparent in this case by the fact that in the latter story, Orson is not even brought up in the Doctor and Clara's confrontation over Danny's death). This treating of season-arc plotting as a lesser priority (which is hardly new; see the entire Matt Smith era and its only partially successful tying up in *The Time of the Doctor*) flies in the face of the usual practice of current science fiction series, and has led to some criticism of Moffat within the hard-core fandom. However, I think that as long as *Doctor Who* retains its paradoxical status as a sci-fi show aimed primarily at a large audience of general viewers who tend not to watch every episode (as is certainly the case in its home country), its structure as a string of separate and more or less self-contained stories is inevitable and right. Still, in this particular case, the discrepancy is such that I wish that the season finale had at least acknowledged it, even if just to wave it away with a bit of "time can be rewritten" dialogue.

Other negative reactions came from those who felt that Clara was threatening to take over the show. After preserving the Doctor's entire timeline in 2013, she now turns out to be part of a crucial formative experience of the Doctor's childhood, and future episodes of this season would dwell heavily on her relationship with the Doctor and its effect on her. However, I think the impression of "Clara overload" is largely a product of her involvement in two quite separate storylines. After *The Name of the Doctor*, a line seemed to be drawn under the whole "impossible girl" business with Matt Smith's Doctor, and it has rarely been even alluded to since; one could easily envisage an entirely new companion being introduced (as a teacher at Coal Hill School) to fill Clara's place alongside Capaldi's Doctor and go through similar experiences. But it is hard to imagine the character arc Clara goes through in this season and the next being better handled than by Jenna Coleman; I can only be glad that such a fine actor ended up staying with *Doctor Who* for a year longer than she originally planned.

Meanwhile, the Doctor's personality continues to evolve. Fortunately, the worst of the grating snipes at Clara's appearance are now past; from now on, they will tend more towards standard comic banter (see, for example, his failure to notice her dressed-up look in the next episode). The avuncular connection he develops with Rupert is the first crack in his dour facade, looking forward to the more relaxed persona he will develop next season. And Clara rewarding him with a big hug – and his "No, not the hugging!" reaction – is a laugh-out-loud moment perfectly placed to lighten the emotional final sequence. Given the stormy weather their relationship will soon be travelling through, it's reassuring to keep in mind that they can be, after all, good friends.

5: Time Heist

Writers: Steve Thompson & Steven Moffat
Director: Douglas Mackinnon
Originally Broadcast: 20 September 2014

Cast

The Doctor: Peter Capaldi
Clara: Jenna Coleman
Ms Delphox: Keeley Hawes
Psi: Jonathan Bailey
Saibra: Pippa Bennett-Warner
Guard: Mark Ebulue
Mr Porrima: Trevor Sellers
Suited Customer: Junior Laniyan
The Teller: Ross Mullan

Over the last couple of seasons, Steve Thompson has established himself as a specialist in producing harmless filler episodes. *Time Heist*, co-written with showrunner Steven Moffat, is another example of the type, but it's distinctly superior to Thompson's previous efforts, avoiding both the overwrought melodrama of 2011's *The Curse of the Black Spot* and the reset-button ending of 2013's *Journey to the Centre of the TARDIS*. With a nicely twisty plot that hangs together well, it provides a pleasant way to spend an hour in the company of the Doctor and Clara.

Not for a long while has there been an episode with so little connection to any ongoing plot threads. Together with the complete absence of the "fairytale" tone that has tended to characterise the Moffat era (albeit less so this season), this gives the opening a very refreshing feel, as the Doctor and Clara are pitchforked straight into the adventure. We open in Clara's flat, as she is getting dressed to go on a date while the Doctor tries to convince her to come with him for a trip in the TARDIS. The police box phone rings, the Doctor picks it up – and without warning they suddenly find themselves in a far future environment, their memories of recent events erased thanks to making contact with a couple of the "memory worm" creatures first seen in 2012's Christmas special, *The Snowmen*. Seated at a table with them are a couple of new associates – a cybernetically augmented human named Psi and a shape-shifter called Saibra (a "mutant human," who involuntarily assumes the appearance of anyone she touches). All four of them, it seems, have willingly agreed to break into the ultra-secure Bank of Karabraxos, the repository of the galaxy's greatest treasures, for reasons known only to the mysterious "Architect" who gives them their instructions by means of a high-tech briefcase which opens with a strange golden glow – a passing nod to a similarly enigmatic case in Tarantino's *Pulp Fiction*.

There's a nice sense of urgency created from the outset, with the team under immediate threat of capture from the bank's security guards even as they are introducing themselves. They have to scramble to get away, while sizing each other up at the same time. (Meanwhile, some necessary exposition is deftly taken care of in an amusing moment when Ms Delphox, the bank's head of security, has to re-introduce herself to the guard captain, and hence us, due to the guard's memory accidentally getting wiped by the worm.) They quickly conclude that their only viable course of action is to follow the path laid down for them by the Architect and carry out the robbery using the items left for them in the briefcase: a data chip that provides Psi with information about the layout of the bank, and a DNA sample that Saibra can use to assume the appearance of a legitimate customer. As they travel down their pre-programmed path, they find other briefcases left by the Architect containing further equipment and information. The obvious question – if the Architect could sneak in to plant the cases, why couldn't he rob the bank himself at the same time? – is raised, but will not be answered until the last piece of the jigsaw-puzzle plot is revealed. The Doctor is more intrigued, though, by the question of *why* they would all have agreed to become bank robbers for the Architect, concluding that there must be treasures within the vault that have a special meaning for each of them: "Picture the thing you want most in the universe, and decide how badly you want it."

Director Douglas Mackinnon has fun indulging in various eye-catching wipes and dissolves to transition between scenes, along with all the usual motifs of caper movies and TV shows – like the ostentatious slow-motion shot of the team striding purposefully into the bank lobby, accompanied by jazzy, up-tempo music. The main floor of the bank is an impressively large and opulent space, matching the striking CGI shots of its imposing pyramidal exterior. The actual mechanics of the heist are plausible enough and sufficiently intricate to maintain the viewer's interest, with a sci-fi "dimensional shift bomb" providing a neat way for them to penetrate to the service levels of the bank. Unfortunately, the pace does flag a little in the middle, with too much running up and down a series of bland corridors which are all too clearly the same set reused – an attempt to disguise the cost saving through the use of lighting of different colours is entirely unsuccessful. Other parts of the lower levels are represented by one of *Doctor Who*'s standard industrial environments (a power station, in this case), and the location and the corridor sets look and feel different enough that the switching between them undermines the believability of the setting – a rare let-down in the production design department, which is usually impeccable on *Who*. Another flaw is that the security guards that initially seem so menacing quickly become unimportant; they never seem to come even close to catching the Doctor's team, and some of the pressure our heroes should be feeling as they are forced to keep progressing towards an unknown objective is missing.

For a story about a bank robbery to really be at home in *Doctor Who*, it needs an element of the monstrous, which is provided by the bizarre-looking Teller, the bank's principal defender. This massive creature, looking like a cross between a minotaur and a giant slug, with eyes at the ends of huge stalks at the sides of its head, is an excellent combination of costume and animatronics. Its deadly telepathic abilities are established in a long scene when the team first enter the bank lobby; they witness it detect the guilty thoughts of another hapless visitor and liquefy the miscreant's brain (and the visual effect of the victim's head looking like a deflated football afterwards is a genuinely disturbing image). The Teller's power to psychically fasten on to the memories of its victims provides a neat justification for the Architect keeping his team so entirely in the dark, and its outfit – a prisoner-orange straitjacket, sometimes with leashes held by a couple of guards – reinforces the impression of a violent and dangerous beast. But there's a certain lugubrious quality to its appearance, too, which nicely defuses its menace once it becomes apparent, at the episode's conclusion, that the creature is acting under duress.

Rather conveniently, in the course of evading the guards the Doctor accidentally leads his team into the room where the Teller is resting in its hibernation cubicle. As he peers through the glass wall and the creature suddenly lunges at him, it's like a fleeting homage to the memorable 2009 *Torchwood* mini-series *Children of Earth*, when Capaldi's character John Frobisher had the task of facing up to an even more unnerving alien, looming over him in a similar fog-filled glass cage. Compared to last week's deep exploration of the Doctor, this episode is relatively superficial, although he once again stays firmly in charge throughout (as he says, "That's *my* special power"), and Capaldi shows the Doctor's thirst for knowledge when he first sees the Teller and realises he doesn't know what it is ("I *hate* not knowing"). As in *Into the Dalek*, he has to deal with the loss of a member of his team, when Saibra is trapped and held by the creature. The only way he can help her avoid the agonising living death of the Teller's victims is to give her one of the items apparently left by the Architect as their "exit strategy" in case of failure – an "atomic shredder" which will destroy her instantly. Saibra's parting shot can't help but trigger memories of the earlier episode:

Saibra: "When you meet the Architect, promise me something. Kill him."
The Doctor: "I hate him, but I can't make that promise."
Saibra: "Oh, a *good* man. I left it late to meet one of those."

But in contrast to his completely indifferent attitude in *Into the Dalek*, he is clearly affected by what happened to Saibra, even if he immediately refocuses on the task at hand, prompting Psi to berate him for his "professional detachment." When Clara tries to calm the situation, Psi sarcastically congratulates her for being "really good at the excuses" for him – an accusation that clearly strikes home. Apart from that moment, though, Clara is mostly stuck in generic companion mode this week; with no special abilities to bring to the team, she has nothing to do but tag along and ask questions. She does seem to form something of a rapport with Psi, sympathising as the young hacker tells her about the holes in his memories which were self-inflicted to protect his family and friends from discovery during a prison interrogation. It was obviously never going to really lead anywhere, given that this adventure is just a momentary interruption in her continuing relationship with Danny Pink (who is seen only briefly at the beginning here but, judging from the preview of next week's episode, is about to assume prominence again); however, the connection between them is enough that Psi is willing to sacrifice himself to save Clara from the Teller. Jonathan Bailey manages to imbue a mostly purely functional character with some emotional depth in his final moments, letting the creature corner him and then using a shredder just as Saibra did.

47

It looks as though the Doctor and Clara have failed: there is still one last lock to the bank vault that Psi could not open. But then the true ingenuity of the Architect is revealed, as a solar storm erupts, disrupting the bank's systems and opening the vault. It's a pity that, as with a similar storm in 2011's *The Rebel Flesh*, what is shown on screen is so ludicrously exaggerated as to shatter the suspension of disbelief – the wave of energy striking the planet is on a scale that suggests an extinction event rather than a survivable episode of electromagnetic interference. Nevertheless, the providential arrival of this natural phenomenon to help them is enough for the Doctor to realise that the whole robbery must have been planned by someone with foreknowledge of future events ("It's not just a bank heist, it's a time travel heist!"). It also provides a clever answer to the objection (raised by the Doctor earlier) of why were they not using the TARDIS, which would make the robbery a trivial task: the storm would have prevented them from landing at the critical moment.

Within the vault, they quickly follow the Architect's directions and locate the promised rewards for Psi and Saibra – a pair of technological MacGuffins capable of restoring Psi's lost memories and allowing Saibra to escape her unwanted shape-shifting. Before they can locate their own reward in the inner "private vault," though, they are captured by the Teller and brought before Ms Delphox. However, what should be a tense confrontation turns out to be a damp squib: rather than do the sensible thing and simply have the Doctor and Clara killed by the Teller, the writers force Ms Delphox to have a Bond villain moment, walking away and leaving them in the custody of two guards – who turn out to be a disguised Psi and Saibra, not dead after all. The reversal itself is clever, but the contrivance required to set it up is made worse by an uncharacteristic lapse from Capaldi, who painfully overplays the Doctor's reaction to seeing them again. Fortunately, he is soon back under control, helped by composer Murray Gold, whose majestic theme for the Twelfth Doctor comes to the fore as the Doctor gives Psi and Saibra their rewards, allowing them to choose freely whether to leave now or stay for the final confrontation in the private vault.

The vault turns out to be occupied by the bank's director, Madame Karabraxos herself, pulling strings from a hidden sanctum just like the reclusive billionaire Max Capricorn in 2007's *Voyage of the Damned*. As the Doctor and his friends are entering, there's a sudden incongruous burst of classical music on the soundtrack – the rarely heard concert ending to the overture of Mozart's *The Abduction from the Seraglio*. Perhaps it was intended as a hidden analogy to the Teller's true circumstances, which are about to be revealed, since the opera concerns the rescue of a woman held captive in a powerful ruler's harem. However, the way the final cadence so neatly sounds just at the precise instant Karabraxos turns around to face the intruders makes the moment seem wholly artificial. (And ironically, despite the direction in the script – which simply says, "Mozart plays" – this particular passage is not real Mozart anyway; it's a makeshift appendage that was added by the opera's publisher to turn Mozart's open-ended overture into a separately performable piece.)

Guest star Keeley Hawes has played Ms Delphox throughout in a deliberately arch and somewhat over-emphasised style, the reason for which becomes clear with the revelation that she is merely a subordinate clone of the bank's director. A most accomplished actor, Hawes does what she can with a dual role that doesn't exactly exercise her full range, adopting a much more natural manner when Karabraxos finally faces the Doctor. Unfortunately, although this climactic scene successfully resolves all the outstanding questions of the plot, the way it plays out is very messy. For no good reason, they make no move to stop Karabraxos from summoning the Teller. Then, it takes a very long time for the Doctor to come to the crucial realisation – which has been obvious since the revelation that the shredders were really teleporters – that the mysterious Architect can only be himself. The journey to that realisation involves some more moments of eccentricity that are atypically overplayed by Capaldi: his bounding around the room, shouting "I *hate* the Architect!" would have been suited to the previous Doctor, but just looks odd with this one. There's also a tediously extended riff on the theme of "Shut up! Shut up, shuttety-up!" which is only included to evoke memories of Capaldi's performance as Malcolm Tucker in *The Thick of It*, his most immediate prior success before taking on the role of the Doctor. Clara, Psi and Saibra have nothing to do but look on, perplexed, as the Doctor gives Karabraxos the TARDIS phone number and lets her make an unopposed exit from the vault. Then the Teller arrives, and the Doctor's confrontation with the creature turns into a flashback that fills in the missing memories from the teaser, leading into a montage laying out all the other details of how he went about setting up the heist. Lastly, the true reason for the Teller's co-operation with Karabraxos is exposed, as one final safe door is opened to reveal its imprisoned mate.

As happened with Celia Imrie in the previous season's *The Bells of Saint John*, Hawes makes the most striking impression in her final scene as, many years later, the dying Karabraxos contacts the Doctor and starts the whole chain of events. Even under heavy ageing makeup, Hawes succeeds in bringing more depth to the character, now sincerely regretful at having kept the Teller's mate chained up and taking the opportunity the Doctor offered to redress the acts of her younger self. As the bank heist which was actually a rescue mission is concluded, the final sight of the two freed creatures lumbering off into the distance in a tranquil, empty landscape is rather amusing, but provides a sweet ending. The Doctor looks on, commenting that after all the memories the Teller was forced to endure, it will now be able to find peace in mental solitude. Despite the few little hiccups noted above, Capaldi's Doctor has become steadily more impressive, especially when (as was also the case with *Listen*) he is allowed to show some warmth and charm. He may have overdone the dour, stern demeanour in his first couple of episodes, but by the end of *Time Heist*, as he is relaxing and joking in the TARDIS with his friends, Peter Capaldi is indubitably the Doctor.

Classic Who DVD Recommendation: 1988's *The Happiness Patrol*, starring Sylvester McCoy and Sophie Aldred, also features a particularly manipulative Doctor – though in this case, bringing down a totalitarian regime rather than masterminding a bank robbery – with a female villain and a bizarre monster at the centre of the story.

Reflections: As I noted above, this is almost entirely a stand-alone episode, with very little impact on the season as a whole except for providing a bit more softening of the Doctor's character. Even the one possible connection to an outstanding plot thread turns out to be a red herring: it looks for a moment as if Karabraxos might be the unknown "woman in the shop" who gave Clara the TARDIS phone number that led to her initial meeting with the Doctor. However, Karabraxos' use of the Doctor's number turns out to be for a different reason entirely, and the mystery woman's identity would remain unrevealed until *Death in Heaven*.

Clara is still managing to keep the Doctor uninvolved in her Earth-based life, but this is the last episode where she will successfully manage that. It's amusing to see that Clara's date with Danny brings out a certain mischievous competitiveness in the Doctor, which she is happy to fall in with, telling him as she leaves not to go robbing any banks without her. More seriously, Psi's accusation about her excusing the Doctor's behaviour passes without further comment here, but is the first portent of her shift away from being the Doctor's "carer" (as *Into the Dalek* described her) to becoming more of a protégé, modelling herself on him – a shift which will end up being of fundamental importance to her fate.

To present, immediately after *Listen*, another tale involving a time-twisting web of cause and effect might seem like a weakness in the season structure. However, the two stories are sufficiently different in tone to avoid any feeling of repetition. *Listen* is very much one of a kind, propelled by the Doctor's own inner impulses until the final surprise, while *Time Heist* is a much more typical Moffat-era "timey-wimey" escapade where the Doctor has to puzzle his way through until he completes the narrative loop. There's no doubt that *Listen* is the deeper and more significant episode, but *Time Heist* has its place, too; every once in a while it's pleasant to relax with a straightforward, undemanding adventure.

6: The Caretaker

Writers: Gareth Roberts & Steven Moffat
Director: Paul Murphy
Originally Broadcast: 27 September 2014

Cast

The Doctor: Peter Capaldi
Clara: Jenna Coleman
Danny Pink: Samuel Anderson
Courtney Woods: Ellis George
Adrian: Edward Harrison
Mr Armitage: Nigel Betts
CSO Matthew: Andy Gillies
Noah: Nanya Campbell
Yashe: Joshua Warner-Campbell
Kelvin: Oliver Barry-Brook
Tobias: Ramone Morgan
Mr Woods: Winston Ellis
Mrs Woods: Gracy Goldman
Mrs Christopholou: Diana Katis
Skovox Blitzer: Jimmy Vee
Seb: Chris Addison

The Caretaker is another mostly light-hearted script from Gareth Roberts, similar to his two episodes for Matt Smith's Doctor, *The Lodger* (2010) and *Closing Time* (2011). But this time, the comedic trappings are intimately intertwined with crucial developments in the ongoing plot threads running through the season (hence another co-writer credit on this episode for Steven Moffat). Although the Doctor has an alien menace to confront and defeat, the heart of the story is the clash with Danny Pink that we have been waiting for ever since Danny first appeared, with Clara caught between them. And while there are plenty of funny lines and moments, they are balanced by important dramatic scenes as it is forcefully borne in upon Clara that she can no longer keep the two strands of her life separate.

At the beginning, though, she is still jumping between madcap escapades with the Doctor and dates with her boyfriend with only the odd unexpected suntan or seaweed-festooned dress to explain away.

The opening "edited highlights reel" of fragments of adventures provides a wonderfully breezy start to the episode, showing just how bizarre her double life has become. It also plants a small foreshadowing of later events as she and the Doctor are shown running down some dark corridors, fleeing laser bolts, the Doctor yelling that he hates soldiers. She hastily agrees with him, making it karmically appropriate that she gets back home exhausted only to find Danny knocking at the door, expecting her to join him for a morning exercise run. Afterwards, she tries to convince herself that "I've got it all under control" – which is, of course, the exact point where her carefully compartmentalised life starts to unravel. When she next walks into the TARDIS, expecting another trip, the Doctor begs off with the excuse that he has a task to do in "deep cover." She is puzzled, but figures that she'll simply have more time to spend with Danny – only to discover, to her alarm, that the Doctor has identified an alien threat in the vicinity of Coal Hill School, and has decided to deal with it without her by changing his coat and passing himself off as a substitute school caretaker.

Both Capaldi and Coleman display superb comic timing throughout. In their initial bantering in the TARDIS, the Doctor simply shrugs off her suspicions before sending her on her way with a snap of his fingers to open the doors (an idea that was used for dramatic purposes in episodes like 2008's *Forest of the Dead*, but becomes amusing here when Clara can snap *her* fingers to close them again). When Clara contrives an excuse to get away from Danny and confront the new caretaker on her own ("So you recognised me, then," he deadpans), all Roberts has to do is slightly heighten the Doctor's already established tendency to brush off Clara's concerns to produce a hilarious scene. Her control freak personality is thrown into exasperated apprehension when he refuses to give her any more than vague reassurances that the school will be safe if she will just let him do his work ("I hate you." "That's fine, that's a perfectly normal reaction") – and even more so when she later observes Danny talking to him. The sequence where she tries to unobtrusively overhear them, but gets repeatedly accosted by other staff and students wanting to talk to her, is a good set piece from director Paul Murphy, featuring lots of jumpy, handheld camera shots to convey her flustered state. Murphy's work in this episode is even more assured than his handling of the similarly comedic *Robot of Sherwood* earlier in the season.

A particularly praiseworthy aspect of this script is the way it smoothly changes gears between comedy and drama as required, without making the Doctor, Clara or Danny act completely out of character just for the sake of being funny. In the first half, Danny is mostly in the straight man role with both Clara and the Doctor, such as when the latter firmly pigeonholes him as a P.E. teacher, refusing to believe a former soldier could be a mathematics teacher – a purely comic idea here, but one that will assume dramatic weight later. But as he becomes more curious about "John Smith," Danny discovers the man is planting small electronic devices in various places around the school, and naturally starts investigating further. Meanwhile, Capaldi is taking advantage of the opportunities offered for physical as well as verbal comedy, such as the very funny moment when he fends off an advancing Clara with a broom. When he sees Clara with another teacher who bears a passing resemblance to his previous incarnation (floppy hair, bow tie and all), he automatically assumes this must be her boyfriend. He gives her his enthusiastic approval – which she imagines means he has worked out who Danny is. The misunderstanding becomes a ticking time-bomb, until it detonates at the most ill-timed moment after Danny unintentionally disrupts the Doctor's attempt to neutralise the alien menace.

The alien itself, a war robot called a Skovox Blitzer, is definitely not among the most convincing monsters the show has ever featured. As it chases people down corridors, legs scuttling like an overgrown wind-up toy, it's very hard to believe the Doctor's contention that the thing is an unstoppable killing machine that threatens the entire planet. He is clearly right when he complains later that if only he had been left alone, he could have dealt with this problem without breaking a sweat. In order to ensure we take it at least a little seriously, the script includes a gruesome sequence where a hapless policeman stumbles upon its hiding place, and it blasts him to smithereens. The ensuing lengthy close-up of a severed, charred and smoking hand is quite shocking, being so out of keeping with not just the rest of the episode but the tone of the show as a whole (it may have been allowed only because *The Caretaker* was originally shown in the UK at 8:30 p.m. – a later starting time than any previous episode of *Doctor Who*). It's a nice touch that it homes in on Coal Hill School because of the "artron emissions" from alien activity in the vicinity over the years, given that this is where the Doctor originally landed in 1963 (and revisted in 1988's *Remembrance of the Daleks*), plus his recent presence there with Clara.

Everything comes to a head at the halfway point, when the Doctor's plan to shunt the Skovox through time into the far future is ruined by Danny's interference. The moment of realisation is comically stretched out as Clara desperately tries to pass off what Danny saw as special effects from a play rehearsal, while Danny has to cope with seeing "a space thing" and jumps to the conclusion that Clara is "a space woman" ("You said you were from Blackpool") and the Doctor can only be her "space dad." The Doctor's indignation at this last finally produces some sort of payoff for his tone-deaf remarks about Clara's appearance in earlier episodes – "How can you think I'm her dad when we both look exactly the same age?" – cleverly turning a previously irritating character trait into something amusing. When he finally realises the truth about Danny, lines like "It's a mistake. You've made a boyfriend error!" could have come straight from Moffat's sitcom *Coupling* (2000-04). But while his berating of Danny is initially hilarious ("Never mind that some people are actually trying to save the planet. Oh, no. There's only room in *my* head for cross-country and the offside rule!"), his pettiness in continuing to refer to him as a P.E. teacher soon becomes not funny at all. This Doctor's visceral dislike of soldiers has been evident since *Into the Dalek*, and here, mixed with his understandable anger at now having only three days before the Skovox returns in which to devise a new plan to deal with it, it produces an entirely unreasonable sneering towards Danny. Given that in the classic series the Doctor's closest military friend, Brigadier Alastair Lethbridge-Stewart, did exactly the same as Danny (in 1983's *Mawdryn Undead*, we learned that after retiring from the army he became a mathematics teacher), the audience is clearly not meant to be sympathetic in any way to this prejudice. Whether it is some carry-over from his experiences in the Time War (although *The Day of the Doctor* seemed to resolve that part of his past), or the hundreds of years he spent on Trenzalore as a warrior defending the town of Christmas before his last regeneration, the show is taking a risk with making the Doctor so disagreeably pigheaded in such a way. Although Danny gets to see inside the TARDIS, the Doctor leaves no doubt he wants nothing further to do with him – he just wants Clara to keep him out of his way.

Ironically, the element of the Clara/Danny relationship that is hardest to swallow is the idea that the pair are deeply in love. Whether it's because their first kiss was only two episodes ago, or because we have only seen small fragments of their time together, or simply because the on-screen chemistry between the two actors is not particularly outstanding, it feels like we've missed something when Clara suddenly blurts out to the Doctor that she loves Danny. In every other respect, though, Coleman and Anderson complement each other well as they show the pair working through the consequences of the evening's events. Not surprisingly, Clara finds there is now a distance between her and Danny; we know from *Listen* how being deceived is a sore point with Danny, and the heartfelt disappointment of his "Really had enough of the lies" is more effective than any amount of anger at making Clara understand how she has hurt him by not sharing her experiences with the Doctor with him. There's a particularly nice piece of direction showing Clara looking into her troubled reflection in a darkened window, rather than facing him directly, as she answers his questions.

The Doctor's severe (in fact, downright unreasonable) declaration to Clara – "You've explained me to him; you haven't explained him to me" – not only marks the point where the comedy drops away as the story turns serious, but also drives a wedge between himself and Clara. Forced to make a choice of which relationship to concentrate on repairing, she clearly decides to side with Danny, and borrows a gadget of the Doctor's he had earlier used against the Skovox – a watch that makes the wearer invisible – in order to get Danny inside the TARDIS so he can observe for himself what she is like when she is with the Doctor. Unfortunately for her, the Doctor has the ability to feel when the invisibility field is being used near him; he rather cruelly feigns boredom and suggests a quick trip elsewhere, to Clara's alarm ("It's a time machine. We can get back straight away, like we always do on your dates"). Danny realises his cover has been blown, and he and the Doctor have an angry confrontation as he scorns the aristocratic implication of the title "Time Lord" and thoroughly annoys the Doctor by pretending to be a subordinate saluting an officer. Capaldi and Anderson both bring great intensity to their heated conflict, with Danny definitely scoring a point by reflecting the Doctor's dislike of soldiers back at him, putting him in an unwanted role. We know that Danny has some trauma in his past, and it seems like he is speaking from experience when he tells Clara, "I'm the one who carries you out of the fire; he's the one who lights it."

The Doctor's allegiance also shifts slightly – or rather, he makes no attempt to be conciliatory towards Clara or Danny, instead forming a connection with a pupil of the school, Courtney Woods (who had made brief appearances in a couple of previous episodes). Capaldi and Ellis George strike up an excellent relationship (similar to the Doctor's scenes with Rupert in *Listen*), as the Doctor evidently recognises a kindred spirit in this girl who has been labelled a "disruptive influence." The joke about the Doctor's "Keep out" sign that, she points out, actually reads "Go away humans" ("Never lose your temper in the middle of a door sign") is a hoot. Perhaps a little reckless in the wake of Clara's temporary abandonment of him, he is quite happy for Courtney to see the inside of the TARDIS, and even tells her, "I may have a vacancy, but not right now," before giving her an actual trip in the time machine at the end, when he disposes of the defeated Skovox. In fact, as the preview for next week reveals, she will be sticking around for at least one more episode.

When the Skovox returns, sooner than the Doctor had expected, he and Clara have to scramble to defeat it, after some fun with Clara and Danny having to come up with excuses to extricate themselves from parent-teacher interviews. The Doctor treats Danny as a useless deadweight while he sends Clara to act as a decoy until he can shut down the Skovox, using a jury-rigged assemblage of machinery to pretend to be the robot's superior. But Danny proves his worth in the end, using the invisibility watch to distract the thing and giving the Doctor the time he needs to transmit the shutdown code. Afterwards, he rather generously (and with little evidence, it should be said) attributes the Doctor's hostility towards him to a concern that he might not be "good enough" for Clara, and when she points out that he did just help to save the world, the Doctor can only grudgingly respond, "Yeah... Good start." However, gaining the Doctor's approval is unimportant to Danny; he is more worried about Clara, pointing out to her that she followed the Doctor's orders to distract the Skovox without question ("You weren't even scared... and you should have been"). He perceptively compares the Doctor to officers he has known who pushed their men into feats they had no idea they were capable of, and makes her promise to tell him if she ever gets pushed too far. Anderson's playing of Danny with a calm and restrained manner throughout this last section reinforces the impression of a seriousness based on hard experience.

And finally the other ongoing plot thread of the season resurfaces, as the policeman killed by the Skovox earlier finds himself in the "Nethersphere" (previously referred to as "the Promised Land") where the mysterious "Missy" dwells. His body is fully intact, so this is definitely some kind of continuation of consciousness after physical death (as has been seen before, for example, with River Song in 2008's *Forest of the Dead*). There are still few real clues as to what is going on here, but with Missy and her realm of the dead already known to be featuring in the season finale, it seems that the Doctor has a nasty surprise waiting for him.

Classic Who DVD Recommendation: 1971's *Terror of the Autons* shows Jon Pertwee's Doctor working with the forces of UNIT (and also introduces Katy Manning as companion Jo Grant and marks the first appearance of the Master, played by Roger Delgado). It provides an interesting contrast to this episode regarding the Doctor's attitude towards the military.

Reflections: As with the end of *Deep Breath*, the final sequence becomes something of an irrelevant appendage once one knows what the deal is with Missy and the Nethersphere. A properly satisfying end to the episode comes with Clara and Danny's quiet conversation just before it. Ultimately, the "Missy arc" proved to be rather like the Harold Saxon arc in 2007 – introduced at the beginning of the season, then briefly popping up in the middle to remind the audience of its existence, but with several episodes being completely unconnected to it, before the payoff arrives in the season finale.

The notion of the companion leading a separate life in conjunction with adventuring with the Doctor is more or less an innovation of the Moffat era. Amy and Rory continued to regularly encounter the Doctor even after they departed the TARDIS in 2011's *The God Complex*, and the idea has been developed much further with Clara. Practically all previous companions were pulled out of their original lives for one reason or another to go travelling with the Doctor, and then after a time found some way to permanently depart his life. While they were with him, there might be occasional references to unseen adventures, but for the most part what was shown on screen was the entirety of their story (not that this has stopped the creators of *Doctor Who* novels and audio plays from wedging new stories into every available nook and cranny of the continuity). About the only case in the classic series of a "part-time" companion in the same vein as Clara is Sarah Jane Smith in the mid-1970's, who on no less than five separate occasions was on present-day Earth with the opportunity to resume her normal life, only to be invited back into the TARDIS by the Doctor for another trip. But while Sarah nominally had an everyday life as a journalist, we saw virtually nothing of it. Only with Clara have we been following the companion's life away from the Doctor as well as her time with him, and doing so was a good idea of Moffat's, with the friction between the two providing a whole string of interesting story ideas.

With the new Doctor now fully established, the relationship between him, Clara and Danny moves to centre stage and becomes important for the rest of the season, influencing all of the episodes from this point on in different ways. Although in this episode, the characters are exaggerated at times for comedic purposes, the drama is played very straight, and is all the more powerful for it. (Next season, *The Girl Who Died* will have a similar jokey feel that suddenly turns serious, while the idea of the Doctor taking Clara's pupils for trips in the TARDIS would be humorously revisited in the tag scene of that episode's companion story, *The Woman Who Lived*.) Danny finally gains an understanding of all the weird happenings he has been troubled by around Clara. Clara emerges with the relief of knowing that she has Danny's support as long as she keeps her promise to remain honest with him – a promise which, of course, will come back to bite her in a couple of episodes' time. As for the Doctor, he will continue to refer to Danny dismissively as "P.E." in future episodes, but the full antagonism will be toned down, and when Clara really needs his help to find Danny again in the finale, he will support her unstintingly. But before then, Danny's intuition that the Doctor would one day push Clara too far will soon come true.

7: Kill the Moon

Writer: Peter Harness
Director: Paul Wilmshurst
Originally Broadcast: 4 October 2014

Cast

The Doctor: Peter Capaldi
Clara: Jenna Coleman
Danny Pink: Samuel Anderson
Courtney Woods: Ellis George
Lundvik: Hermione Norris
Duke: Tony Osoba
Henry: Phil Nice
McKean: Christopher Dane

Kill the Moon is clearly a tremendously important episode in the arc of this season, ending with a wrenching emotional crisis that marks a major turning point in the relationship between the Doctor and Clara. Unfortunately, the story leading up to that crisis (written by Peter Harness, a newcomer to the series) rests on a hopelessly compromised foundation – not just one but a whole string of ludicrous scientific concepts that, as the famous physicist Wolfgang Pauli might have put it, are so not right that they're not even wrong. In these pieces, my normal practice is to go through the salient aspects of an episode more or less in order of appearance, but in this case it's impossible not to take notice right at the start of the elephant in the room – or rather, the bat in the moon.

When the Doctor, Clara, and Courtney Woods (the student from Clara's school who played a part in last week's episode as well) land on the moon in 2049, they encounter a small group of astronauts trying to discover why the satellite is in the process of breaking apart. The rather surprising answer is, in the Doctor's words (which even he seems to have trouble believing he's saying): "The moon is an egg!" A world-sized creature has been incubating inside the moon for millions of years and is about to hatch – an event which is already causing devastation on Earth, and could result in total disaster for all human life on the planet. It's a mind-boggling "high concept" straight out of the pulp magazine era of science fiction. There's a rule of thumb often cited (in literary SF circles, at least) that television and movie science fiction lags behind the printed variety by about three decades in terms of storytelling sophistication. In this case, though, we need to go half a century further back: a novelette by Jack Williamson called "Born of the Sun" (published in the appropriately named *Astounding Stories*) presented the same basic idea as long ago as 1934. Even then it was a notably *outré* notion; to employ it completely seriously in 2014, without any kind of ironic or humorous twist, is one of the most bizarre writing decisions ever made on *Doctor Who*.

As if that wasn't enough, the episode also mixes in so-called "germs" that look like tarantulas the size of dogs (but nevertheless are apparently still single-celled), a pool of "amniotic fluid" unaffected by the vacuum of the lunar surface, and the completely inexplicable gain of billions of tons of mass by the growing creature (without any consequent loss of mass in the surrounding moon). And for the crowning touch, when the creature finally hatches and flies away, it somehow leaves behind within seconds another egg, a "new moon" – an identical-looking replacement satellite seemingly as large as itself! Of course, *Doctor Who* has never been renowned for particularly careful adherence to scientific rigour in its storytelling; it is, after all, a show about an alien who travels through time and space in a phone box that's bigger on the inside. But there are limits to any viewer's suspension of disbelief, and for most people this episode will zoom so far past those limits it achieves escape velocity. Worse, the script insists on trying to integrate these preposterous concepts into a very un-fantastic milieu of space shuttles, lunar bases, spacesuits, etc. based on current technology, and tell an earnest, character-based story. With elements pulling in such different directions, every time the episode tries to get serious, another ridiculous scientific gaffe comes along to cause painful cognitive dissonance, making the whole story a disagreeable experience for all but the most forgiving of viewers.

It's a pity, because if only one can get past the jarring silliness at the heart of the story, there are certainly things to appreciate in this episode. Thanks to a location shoot on the volcanic island of Lanzarote, director Paul Wilmshurst (another newcomer to *Doctor Who*, acquitting himself well here) is able to present a convincingly vast and arid moonscape. In the first half, before the big reveal of the creature within the moon, an effectively creepy atmosphere is evoked as the characters explore an abandoned base belonging to a previous expedition. They may make very little sense, but the cobwebbed, dark rooms and the sudden attacks by the scuttling "spider-germs" evoke memories of the classic series' mid-1970's peak, when the stories would regularly draw inspiration from old Universal and Hammer horror movies. Harness is clearly a fan of this period – the scene where the Doctor first meets the astronauts has multiple callbacks to the opening of 1975's *The Ark in Space*, with the Doctor talking of a "Bennett oscillator," taking a "gravity reading" and playing with a yo-yo (which gets used in a couple of other places during the episode, too). The spider-germs are really just a means of padding the story – they could be completely removed with no effect on its ultimate course – but they do provide an exciting action/horror element that punches up what would otherwise be an extremely talky script. It's unfortunate, though, that the first appearance of one results in Peter Capaldi being saddled with the line, "It's a prokaryotic, unicellular life form with non-chromosomal DNA" – not only is it a tongue-twisting tautology, but he botches the pronunciation of "prokaryotic" as well.

Young Ellis George follows up her solid work in *The Caretaker* with another good performance as Courtney. According to Clara, Courtney has apparently "gone off the rails" after the Doctor, annoyed about her throwing up in the TARDIS at the end of last episode's trip (and on subsequent unseen occasions as well), dismissed her with a remark that she wasn't special. Finding her back inside the TARDIS with some cleaning fluid, he reacts to Clara's demand that he tell Courtney she's special by somewhat irresponsibly offering to make her the first woman on the moon – leading to them arriving in 2049 aboard a space shuttle carrying three astronauts that is about to make a bumpy landing there. Although Clara seems to think she is some kind of problem child, Courtney's behaviour is really just typical teenage self-centeredness – when she gets the chance to be the first out of the shuttle, she can only come up with, "One small thing for a thing, one enormous thing for a thingy-thing." She demonstrates bravery and quick thinking, however, when she uses her cleaning fluid to deal with an attacking spider-germ (although it's best not to ask how and why she carried it with her out of the TARDIS). The plight of the moon-creature, and the debate on what to do about it, gets her to look outside herself (a nice echo of its larger effect on humanity itself), and by the end, according to the Doctor she has a great future ahead of her.

Guest star Hermione Norris plays the leader of the astronauts, Lundvik (rather carelessly, the script doesn't bother to mention her name except once in passing, towards the end), with a worn-down fatalism that gives the impression that she doesn't really believe her group are capable of dealing with the problem; after an initial perfunctory challenge, she readily falls in behind the Doctor and passively follows his lead. The astronauts are all deliberately played as lethargic, past it, not up to the job, but they're all that humanity has to offer, like the museum-piece space shuttle they used to get to the moon. "We'd stopped going into space... Nobody cared," she tells the Doctor. When her colleague Duke (played by Tony Osoba, making a third appearance in *Doctor Who* after 1979's *Destiny of the Daleks* and 1987's *Dragonfire*) is killed by a spider-germ, she notes, "We were both given the sack on the same day." Fortunately, the tremendous progress now being made in the non-government space sector makes the future shown here very unlikely. But if one were to judge only by the general public's current lack of interest in space travel, it could well be thought that by 2049 (less than thirty-five years away) a bunch of ageing has-beens and an antiquated shuttle might be the only ones available (although they did at least manage to soup up the shuttle enough to reach the moon – in reality, that vehicle was designed for low Earth orbit operations only). Lundvik only really comes alive when she faces the decision of whether to go ahead with detonating an arsenal of nuclear bombs the astronauts brought with them to destroy whatever alien threat is causing the changes in the moon.

There's an ironic counterpoint between this story and *The Waters of Mars*, the 2009 David Tennant episode which is set just ten years further in the future. In that story the Doctor was helpless to prevent a cataclysm because it was a fixed point in time – an event which had to happen. Here, the crux of the story is that exactly the opposite is true, as he goes to some pains to explain to Clara when she wants to leave – since, after all, doesn't he already know the moon didn't break up in 2049?

The Doctor: "Clara, there are some moments in time that I simply can't see... They're not clear – they're fuzzy, they're grey. Little moments in which big things are decided. And this is one of them. Just now, I can't tell what happens to the moon, because whatever happens to the moon hasn't been decided yet. And it's going to be decided here and now. Which very much sounds as though... it's up to us."

When the true nature of the problem becomes apparent, Lundvik's immediate reaction is, "How do we kill it?" Despite the Doctor's attempt to make her feel guilty ("You'd have an enormous corpse floating in the sky. You might have some very difficult conversations to have with your kids"), and Clara's and Courtney's distress at the idea of killing a possibly unique life form, she stands firm on the idea of using the bombs, and it's difficult to disagree with her point of view. We have already heard that the changes in the moon have caused gigantic tides that have swamped whole cities. Now, she fears, when the moon finally breaks up as the creature emerges, huge chunks of debris will rain down on Earth. As she tells Courtney, "Look, when you've grown up a bit, you'll realise that everything doesn't have to be nice. Some things are just bad."

But the true shock comes when the Doctor, despite his earlier words ("It's up to us"), voluntarily removes himself from the debate. He has sensed that what happens at this point will somehow be vital to the whole future of humanity, and being non-human himself refuses to influence it – and so he departs in the TARDIS, leaving Clara, Courtney and Lundvik behind, and will only return after the decision to kill or spare the creature is made. In principle, it's a marvellous idea for a plot turn, giving both Clara and Courtney the opportunity to show their true character, but there are several things wrong with the execution. The debate is interspersed with an irrelevant action climax as they are threatened by a horde of attacking spider-germs, a breach in the base wall and more moonquakes as the ground continues to break up. Rather than being exciting, this simply makes the Doctor look appallingly uncaring about leaving them in danger. Then, Clara and Courtney trying to work out what the Earth would be like without the moon is very hard to take seriously ("I have a physics book in my bag. There's a thing on gravity") – it feels as inadequate a response to the situation as Amy negotiating with the Silurians about partitioning the Earth in 2010's *Cold Blood*. Finally, a fortuitous moment of contact with the Earth allows Clara to make a broadcast asking humanity to vote on whether the creature should be killed. (This speech also provides the episode with its flash-forward teaser, ending with a wink to the audience: "We have 45 minutes to decide.") But while it's natural for her to want the decision to be made democratically, the idea doesn't stand the slightest scrutiny. Since people are supposed to turn off their lights to indicate they agree with killing the creature, the half of the planet she can't see doesn't get a vote. And in practice, the "votes" would be in the hands of whoever controlled the power systems of the world's cities. In the event, it doesn't matter as she resorts to her own intuition: the lights go out on Earth, but Clara ignores them anyway, hitting the cut-out to stop the countdown as the Doctor returns for them.

He takes them to a bright, sunny beach – a lovely contrast to the darkness of the episode up to this point – where the denouement plays out. It seems that Clara made the right decision: when the creature hatches, the remains of the "egg" disintegrate without harming Earth and the creature flies off and leaves a "new moon" behind. The effects showing the moon's disintegration and the creature emerging are actually quite impressive, but the best part is Capaldi's performance as he shows the Doctor sensing the future timeline; with the human race's interest in space reignited by this event, their destiny is now settled, to expand out into the universe and endure "till the end of time." It's an unexpectedly uplifting ending – except that when the TARDIS returns to the present day, Clara makes it clear just how angry she is at being put on the spot by the Doctor in such a fashion. She is quite right to point out that she didn't have enough information to have a fair chance of making an informed decision ("I nearly didn't press that button. I nearly got it wrong"). It makes him seem dangerously unpredictable rather than a mentor giving her a chance to stretch herself.

The Doctor tries to explain that from his viewpoint as an outsider, he was respecting Clara and humanity by not influencing their actions, but together with his rather patronising earlier remark about "taking the stabilisers off your bike," this leads to her rounding on him furiously. Coleman is absolutely brilliant here, showing Clara shaken and sobbing with both distress and rage, reaching a level of raw emotion almost never seen in *Doctor Who*. At last, she sends the Doctor away and gives the impression she would be glad never to see him again, before unburdening herself to Danny Pink, who only last episode had suggested to her that a day might come when the Doctor would push her too far. Wisely, he tells her she won't be finished with the Doctor until she can leave him calmly. It's a tremendously powerful ending which, had it not arisen from such an egregiously nonsensical story, would have been even more effective.

Classic Who DVD Recommendation: A previous visit to Lanzarote in *Doctor Who*, with the island playing both itself and the surface of an alien planet, can be found in 1984's *Planet of Fire*, starring Peter Davison, Mark Strickson, and Nicola Bryant.

Reflections: As one would expect, *Kill the Moon* aired to strongly negative reaction, with its numerous scientific howlers receiving widespread derision. Certainly, when watched again it cries out for *Mystery Science Theater 3000* treatment. (If you're unfamiliar with this icon of 1990's geek culture, in which a guy and his robot sidekicks are trapped in space, subjected by evil scientists to an endless string of bad movies, and keep their sanity by wisecracking about the nonsense they're forced to watch, do yourself a favour and look it up.) Some of the episode's junk science would be right at home in the ancient 'B'-movies lampooned by *MST3K*: for me, the "spider-germs" prompted memories of how 1957's *The Amazing Colossal Man* expects the audience to accept the weird idea that the human heart is "made up of a single cell"(!), while the "amniotic fluid" lying in the open on the lunar surface led me to recall Tom Servo's increasingly exasperated cries of *"There is no steam in a vacuum!"* while watching the 1960 yawner *12 to the Moon*. Add to those a space shuttle landing scene only slightly less ridiculous than the one in *Airplane II*, and the jaw-dropping line "The moon isn't made of rock and stone... It's made of eggshell!" (and kudos to Jenna Coleman for delivering that one with a straight face), and the result is something that would be well suited for mockery by the revival of *MST3K* which is in production even as I write this in 2016.

In the same way as *Robot of Sherwood* was ahistorical, deliberately flouting known history in order to tell a story which it nevertheless insisted really happened, *Kill the Moon* could be considered "ascientific" – it expects viewers to simply ignore the contradictions with known facts about the moon, accept the "facts" of the situation as presented, and allow them to form the basis of the drama between the characters. (Oddly, just three episodes later, *In the Forest of the Night* would test the audience's goodwill again in a very similar way. Its more fantastical atmosphere meant its "weird science" was not quite as discordant as in *Kill the Moon*, but various other problems led to it being an even weaker episode overall.) But despite the bizarre and uncomfortable conflict of tone, the character development, especially the final confrontation between the Doctor and Clara, still makes an impact. The effects of their quarrel will ripple through the rest of the season; even though the immediate rift is patched up in the next episode, Clara can no longer just blithely run from adventure to adventure. Also, her pointing out to the Doctor that she has a duty of care to Courtney will find an echo in the Doctor's own attitude to

Clara in the finale of the next season.

The episode also garnered criticism (particularly in the US) when some saw it as making allusions to arguments about abortion. In interviews, Harness later denied any such intention, and certainly there's no obvious, on-the-nose allegory – the creature's parent, for instance, is conspicuously absent, and the debate about killing it is centred on trying to decide what level of threat it poses to humanity. Still, with questions about killing babies and whether Clara wants to have children, and the Doctor leaving the decision in the hands of Clara, Lundvik and Courtney ("It's your moon, womankind"), it's easy to see how the impression could arise. Fortunately, Harness would get another chance to combine a hard-edged thriller story with important character development, in his Zygon two-parter in the next season – and would make a much better job of it, including a far more deliberate usage of a contemporary hot-button political issue. But this first attempt simply demonstrates that while there's a good story in the idea of a wondrous, world-shattering event providing a numinous experience that shocks the human race out of insularity and reorients it towards the wider universe, having a giant bat hatching out of the moon is probably not the way to do it.

8: Mummy on the Orient Express

Writer: Jamie Mathieson
Director: Paul Wilmshurst
Originally Broadcast: 11 October 2014

Cast

The Doctor: Peter Capaldi
Clara: Jenna Coleman
Danny Pink: Samuel Anderson
Perkins: Frank Skinner
Captain Quell: David Bamber
Gus: John Sessions
Maisie: Daisy Beaumont
Mrs Pitt: Janet Henfrey
Professor Moorhouse: Christopher Villiers
Singer: Foxes
The Foretold: Jamie Hill

Mummy on the Orient Express is a particularly satisfying episode, successfully striking a balance between telling a suspenseful story in its own right and continuing the development of the tension that has grown up between the Doctor and Clara. New writer Jamie Mathieson provides a rich and rewarding script, and the fact that he is also responsible for next week's episode makes it one to look forward to as well. Right from the teaser it's clear than we are in traditional "monster of the week" territory, but after all the narrative trickery employed in previous episodes (with varying levels of success), it's a nice change to be presented with a simply told but very *Doctor Who*-ish story: sharply written, scary and funny in all the right places, and produced with a high degree of polish.

That teaser perfectly does its job of grabbing the viewer's attention. We appear to be in the dining car of the renowned Orient Express, sometime in the 1920's. An old woman, Mrs Pitt (Janet Henfrey, whose previous *Who* appearance in 1989's *The Curse of Fenric* saw her play a character who suffered a similar fate) becomes disturbed, and then terrified, as a horrifying, bandage-wrapped mummy shambles through the car towards her, hands outstretched. But only she can see this apparition; to everyone else, her babbling about "that man, right there, dressed as a monster" refers only to thin air. The mummy reaches out to touch her, and she apparently dies of a heart attack. Then, the camera pulls back – to show that the train is not on Earth at all, but hurtling through the blackness of space on hyperspatial rails.

As with the imitation *Titanic* in 2007's *Voyage of the Damned*, placing the story aboard a futuristic recreation of the famous luxury train provides the perfect excuse to combine a period setting (always a strong point of BBC productions) with sci-fi trappings. The art deco production design is beautifully done, with the elegant costumes of the characters (including Clara in a striking flapper outfit) flawlessly creating the pseudo-1920's feel. But after last week's explosive argument, there is a bittersweet start to the episode, with the Doctor bringing Clara here as a special treat for what they have agreed will be their last time together. He looks particularly formal, in a white dress shirt with a black cravat that recalls one worn by William Hartnell's original incarnation. For Clara, it is now several weeks after she stormed out of the TARDIS at the end of *Kill the Moon*; she has worked through her thoughts about him and come to a firm conclusion ("I could never hate you... but I can't do this any more. Not the way you do it"). Even though as viewers we know that Clara will not be leaving the show in this episode, their quiet conversation is filled with a genuine and affecting regret at ending their partnership – on Clara's side, at least; while she wants to air her feelings, the Doctor, amusingly, is confused by her mixture of emotions and would prefer to talk about what they can see out of the train windows.

But as soon as they learn about the death of Mrs Pitt earlier, their determination to stop is thrown into doubt. The Doctor wonders if Clara actually *wants* another adventure; her denial is not entirely convincing, but they retreat to their compartments, deciding that the "mummy" must have been a hallucination of the dying old woman. Coleman gives a wonderfully nuanced portrayal of Clara's conflicting emotions throughout this section as she and the Doctor dance around each other, toasting their "last hurrah" but with neither of them now willing to definitively state that after this trip, they will never see each other again. Clara takes refuge in a phone call to Danny Pink who, now that she has confided in him, has no problem with her enjoying her "space train". Meanwhile, the Doctor, after some humorous debate with himself (which at one point shows off Capaldi's ability to accurately impersonate Tom Baker's distinctive tones), realises that what he has heard about the mummy fits the description of the

Foretold, a five-thousand-year-old myth. And so he sets off – without Clara, in accordance (so he thinks) with her wishes – on an investigation that will soon turn into a tense struggle for survival as the mummy keeps reappearing at intervals to pick off another victim.

Just like the movie that is its clear inspiration, 1974's *Murder on the Orient Express*, this episode boasts an excellent ensemble cast. With the mummy on the rampage, quite a few of them don't make it to the end, but Professor Moorhouse (Christopher Villiers, who previously appeared on *Doctor Who* in *The King's Demons* back in 1983) and Captain Quell are both sharply delineated characters who make an impression in their brief time on screen. Daisy Beaumont is a good foil for Jenna Coleman as Maisie, Mrs Pitt's granddaughter, who is befriended by Clara and ends up being the key to the Doctor's final victory. There are also a couple of guest stars; the singer Foxes has a brief early cameo, performing Queen's "Don't Stop Me Now" in the style of a 1920's jazz number. By contrast, comedian Frank Skinner has a substantial part as Perkins, the train's chief engineer. Despite the slight whiff of stunt casting, he plays well opposite Capaldi, as the Doctor finds Perkins almost suspiciously eager to help with his enquiries. This turns out to be a red herring, though, and his final wry refusal of the Doctor's offer to bring him on board to help with maintaining the TARDIS ("That job could... change a man." "Yes it does. Frequently") is a sweet ending note for the character.

The episode certainly brings the suspense and terror; the inexorable advance of the mummy is chilling every time it occurs, even though essentially the same set piece is being repeated half a dozen times. From the moment it appears to the victim's inevitable death is exactly sixty-six seconds, with the stylish touch of a ticking countdown clock superimposed on screen in each case to emphasise that we are seeing the attack in real time. This must have posed some unusual problems for director Paul Wilmshurst in making the dialogue and action of each attack sequence flow naturally while still ensuring that the mummy's hands close around the victim's head precisely as the clock reaches zero. The costume design and makeup work for the mummy is impressive, with the creature's decayed, skeletal form covered in ancient, frayed bandages, falling off in places. The design work is matched by an excellent physical performance from Jamie Hill, with details such as the slight tilt to his body and the dragging of one foot behind him as he walks producing a total effect that really pushes the limits of how scary *Doctor Who* can be, given the number of young children in the audience. Indeed, the mummy was deemed sufficiently scary that it was deliberately left out of the pre-season trailers, and was apparently one factor in the BBC's decision to shift the broadcast time of the last few episodes to 8:30 p.m. – the latest regular timeslot the show has ever had in the UK.

It turns out that the passengers consist of a group of experts (like Professor Moorhouse) that have been assembled (without their knowledge) by some entity known only as "Gus" in order to capture the Foretold and understand its abilities. Gus communicates only through the displays of the train's computer system (or perhaps *is* the computer – it's deliberately left unclear), and has caused an ancient scroll near which the Foretold always appears to be brought on board. He (it?) stops the train in deep space, so that the passengers have no choice but to solve the mystery. John Sessions imbues Gus with an affable demeanour throughout, but the villain shows his true colours when the Doctor refuses to do as ordered. He depressurises a section of the train, killing a number of the staff; the Doctor gets everyone back to work immediately. The investigation scenes do, by the way, display the only directorial blemish of the episode: because of the confined space in the train car set, the numerous background artists playing the other passengers are unavoidably present in nearly all of the shots, crowded around the principals. It becomes rather amusing when (because they're non-speaking extras) they can't make any contribution – not even facial reactions – but just stand woodenly while the Doctor is haranguing everybody around him to help him get answers.

Even by the end of the episode we have no further information about Gus – he might be a part of the ongoing "Missy" arc plot, or he could be completely separate. As the Doctor tells Clara, Gus has tried to entice him here before, even phoning the TARDIS once, as we saw at the end of 2010's *The Big Bang*. (Like several other Moffat-era callbacks, though, the precise details don't quite match up, reflecting the fact that the reference to "the Orient Express... in space" back in 2010 was simply a throwaway gag, with no intention at that time to follow it up.) Clara's anger at realising that he had ulterior motives for coming here ("You see, this... this is why I'm leaving you... because you lied") is rather ironic in view of what she will do at the end of the episode.

Mathieson takes care to remove the Doctor's access to both the sonic screwdriver and the TARDIS, making it more difficult for him to gain information about a foe that can only be seen by the person it is about to kill. One gets the sense of the Doctor really having to work hard to solve this problem; each death gives him a little more information even as it makes the mummy seem more and more inescapable. The second attack (on a chef in the train's kitchen) shows it cannot be escaped by barricading oneself behind a door – it can simply teleport from place to place. The third (on a train guard) shows bullets don't affect it. The fourth (on Professor Moorhouse) shows it cannot be placated or reasoned with; there is nothing it wants except to kill its selected victim. The fifth (on Captain Quell) again shows it teleporting and gives the Doctor enough clues to understand the technology it is using – as well as providing one especially spooky shot of the "out of phase" mummy walking straight through the Doctor, with its outstretched hand appearing to emerge from his eyes.

Peter Capaldi's performance has grown more and more impressive over the season so far, and the early difficulties at finding the right balance between harshness and warmth for his Doctor are now long gone. Apart from the sweet melancholy of the initial scenes with Clara, he makes the most of some good comic material – the hilariously inappropriate "Are you my mummy?" joke, the cigarette case containing jelly babies he produces from his pocket at one point (an idea apparently contributed by Capaldi himself), playing along when his psychic paper causes the captain to mistake him for a "mystery shopper" – while also effortlessly taking command in the fight against the mummy. The hard edge is still there; like Tom Baker's Doctor in a similar desperate situation in 1975's *Pyramids of Mars*, he refuses to be distracted even as the mummy is attacking Moorhouse and then Quell, instead pressuring them to make their last seconds count by passing on information that might help the next victim, and refusing to stop to mourn their deaths. When he realises that the creature is not choosing its victims at random, but in order of weakness (either physical or psychological), and that Maisie's guilt over daydreaming about her grandmother's death means she is next in line to die, he impatiently tells Clara to lie to Maisie in order to get her to come to him. He ignores Clara's seething even as he saves Maisie almost in passing, using a brain scanning device to transfer her guilt into himself in order to get the mummy to turn its attention to him instead.

Everything comes together with the revelation that the mysterious "scroll" is actually a tattered flag; the mummy is the last remnant of a soldier from some ancient, forgotten war, forced to remain in this state by another instance of malfunctioning advanced technology. Like several other adversaries the Doctor has encountered this year, the creature echoes an aspect of himself, thousands of years old and unable to stop existing. It's an unexpectedly affecting moment when, at the last possible instant, the Doctor finds the key phrase to make it stop – "We surrender!" – and it struggles to shape a final salute before disintegrating. Of course, now that Gus has the answers he wanted about the Foretold, he begins to remove the air from the train ("Well, there's a shocker," is the Doctor's sardonic comment), and the Doctor has to quickly adapt the teleportation device from the remains of the ancient soldier to get everyone into the TARDIS.

In a small but very effective moment of non-linear narrative in this otherwise completely straightforward tale, we first see the train blowing up in space before cutting to the Doctor and Clara alone on a beach, where he assures her that he managed to rescue everyone before Gus destroyed the train, and dropped them off while she was still unconscious. Drolly, he points out that he could be lying ("No, I just saved you, and I let everyone else suffocate... This is just my cover story") – but actually, his earlier behaviour means we can't be fully confident that he *did* really save the others until we see Perkins alive and well later. This conversation is an important moment, and Capaldi and Coleman navigate its shifting moods perfectly. When Clara seizes on the idea that he couldn't risk Gus learning about his plan to use Maisie as the reason he made her lie to the girl, he refuses to take the easy way out and reassure her: "Would you like to think that about me? Would that make it easier?" Although in the last episode he claimed to be respecting Clara, it's here that he shows actual respect towards her by being completely honest about his apparent heartlessness, in a speech which does a far more convincing job than the equivalent one in *Kill the Moon* of conveying his point:

The Doctor: "I didn't know if I could save her. I couldn't save Quell, I couldn't save Moorhouse. There was a good chance that she'd die too. At which point, I would have just... moved on to the next... and the next... until I beat it. Sometimes the only choices you have are bad ones. But you still have to choose."

By the time the Doctor and Clara are back in the TARDIS, it seems like the trip to the Orient Express has achieved its purpose of bringing

Clara to the point where she is ready to say goodbye. On the phone to Danny, she declares "mission accomplished." But then the rug is pulled out from under us: having previously wondered if the Doctor is addicted to his adventuring life ("Well, you can't really tell if something's an addiction until you try and give it up," he replies), she now demonstrates that she is addicted at least as much as he is. Coleman's performance marks this as a crucial turning point in Clara's journey. She takes a deep breath... and flat-out lies to the Doctor, telling him that Danny is fine with her continued travelling ("Look, as long as you get me home safe and on time, everything is great"). The Doctor is delighted, they grin excitedly at each other, and the swelling music tries to convince us it's a happy ending. But re-establishing the compartmentalised life she enjoyed before it was disrupted in *The Caretaker* will require Clara to keep on lying to both Danny and the Doctor, and it seems most unlikely that anything good will come of this.

Classic Who DVD Recommendation: The classic series also did "Agatha Christie in space" with 1977's *The Robots of Death*, starring Tom Baker and Louise Jameson. Strongly influenced by Christie's *And Then There Were None* (1939), it's another story set aboard an isolated opulent but futuristic vessel, with a technological menace picking off the occupants one by one.

Reflections: *Doctor Who* has always been spoken of by those responsible for coming up with its scripts – from classic series script editors like Terrance Dicks to modern-day showrunners like Steven Moffat – as a voracious devourer of story ideas, with its constant demand for variety in the settings, characters and creatures the Doctor and his companions encounter. In all eras of the show the producers have felt a need to bring new writers on board, to keep on introducing originality and fresh approaches to the storytelling. The show is a notoriously tricky one to write, however, requiring its scripts to work on multiple levels for an audience of both adults and children, which creates an opposing pressure to not risk placing too many episodes in a season on the shoulders of untried writers. This season, in which four episodes come from new writers, is an exception in the Moffat era; nowhere else does he use more than two rookies in any given year. It's very rare for a new writer to capture the tone of the show quite so successfully as Jamie Mathieson does in both of his scripts this season.

74

For example, Richard Curtis (in 2010's *Vincent and the Doctor*) and Catherine Tregenna (in next season's *The Woman Who Lived*) both delivered excellent character-based drama, but also included alien creatures (a space chicken and a space lion, respectively) whose treatment was quite perfunctory, in the latter case noticeably weakening the overall effect of the story.

Both the mummy in this episode and the Boneless in *Flatline* demonstrate Mathieson's ability to come up with strong and memorable imagery for his stories. What's more, the creatures are placed at the centre of their stories, and drive the bulk of the action – they haven't been included simply out of a sense that every *Who* story must have a monster or alien of some kind in it. Together with his sure handling of the dramatic through-line of the Doctor and Clara's story, and his equally deft ability to be funny, the result is two very good episodes that work on all levels. Although his contribution to the following season, *The Girl Who Died* (co-written with Steven Moffat) wasn't quite as big a hit, it was still good enough to make one hope that he becomes a fixture in the show's stable of regular writers.

Clara's lie in the final scene is obviously the most important connection with later episodes, and its consequences will soon appear, with the Doctor finding out in the next episode, and Danny in the one after that. Meanwhile, although it seemed at the time as if the mysterious "Gus" might have a part to play in the rest of the season, in fact he has never been so much as mentioned again since. It's always possible that the Doctor could encounter him again in the future, but for now this episode's villain remains an annoyingly unresolved plot thread. Apart from that one flaw, though, *Mummy on the Orient Express* is a superior stand-alone story, of the sort that has always formed the bedrock of the Doctor's adventures.

9: Flatline

Writer: Jamie Mathieson
Director: Douglas Mackinnon
Originally Broadcast: 18 October 2014

Cast

The Doctor: Peter Capaldi
Clara: Jenna Coleman
Missy: Michelle Gomez
Danny Pink: Samuel Anderson
Rigsy: Joivan Wade
Roscoe: John Cummins
PC Forrest: Jessica Hayles
Fenton: Christopher Fairbank
Al: Matt Bardock
George: Raj Bajaj
Bill: James Quinn

Flatline is a second very successful episode for new writer Jamie Mathieson, hot on the heels of last week's *Mummy on the Orient Express*. Again, he delivers a funny, intriguing and suspenseful stand-alone story with a highly successful and original monster design, which also contains very important, meaningful character development for the Doctor and Clara. He shows again that he knows how to start a story with a good visual hook, as the low-key but tense teaser sees a frightened man making a phone call to the police, quietly babbling about how "They are everywhere. All around. We've been so blind." But before he can say anything further he is reduced by an unknown force to a distorted, screaming picture on the wall. Then, after the opening titles, we have an even more surprising image as the Doctor and Clara land in present-day Bristol, and find themselves struggling to emerge from a police box that has suddenly shrunk to half its normal height.

There's a refreshingly old-school feel to the story in that the Doctor starts off completely clueless about what is going on, in contrast to much of the past few seasons (as he says to Clara, "Could you not just let me *enjoy* this moment of not knowing something? They happen so rarely"). He decides there must be some "dimensional leeching" originating nearby causing the TARDIS's reduction in size – and the problem soon becomes even more acute after Clara has done some initial investigating of the area, and returns to find the TARDIS has shrunk even further, down to only about twenty centimetres high. There is no way for the Doctor to get out; trapped for almost the whole episode, he is only able to offer advice and the occasional bit of equipment as Clara does the legwork, carrying the TARDIS with her in her handbag. As with 2011's *The Girl Who Waited*, the story was deliberately structured so that the Doctor spends nearly all of his time in the TARDIS, and for the same reason: to reduce the number of days the lead actor was required for this episode, enabling it to be filmed simultaneously with others (in this case, the block containing *Kill the Moon* and *Mummy on the Orient Express*).

The "high concept" of having the Doctor stuck inside a toy-sized TARDIS leads to some wonderfully inventive visuals. It's not the first time *Doctor Who* has played with TARDIS dimensions; in 1965, *The Time Meddler* saw the Doctor, for the first time, coming up against a fellow Time Lord (although that name hadn't been invented yet), the Monk. In a reverse of the idea used here, the Doctor finally triumphed by sabotaging his enemy's TARDIS so that the interior dimensions shrank to match the exterior, making it impossible for the Monk to enter it. Later, in 1981's *Logopolis*, the Doctor was trapped inside a shrinking TARDIS by the Master – which, as here, led to the amusing sight of a small police box being carried around from place to place. Of course, in the days of the classic series, the available special effects were not able to show any direct interaction between the inside and outside of the TARDIS even in its normal state, never mind shrunken. *Flatline* makes full use of the much more extensive technology available now to convincingly show that the Doctor truly is inside there; the shots of his face filling the tiny TARDIS doorway, or his hand reaching out of the little police box, are equal parts funny and slightly disturbing ("Please don't do that, that's just wrong," comments Clara). His ability to pass pieces of equipment to Clara is even used at one point for a great sight gag when she appears to pull a full-sized sledgehammer out of her bag.

In the sort of mundane urban environment often seen in the first few years of the modern series, but which has been a rarity since Steven Moffat took over the show, Clara encounters a group of council workers along with Rigsy, a graffiti artist serving a community service order. They are here to clean off a strange mural that suddenly appeared on an underpass wall, which seems to contain representations of people who have disappeared from a nearby housing estate. Thanks to a small earpiece-like device which allows him to see what Clara sees and communicate with her, the Doctor is able to participate in her investigation (as in *The Girl Who Waited*, where a pair of souped-up spectacles performed the same function). Jenna Coleman takes centre stage as Clara enjoys waving his sonic screwdriver and psychic paper around and passing herself off as "the Doctor… Doctor Oswald – but you can call me Clara," to his comical annoyance. The Doctor dismisses Rigsy as a "pudding brain" – an early favourite epithet of this Doctor, which had gone missing since *Robot of Sherwood* – but then concedes he might be useful as he takes Clara to the scene of one of the disappearances. Rigsy effectively becomes a companion to "Doctor Clara" after she shows him the tiny TARDIS and tells the Doctor to open the doors ("You really do throw your companions in at the deep end, don't you?" he says, exasperatedly), falling into the traditional companion role of following her around, being baffled and asking questions.

In the empty flats, they find more strange pictures on the walls, and a policewoman with them suddenly meets a bizarre fate, being pulled straight into the floor. The Doctor realises that all the strange events (including the shrinking of the TARDIS) are the work of two-dimensional aliens with the power to "flatten" objects and people. Director Douglas Mackinnon seizes the opportunity for startling visuals throughout the episode as characters are warped out of shape and vanish, door handles and pieces of furniture are flattened into uselessness, and the aliens themselves appear as a set of creepy distortions slithering across walls and floors. The script presents some inventive and macabre ideas on how two-dimensional aliens would interact with our world. All that is left of the unfortunate policewoman is an image of her nervous system, stretched out on the wall; another weird mural turns out to be a magnified slice of human skin. The Doctor hypothesises that the aliens have been "dissecting" humans in an attempt to understand them. The motivation of the creatures remains a complete mystery; in fact, the Doctor never manages to find out whether they are killing people deliberately, or whether they are making an attempt to communicate which they simply don't realise is lethal.

Finding themselves trapped by the aliens, Clara and Rigsy manage to take advantage of a rather convenient bubble chair to allow them to escape the room while keeping clear of the floor. Unfortunately for Clara, the lie she told last week about her boyfriend Danny being happy with her continued travelling aboard the TARDIS now catches up with her at a most inopportune time, as Danny phones her for a lunchtime meet-up. She manages to extricate herself without arousing his suspicions, but the Doctor, eavesdropping over the earpiece link, is not pleased. With the perspective of one whose "Rule One" in previous years was "the Doctor lies," he tells her lying is a vital survival skill – and a terrible habit – and comments acidly about how she is getting good at it.

Clara and Rigsy return to the council workers at the underpass mural as the aliens attack, wearing the appearances of the people they have taken. With the Doctor's advice, Clara takes charge as they all flee into some nearby train tunnels. Trapped underground and with the aliens closing in, Clara shows that she is up to the role of leading the group. She manages to deflect their resistance to being ordered around by this stranger and keeps them focused, even when people start dying – and if she has to lie to them to give them hope, she is fully prepared to do so. It's an unsettling moment for the Doctor, hearing his own pragmatism coming from someone who in *Into the Dalek* he described as caring so that he didn't have to.

Unlike the mummy in last week's episode, which repeated the same attack over and over again, the aliens here are constantly learning more about humans and developing new methods of dealing with them. The Doctor provides Clara with a gadget for restoring a door handle flattened by the aliens (naming it with a groan-inducing pun: the "2-Dis") so that they can escape to another tunnel, and which can reverse the process afterwards to prevent them from following. The aliens respond by firing dimensional energy into the flattened handle to restore it to usable form. There's an effective "jump" moment as the aliens learn how to achieve three-dimensional form, suddenly snatching one of the workers and dragging him away. Then they assume the forms of their victims and shamble towards Clara and the others in an effectively bizarre pseudo-stop motion fashion. When Clara suggests using an empty train to try to ram the aliens, Rigsy thinks he needs to drive it into them himself, only for her to amusingly deflate his noble self-sacrifice by using a hair band to hold the dead man's handle. Not that it succeeds, anyway – the aliens flatten the whole train into an image on the tunnel wall.

Aside from Rigsy, the supporting characters are a nondescript bunch, except for Fenton, a deeply unpleasant council worker who hardly has a single line that isn't a sneer. So stolidly unimaginative that even the psychic paper doesn't work on him, he tags along with Clara and Rigsy, sniping at them and complaining every step of the way. Christopher Fairbank, best known for *Auf Wiedersehen, Pet* (but who also has some notable sci-fi credits ranging from *Alien 3* and *The Fifth Element* to *Sapphire and Steel*) is an actor of greater stature than this part really needs. The only action he takes of significance to the plot is when he stupidly causes the shrunken TARDIS to fall out of Clara's bag onto some train tracks. Even the Doctor is disappointed when, after so many others have died, Fenton is still alive at the end and crassly comparing the aliens' victims to brushwood destroyed in a forest fire. ("They were community-payback scumbags, I wouldn't lose any sleep." "I bet you wouldn't.") Like the cartoonish businessman Rickston Slade in 2007's *Voyage of the Damned*, his only function is to prompt the Doctor's rueful reflection that sometimes the wrong people manage to survive. Presumably the aliens refrained from flattening him out of professional courtesy towards a fellow two-dimensional character.

By the end, Clara no longer has access to the Doctor's advice; he has been forced to activate the TARDIS's "siege mode," reducing its external appearance to a small metallic cube – completely sealed, with no way in or out. But she manages to come up with a solution that is ingenious enough to catch viewers by surprise, yet is still a completely logical development of the plot – a very satisfying piece of writing. She gets Rigsy to use his graffiti skills to produce a depiction of a door and tricks the aliens into firing dimensional energy at it uselessly; as she says, "Rule number one of being the Doctor – use your enemies' power against them." The energy they expend trying to give three-dimensional form to a door that never existed is instead able to be used by the Doctor to restore the TARDIS. It was established earlier that the Doctor had a solution to the problem (and believably so, since the Time Lords are known to be masters of dimensional engineering), so it's not really a surprise that once the TARDIS is back, the threat is ended almost immediately. He simply uses the TARDIS as a massive version of the device he gave to Clara, to expel the aliens back to their own two-dimensional universe.

Despite being confined to the TARDIS control room for the bulk of the episode, Capaldi still gives the Doctor plenty of memorable moments. Often they are comic, like his little dance after he thinks he has successfully dragged the TARDIS out of the way of an oncoming train (in a hilarious effect, looking like Thing from *The Addams Family*), only for it to topple back onto the rails. Unlike the previous episode, Mathieson started writing this one before learning who had been cast as the new Doctor, and at certain points such as when the Doctor is rushing around the room, expounding on the nature of the aliens, the influence of Matt Smith is clearly visible. In particular, after the TARDIS is restored, he emerges and sees off the aliens with the kind of bombastic set-piece speech that Smith's Doctor specialised in, taking the opportunity to finally give them a name at the same time – "the Boneless". He has tried to give them the benefit of the doubt, but since they seem to be indifferent to the fate of the humans they are killing, he ostentatiously steps back into his accustomed role, as "the man that stops the monsters."

Earlier, when facing apparent death with the TARDIS life support failing, and not knowing whether Clara could still hear him or was even still alive, the Doctor said that she "made a mighty fine Doctor." She teases him about it afterwards, but he is troubled by the ease with which she looks past the deaths that happened, to the big picture of saving the world. ("That's how you think, isn't it?" "Largely so other people don't have to.") When she wants him to agree that "I was the Doctor today, and I was good," he gets the last word: "You were an exceptional Doctor, Clara... Goodness had nothing to do with it." And just to drive home the point, the episode ends with a quick cutaway to the mysterious Missy, watching Clara on a screen and chuckling to herself that she has "chosen well." It seems that if the Doctor is worrying over the effect he is having on Clara, he is right to be uneasy.

Classic Who DVD Recommendation: For a story where not only the TARDIS gets shrunk but its occupants as well, see 1964's *Planet of Giants*, starring the original TARDIS crew of William Hartnell, William Russell, Jacqueline Hill and Carole Ann Ford.

Reflections: Both of Jamie Mathieson's episodes place an emphasis on showing the Doctor working his way through the process of investigating a problem, and then using his ingenuity to come up with a solution. In *Mummy on the Orient Express* he quickly recognised that the situation matched his knowledge of the Foretold, which gave him a starting point for his enquiries, but gathering information in search of a way to stop the creature was the focus of the whole remainder of the episode. In *Flatline*, as I noted above, the two-dimensional aliens are completely unfamiliar to him; he is forced to start from scratch, and he and Clara have to work hard to get an understanding of the aliens' capabilities, which eventually allows them to defeat them.

Actually showing the Doctor in "exploration and investigation" mode in this way is more characteristic of the classic series; the 21st-century version has sometimes found it difficult to do, simply because it takes up time. With a typical story needing setup, development, and resolution entirely within a single 45-minute episode – as well as including any dialogue and action relating to ongoing season arc threads, which was almost never a consideration in the classic series – the pressure is always on the writer to take short-cuts. Hence, the number of times when the Doctor already has all the pertinent knowledge of what he is dealing with (see, for instance, his sudden info-dump about Hila Tacorian in 2013's *Hide*), or fortuitously encounters someone who will give him all the information he needs with just a few simple questions (2010's *The Vampires of Venice* is a particularly egregious example of this). Mathieson's episodes very skilfully make room for "working out" scenes without skimping on action or making the climax seem rushed. The image of the Doctor working away at a lab bench in the TARDIS, putting together some new gadget he needs to deal with whatever problem he is facing this week (something which also occurred in *The Caretaker*) brings back memories of Jon Pertwee's Doctor in particular, reminding us that the Doctor is a scientist and engineer, as well as an action hero.

The Doctor's closing remark to Rigsy ("I can't wait to see what you do next") is amusingly prescient; it was probably not planned at the time it was written that Rigsy would return next season in *Face the Raven*. In that episode, he will resume his role as Clara's companion, at a time when the influence of the Doctor's lifestyle on her – just starting to fully emerge in *Flatline* – has almost run its course to its devastating ending. Although plenty of previous companions had departed in sad or even tragic circumstances, in few other cases was the Doctor left feeling such culpability for their leaving. In the classic series, there is Tegan's exit in 1984's *Resurrection of the Daleks*: a story with an incredibly high body count, with supporting characters being massacred left and right. Its ending saw her sickened enough by the carnage to refuse to travel with the Doctor again and simply run off, to his distress. But encountering death and destruction is only an external consequence of staying with the Doctor; what happened to

Clara was more like learning too well from him.

After *Death in Heaven* showed that she could equal his facility with pragmatic lying, the next season would show her more and more imitating his recklessness and thinking herself able to cope with any possible situation – with inevitably disastrous results. Before his last regeneration, the Doctor would take comfort in the fact that he had chosen his name as "the man who makes people better." This latest incarnation still has hanging over him the question he asked Clara in *Into the Dalek* – "Am I a good man?" In this episode, the chance to effectively see himself from the outside does nothing to reassure him.

10: In the Forest of the Night

Writer: Frank Cottrell-Boyce
Director: Sheree Folkson
Originally Broadcast: 25 October 2014

Cast

The Doctor: Peter Capaldi
Clara: Jenna Coleman
Danny Pink: Samuel Anderson
Maebh: Abigail Eames
Samson: Jaydon Harris-Wallace
Bradley: Ashley Foster
Ruby: Harley Bird
Missy: Michelle Gomez
Maebh's Mum: Siwan Morris
George: Harry Dickman
Minister: James Weber Brown
Neighbour: Michelle Asante
Emergency Services Officer: Curtis Flowers
As herself: Jenny Hill
Paris Reporter: Kate Tydman
Accra Reporter: Nana Amoo-Gottfriend
Annabel: Eloise Barnes

Whereas the previous two episodes demonstrated how it's occasionally possible for a new writer to click with the show immediately, this week provides an example of the opposite: a prestige writer, already highly successful in another field, is invited to contribute an episode in his own personal style, which turns out to be wildly out of sync with the show's usual tone. Keeping up the tradition of placing the most off-kilter episodes just before the season finale, Frank Cottrell-Boyce's *In the Forest of the Night* is one of the oddest things ever broadcast under the *Doctor Who* banner. It's trying to be a lyrical parable about trust and fear of the unknown, making the refreshingly unusual choice to have a plot with no villain at all; the Doctor triumphs by understanding what is going on rather than fighting it. Offering a novel type of story is no bad thing – variety is one of the defining characteristics of *Doctor Who* – but unfortunately, the wild implausibility of the events and the Doctor's passivity for the majority of them, together with a tedious and uninspiring group of supporting characters, makes for a lacklustre viewing experience.

Cottrell-Boyce, apart from having one of the few recent British writing credits even more high-profile than *Who* – he scripted the opening ceremony for the 2012 London Olympics – is an acclaimed author of children's novels. So it comes as no surprise that a gaggle of schoolchildren, under the supervision of Clara and Danny Pink, are at the centre of the tale. After a sleepover in the London Zoological Museum, they wake up to discover a startling transformation: a dense forest has inexplicably appeared overnight to cover all of London (and, it soon becomes apparent, the rest of the world). Coincidentally, the TARDIS has landed nearby, containing an equally baffled Doctor, who starts investigating after he encounters one of the pupils who has strayed from the group.

The production design deserves praise for successfully creating an impression of the whole city swallowed up by the forest, with pieces of familiar iconography (street signs, lampposts, phone boxes, etc.) strewn around the extensive location. Seeing one of the stone lions of Trafalgar Square surrounded by greenery is a particularly memorable image. It's immediately apparent, however, that this London is completely deserted, in defiance of any realistic expectations. This is obviously a deliberate choice on the writer's part, sacrificing realism in favour of a heightened, stylized feel. Apart from a few perfunctory news clips and one sequence with some workmen attempting to burn a path through the forest, the outside world is kept firmly offstage. The episode is not attempting to portray a plausible response to a worldwide crisis; its forest-covered London is an arena where events play out according to the logic of fairytale.

The young girl who finds the TARDIS, Maebh Arden, is at the centre of the story, and will eventually lead the Doctor to the realisation that the forest is the work of an ancient, benign intelligence that has dwelled on Earth unnoticed for millennia. She is apparently the only person able to sense the strange entity, after the trauma of her older sister going missing a year ago has left her mentally receptive to it. Director Sheree Folkson ensures that we share Maebh's point of view with heavy use of fisheye lenses and low-angle shots (particularly when the Doctor looms over her), and Abigail Eames gives a winning performance, showing Maebh overcoming her fears and growing in confidence over the course of the story. Cottrell-Boyce is clearly adept at presenting the particular mix of questioning and acceptance that comprises a young child's view of the world, as with Maebh's calm reply when the Doctor points out her nonchalant response to the TARDIS interior ("I just thought it was *supposed* to be bigger on the inside, so I didn't say anything"). She and Peter Capaldi share a good rapport right from the start, although for the purposes of this story the Doctor is not so much a dangerous, unknowable alien as a harmless, child-friendly wizard figure, with a suitably eccentric home – the TARDIS console suddenly has a GPS navigation-style voice introduced solely for the sake of a rather leaden "You have reached your destination" gag.

A phone call from the Doctor to Clara results in her and Danny leading Maebh's classmates, the euphemistically named Coal Hill School "gifted and talented" group, through the forest to meet up with the Doctor and retrieve the girl. The kids receive a lot of screen time over the course of the episode, but unfortunately bring the momentum to a halt whenever the story focuses on them. The young actors are adequate, but no more than that; the problem is that nothing they are given to say or do is interesting, especially when the episode resorts to unnecessary flashback scenes back in the classroom that feel like pure padding. Once the party arrives at Trafalgar Square, there is some laboured comedy with the Doctor's dismay at finding his TARDIS suddenly invaded. A little of this goes a long way, and there's more than a little of it. The imperious Time Lord, so forcefully commanding last week as he defeated a powerful alien threat, is reduced to flapping ineffectually at a bunch of schoolkids playing with the TARDIS console. In a tiresomely stretched out sequence where the Doctor tries to identify Maebh by peering closely at each child in turn, Capaldi's face-pulling is reminiscent of the sort of pointless hyperactivity that characterised Matt Smith's Doctor in his wackier (and weaker) moments.

A particularly blatant case of idiot plotting induces Maebh to hide and then run away for no reason at all when they all go into the TARDIS – without the Doctor, Clara or Danny noticing, even though the latter two have come here specifically to collect her. The Doctor and Clara have to go searching for her, and Clara feels a sudden fear as they make their way through what is effectively the primal forest of old myths and legends. There are some loose ends in the scripting; the Doctor's earlier comment that "You can't create an overnight forest with extra special fertiliser. You have to mess with the fabric of time" suggests for a moment that some kind of temporal trickery will ultimately be invoked to explain the forest. But this isn't a Steven Moffat episode, and the writing concentrates instead on establishing a fairytale feel with items like Maebh's red jacket alluding to Little Red Riding Hood (not to mention her surname, which recalls the Forest of Arden in Shakespeare's *As You Like It*). After Maebh encounters a pack of wolves escaped from a zoo (the sudden appearance of wolf eyes in the undergrowth watching her being a lovely spine-chilling moment), a tiger appears to chase them away, justifying the William Blake-inspired episode title. The tiger, in turn, is driven off by Danny, who has led the children out of the TARDIS to find them.

The mystical mood peaks as they enter a glade filled with light where the intelligence appears and speaks through Maebh as firefly-like motes that surround her. To the Doctor's surprise, it shows no interest in him and denies sending Maebh to find him: "We don't know you. We were here before you and we will be here after you" (a statement which is actually unlikely to be true in the Doctor's case!). The exact nature of Maebh's telepathic connection with the intelligence remains frustratingly ill-defined; she says the thought of contacting the Doctor came from "Miss" – implying that she picked it up from Clara (even though Maebh arrived at the TARDIS before Clara became aware of the forest). Another possibility might be an intervention by the mysterious "Missy" – but she appears in a brief cutaway at the end, with a wry comment as she watches the resolution of the threat ("Well, *that* was a surprise") that indicates she had no prior knowledge of what would happen. The said threat turns out to be an imminent massive solar flare that seems like it will destroy all life on the planet (which prompts one of the script's more memorable lines from the Doctor: "Catastrophe is the metabolism of the universe").

The best moment of real character-based drama in the episode comes when Clara convinces the Doctor to return to the TARDIS so they can all escape the (so they think) doomed Earth. When they arrive there, she reveals that it was a ruse to give *him* the opportunity to get away: "It was the only way to get you back to the TARDIS – make you think you were saving someone." Possibly the most fascinating thread of this season has been how travelling with the Doctor is changing Clara; she is still deceiving Danny about her continuing adventures, and is becoming adept at using pragmatic, Doctor-like lying to get her way. The Doctor, though, takes Clara's furious words to him at the end of *Kill the Moon* ("You walk our earth, Doctor; you breathe our air") and neatly turns them back on her, prepared to take the whole group with him ("This is my world, too"). However, she knows that taking the children somewhere else would never work, and Danny will never abandon them, so her choice is to stay as well. Coleman is superb as Clara rejects the offer to join him with brutal honesty: "I don't want to be the last of my kind."

Danny gets some decent screen time here, and Anderson gives a convincing portrayal of a man who has successfully surmounted the bad experiences of his past, and is now calm and centred, with plenty of patience to cope with the kids' wrangling and complaining. He proves a capable leader, always putting the children's interests ahead of his own (although the script undermines him a couple of times by making him fail to notice Maebh's absence). When he confronts Clara with proof that she still has regular contact with the Doctor, his palpable disappointment shames her into agreeing to be honest with him from now on, in a moment which reflects the theme of the larger story ("Fear a little bit less, trust a bit more"), and makes good use of the music from Clara's "fear" monologue in *Listen*. The chemistry between the two actors is still only mild, but the low-key romance has been built up well over the season, despite our view of it being mostly restricted to small flashes squeezed into the interstices of the adventures. With it receiving a more central focus here, it's finally possible to understand what Clara sees in him.

With the Doctor's talk of Ice Ages happening overnight, trees making themselves flameproof by controlling the oxygen in the atmosphere, and his realisation that the worldwide forest will provide a "planetary airbag" against the solar flare, *In the Forest of the Night* is down there with *Kill the Moon* in terms of scientific verisimilitude. But unlike that episode, where the stream of scientific nonsense clashed badly with the high-tech setting, these concepts seem less objectionable set against a magical forest which disappears when its job is done as unaccountably as it arrived. Or perhaps it would be better to say that spending effort on providing scientific justifications would be beside the point; whatever success the story has comes from emphasising the sheer strangeness of what is happening, rather than trying to explain it away. Its scale widens even more when the Doctor realises that the intelligence has saved the human race before ("You remembered the fear, and you put it into fairy stories") – even though this unwisely draws attention to the fundamental incompatibility between this story and the numerous other threats to Earth and the human race the Doctor has encountered throughout history.

As mentioned above, finding a way to give the children an active involvement, rather than having them simply trailing after Clara, Danny and the Doctor from place to place, is a problem which the script never really finds a solution for. Near the end, the Doctor sets up a "worldwide phone call" so that the children can put together a message telling everyone not to attack the trees, which feels like a rather desperate attempt to give the kids some relevance. It's also, interestingly, the Doctor's one positive action in the episode – in the face of a world-covering forest, he is unusually helpless (a clever use of the old "sonic screwdriver doesn't work on wood" gag). Fortunately for him, his enforced inaction – and trust that the entity behind the forest has everything under control – is just what the situation requires.

The only other character in the story is Maebh's hapless mother, who is included to represent the multitude of parents who, in reality, would be in the same situation. Her only role is to wander through the forest by herself in search of her daughter, whom she conveniently finds at just the right moment to bring the tale to an end. However, a final twist is offered, rather akin to the tacked-on, bogus happy ending of the 2011 Christmas special *The Doctor, the Widow and the Wardrobe*. As they arrive home, in a bafflingly obscure scene, Maebh's missing elder sister suddenly materialises in front of them. Judging from Maebh's line ("I knew you'd be here. The thought of you came to me"), the intended inference seems to be that the intelligence took her in order that Maebh would become a channel it could use to communicate, and is now returning her unharmed.

Earlier, the Doctor was made to express disgust at Maebh being given medication to quiet the "voices" in her head – as if using drugs to combat mental illness was somehow a stupid and harmful thing to do. It's an attitude unworthy of the Doctor, a piece of poorly thought out scripting recalling the similar ham-fisted treatment of child abuse in the 2006 clunker *Fear Her*. There's an equally careless glibness in this final sequence, with the trauma of poor Annabel's abduction being left totally unexamined; she doesn't even get so much as a line to tell us how she feels about being taken away for a year. In a way, it's an ending which fits the episode as a whole: aiming for emotion and profundity, it collapses into frustrating incoherence.

Classic Who DVD Recommendation: For another forested world that seems sinister and threatening while being ultimately benign, see

1982's *Kinda*, starring Peter Davison, with Janet Fielding, Sarah Sutton and Matthew Waterhouse.

Reflections: The classic series story *Kinda*, recommended above, has more in common with *In the Forest of the Night* than just a similarity of setting. It was another case of a new writer bringing an extremely unconventional approach to the show. Christopher Bailey's very inward, psychological tale, in which human colonists in an alien forest disrupt the peaceful existence of the native inhabitants thanks to their own inner demons, while one of the Doctor's companions becomes a conduit for an evil, disembodied intelligence taking advantage of the situation, is one of the most adult-oriented stories the series ever presented. Its director, Peter Grimwade, accused the writer of "trying to do *Play of the Month* in the *Doctor Who* slot"; nevertheless, enough "normal" *Who*-style plot elements were able to be grafted on (the Doctor is an active presence throughout, ultimately taking charge and defeating a giant monster) that the story still worked well within the context of the show. When Bailey returned the next year with a follow-up story, *Snakedance*, the integration of his complex and original ideas into *Doctor Who*'s usual idiom went much more smoothly, resulting in an even greater success.

The early 1980's was a particularly experimental time for the show; just a year before *Kinda*, *Warriors' Gate* – another first story by a new writer (Stephen Gallagher, who would go on to considerable success as both a novelist and a screenwriter) – presented a situation where the Doctor's correct course of action at the climax is to do nothing. Another story aimed more at the adults in the audience than the children, *Warriors' Gate* saw the TARDIS hijacked and the Doctor drawn to a nexus point between universes by Biroc, a member of the time-sensitive Tharil race trying to free his people from slavery. The plot keeps the Doctor busy with a journey filled with richly surreal imagery and visions of the Tharils' past glories, but in fact his mere presence is what is important. Biroc's ability to foresee and navigate among possible future timelines has enabled him to place the Doctor at the precise point where he will act as a catalyst, prompting a series of events that that will end with the Tharils being freed without needing his direct action.

Much later, Steven Moffat's first season in 2010 contained an example of an episode by a high-profile, special guest writer, in Richard Curtis's *Vincent and the Doctor*. Like *In the Forest of the*

Night, it centred around a mentally fragile character, whom the Doctor is unable to help (and has a rather more realistic portrayal of such a condition than the one in *Forest*). Again, it's a story oriented towards the older audience, with the usual *Doctor Who* monster-chasing being a very secondary concern. And the emotional, if slightly indulgent, ending where the Doctor gives Vincent a quick trip to the present day is one that shows a writer looking at the series with a fresh eye.

I bring these three stories up to show that despite its idiosyncratic approach, there's not much in *In the Forest of the Night* that hasn't been done before – and done better – elsewhere, and because the episode is frankly too dull and inconsequential to offer much food for thought in itself. It tries for a note of mystical awe, and there are some individual moments and cleverly written lines to be appreciated, but on the whole the characters are uninteresting, the situation is totally preposterous and the resolution too unbelievable to stir any sense of wonder in all but the youngest of viewers. Not only is it uninvolving, with the Doctor kept almost entirely inactive, it is totally irrelevant to the overall season plot, except for Danny finally bringing Clara to accept that she needs to tell him the truth, which leads into the beginning of the next episode – a small moment that has nothing to do with the story proper. *In the Forest of the Night* might best be thought of as the sort of magical fable a parent might spin for a small child at night to help them get to sleep. It's not a *Doctor Who* story – it's a *Doctor Who*-flavoured bedtime story.

11: Dark Water

Writer: Steven Moffat
Director: Rachel Talalay
Originally Broadcast: 1 November 2014

Cast

The Doctor: Peter Capaldi
Clara: Jenna Coleman
Danny Pink: Samuel Anderson
Missy: Michelle Gomez
Woman: Joan Blackham
Gran: Sheila Reid
Seb: Chris Addison
Dr Chang: Andrew Leung
Boy: Antonio Bourouphael
Cyberman: Jeremiah Krage
Mr Armitage: Nigel Betts

In *Dark Water*, Steven Moffat begins the process of drawing together the threads of this season. Being the first half of a two-parter (the first time the show has spread a story across multiple episodes since 2011's *The Rebel Flesh* and *The Almost People*), it has the luxury of being able to draw the Doctor and Clara into the schemes of "Missy" and leave them entangled there, without as yet needing to provide solutions or explanations. This is an episode in which everything goes wrong for them, starting with an exceptionally brutal blow in the opening minutes: Danny Pink is killed in a road accident while talking to Clara on his phone. Having finally nerved herself to confess to him everything about her travels with the Doctor, Clara only gets as far as a preliminary "I love you" before the ominous, prolonged silence at the other end of the line tells her something has gone badly wrong.

Coleman handles this pivotal moment superbly, with Clara's bafflement at suddenly hearing a strange woman's voice on the phone turning to face-freezing realisation as the woman babbles about finding the phone thrown away and "the car, it just came out of nowhere." The stone face remains throughout the ensuing montage of police sirens, massed onlookers, memorial messages and condolences from her colleagues, until she is back home with her grandmother (who, as we know from her previous appearance in *The Time of the Doctor*, is the family member she feels closest to). Gran offers some words of comfort which Clara shrugs off; she has moved on from denial into a cold anger at the meaninglessness of Danny's death. "I am owed better," she declares with unsettling determination, putting in a call to the Doctor. He answers, with a cheery "So, what can I do for you, Clara?" – a particularly unfortunate choice of words as she enters the bargaining phase of her grief.

The first ten minutes after the opening titles comprise a self-contained showcase for Capaldi and Coleman, as the Doctor and Clara have an incredibly tense confrontation. Using all the pragmatism she has learned from the Doctor this season, she puts on a smiling face as she bounds into the TARDIS and asks him to take her to see an active volcano. While he is doing so, she gathers up all of his TARDIS keys, then uses an anaesthetic "sleep patch" to knock him out. When he recovers, they are outside and she is holding the keys over the lava, threatening to destroy his access to the TARDIS forever unless he helps her recover Danny. She throws a couple of them in to establish her control, but he still refuses, pointing out that doing as she wants would cause an unresolvable paradox – if he reverses Danny's death, then she will never bring them here and demand that he reverse it. But with her "control freak" personality (remarked on by the Doctor as long ago as *Deep Breath*), his attempts to gain the upper hand only make her more intransigent. She destroys all but one key, holding the last one up like Frodo with the Ring at Mount Doom. One last refusal from the Doctor, and it disappears into the lava – and Coleman is amazing as she shows Clara crumpling instantly, sobbing at the realisation of what she has done.

However, the Doctor was one step ahead of her and in control of the situation all along; the sleep patch didn't work on him, and he turned it back on her instead. They are still inside the TARDIS; he let her play out her whole scenario in a dream state, to see just how far she was willing to go. Coleman is again pitch-perfect as Clara hits her lowest point; when she asks the Doctor what the two of them do now and he simply replies "Go to hell," she can only nod numbly and move to leave. But driving home a major theme of the season – that although the Doctor may look human, he does not react in human fashion – he has already moved past Clara's duplicity. With the superb line "Do you think I care for you so little that betraying me would make a difference?" he sets off on the trail leading to Danny – to hell, or wherever else it might take them. Of course, the problem is that there *is* no trail in the conventional sense, no clues to be followed. But Moffat has a neat solution that short-circuits the need for an "investigation" phase of the story; using the TARDIS's telepathic interface (as seen in *Listen*) to draw on Clara's connection to Danny, she and the Doctor are taken straight to the enemy's base of operations.

They arrive in the headquarters of the 3W Institute – a dark and gloomy mausoleum containing dozens of glass-enclosed tombs, each one full of water and containing what looks like a seated skeleton. In a macabre moment, one of the skeletons turns its head to follow them as they go by. But the mood soon lifts as Missy makes her long-awaited move out of the shadows to confront the Doctor and Clara directly, hilariously pretending to be a "multi-function, interactive welcome-droid" ("Mobile Intelligent Systems Interface") whose intimacy settings have been somewhat mis-calibrated; she forcefully snogs the Doctor, complete with fond little kisses on the end of his nose. Michelle Gomez is clearly having a whale of a time with Missy running rings around the stunned Doctor; her pretend-robotic head movements on "Helping you, to help me, to help you" are a delight. Despite the circumstances that brought them here, even Clara gets some amusement out of the Doctor's bewilderment. Later revelations shed more light on Missy's behaviour, but at this point her complete unpredictability is itself enough to provide great enjoyment, such as her sudden yelling for her minion, Doctor Chang, which punctures an intimate close-up.

Meanwhile, Danny has arrived in the Nethersphere, the "afterlife" which has claimed many characters this season, and is being dealt with by Seb, the bureaucratic flunky previously seen in *The Caretaker*. With a great deal of exposition about Missy's complicated scheme to get across, Moffat skilfully interleaves the two strands of the story; Danny learns more about the Nethersphere at the same time as Doctor Chang, under the mistaken impression that the Doctor and Clara are government inspectors, obligingly fills in the details of the operation at 3W for us. It is soon clear that there is not any kind of supernatural element to what is going on: as Seb says, "This isn't really an afterlife; it's just more life than you were expecting," making an analogy between Danny's former life and an embryo, unaware of the next stage of existence. But even as he plays the part of a concerned functionary trying to help a new arrival settle in, Seb's objective is actually to increase Danny's disorientation and confusion, by making him face the event from his past that has cast its shadow over him for the whole season, and caused him to give up his army career. We see a flashback of his unit engaged in urban combat in the Middle East, in the course of which he breaks down the door of a house, unleashing a burst of gunfire that kills a young civilian boy. Now, after his own death, he is forced to meet with the child he killed, with no idea what he can possibly say to him – even as he starts to blurt out a halting apology, the boy simply runs off.

But being brought face to face with your own victim is only one of the ways the Nethersphere has to horrify its inhabitants. Danny hears a sudden agonised scream, to which Seb merely remarks, "Sounds like somebody left their body to science." Then he realises he can't stop shivering – which Seb explains as being due to his body being kept in a cold place. Moffat stretches out the full revelation for as long as possible – almost too long, in fact, with Doctor Chang's repeated warnings that what he is about to reveal "will change your life." The Doctor is unimpressed by his reticence, but the truly hellish concept Moffat has come up with actually lives up to the anticipation: "The dead remain conscious. The dead are fully aware of everything that is happening to them." The name 3W stands for the three words "Don't cremate me," which have supposedly been detected as a recurring psychic message from the recently deceased.

While Missy eavesdrops on their conversation, the Doctor dismisses the whole thing as some kind of fakery – it's a scam, and "all these poor souls down there in these tanks… they're not coming back." With a grin, she responds by activating them: all the skeletons stand up and prepare to exit their tanks. Earlier, Doctor Chang had described how the fluid in the tanks is actually a special kind of "dark water" which only shows organic matter; the bodies are encased in a "support exoskeleton" which is invisible while submerged. This is simply a convenient plot device, a bit of bogus science by which Moffat delays the crucial revelation until the tanks are being drained – that the dead bodies have been turned into Cybermen. It's a neat twist, but rather clumsy by comparison with earlier hints such as the Cyberman eye, with its distinctive "tear drop" in one corner, being present as a design feature throughout 3W; the moment when a pair of doors close to form a Cyberman face after the Doctor says "I feel like I'm missing something obvious" – as Murray Gold's six-note Cyber-fanfare blares out – is more likely to raise the hairs on the back of the neck.

Now that Doctor Chang has served his purpose, Missy takes charge, showing off her twisted humour as she orders him to "Say something nice" before casually disintegrating him. She happily leads the Doctor through the rest of her scheme: the Nethersphere is actually a piece of Time Lord technology, a data storage device being used to hold and edit the minds of the dying, prior to them being downloaded into the "upgraded" bodies. "Cybermen from cyberspace – now why has no one ever thought of that before?" she says, with understandable pride, since it's a very neat idea. The Cybermen have always worked best when writers have focused on them not as simple monsters but as transformed human beings. In earlier stories, the Cybermen's efforts were directed at converting living humans, but giving them a way to make use of the dead creates an even greater menace – as Missy says, the dead vastly outnumber the living. As these new Cybermen activate, Moffat recaptures something of the chill of 1967's *The Tomb of the Cybermen* with its famous scene of an army of the creatures emerging from serried ranks of holding cells. The Doctor escapes from the mausoleum – only to discover that 3W was contained within St. Paul's Cathedral, in the heart of London.

But the climactic action is intercut with another standout emotional sequence for Coleman and Anderson. Clara gets an opportunity to talk with Danny again, but with the Doctor's admonition to be sceptical and critical in mind, she can find no way to convince herself that she really is talking to the man she knew, and the result is even more pain for both of them. Danny is lost and bewildered, unable to do anything but repeat "I love you." Previously, that phrase was the most important thing for Clara to say; now, she simply brushes it off as irrelevant if she can't be sure who she is talking to. She is determined to somehow be with him again, and so he steels himself to keep repeating "I love you" until she finally cuts the connection, her face as frozen as when she first lost him. Until now, Chris Addison has had fun playing Seb mostly as a comedy bureaucrat, but now he takes the opportunity to make him a sly and subtle tempter as he achieves his objective. As Danny breaks down in tears, Seb presents him with the option to delete these "difficult feelings" and quietly leaves him to think it over.

The ultimate revelation of Missy's true identity, the Mistress ("Couldn't very well keep calling myself the Master, now could I?"), is almost unnecessary by the time it arrives, as throughout her scenes with the Doctor she has demonstrated the very same kind of demented playfulness that John Simm's Master indulged in opposite David

Tennant. Just how this transformation squares with the fate of the Master the last time we saw him, sealed away with the rest of the Time Lords in Tennant's finale *The End of Time* (2010), remains to be explained (presuming that it will be – in the classic series, the Master's repeated escapes from certain death became almost a running joke). The bright sunshine of this scene, and Missy's enjoyment at pulling the rug out from under the Doctor, make for a strangely upbeat moment after the grimness of what has gone before. But while the episode may climax with a force of Cybermen striding down the steps of St. Paul's Cathedral, and the Doctor face to face with a nemesis he had thought long gone, it's the final shot of Danny with his finger poised over the DELETE button that will end his pain which is the most ominous image of them all.

Classic Who DVD Recommendation: The cliffhanger with the Cybermen on the steps of St. Paul's is a conscious homage to the 1968 classic *The Invasion*, starring Patrick Troughton, with Frazer Hines and Wendy Padbury. Although two of its eight episodes are still currently missing (they are recreated in animated format on the DVD release), it's still well worth watching.

Reflections: It was a very welcome move for Moffat to reintroduce two-part stories into the series after a gap of three and a half years. In all of that time, beginning with the 2011 mid-season finale *A Good Man Goes to War*, the only stories longer than the (approximately) 45 minutes of a standard episode were the regular Christmas specials, the Fiftieth Anniversary special, and Capaldi's first episode (*Deep Breath*). The positive side of having more stand-alone episodes is that the show can present a greater variety of times and places, but there is also the danger of a certain staleness because of the constraints imposed on the storytelling by the restricted running time. When, every week, the show has to introduce a whole new background, set up a problem, get the Doctor and companion involved, develop the situation, bring the action to a climax, resolve it, and send the Doctor on his way, it's difficult to avoid the stories falling into an over-familiar rhythm, thereby reducing their effect. This season's stories have already seen a slower tempo introduced into the writing, making time for extended scenes of conversations between characters (see *Listen*, in particular) in contrast to the frequently more frenetic Matt Smith years, but having a two-parter really allows the scenario to grow and develop at its own pace. It also enables the show to tell a story (like this one) that is simply too big to fit in a single episode, and the idea of telling fewer, but larger and more complex stories would be an important characteristic of the next season.

Of course, the most immediately memorable aspect of this episode was the revelation of Missy's true identity – not only as the Master (and I correctly predicted that Moffat would keep up the tradition of not bothering to explain how the Master got away from his/her previously certain doom) but as the Master in female form. The idea that Time Lords can change gender when they regenerate has been a part of the speculation in both fandom and the media for decades whenever a new Doctor has been cast. It was alluded to in passing in Neil Gaiman's *The Doctor's Wife* in 2011, but only here does the possibility indisputably become part of the show's canon. With the calls for a female Doctor only likely to increase in the future, Moffat's decision to try out the idea by making the Master female is a brilliant one. (It should be noted that he had already briefly written for a female Doctor, albeit only as a deliberate comedy, in his excellent spoof of the show for the 1999 Comic Relief telethon, *The Curse of Fatal Death*, when Joanna Lumley took on the role as the culmination of a whole line of well-known actors playing short-lived incarnations, and did it very well.) A certain amount of controversy was inevitable, but accusations of tokenism or political correctness were refuted in the best possible way – simply by the power and quality of Michelle Gomez's performance. She clearly showed in this two-parter that she fits perfectly alongside the other actors who have portrayed the Master, to such an extent that by the time Missy returned at the beginning of the next season, the fact that the Master was now in female form had become a complete non-issue.

"If you've had a recent loss, this might be... this *will* be disturbing," says Doctor Chang, and he's not wrong. The question of what happens after death is a very unusual area for *Doctor Who* to venture into, and an uncompromising tone is set from the start by the dreadfully real manner of Danny's off-hand demise. As would be expected for a show that is (at least nominally) science fiction, the ultimate explanation for the "afterlife" we have been shown throughout the season is completely non-supernatural in nature, and Moffat is careful to avoid contradicting any personal beliefs that viewers may hold by making it clear (even more so in the second half) that the whole Nethersphere set-up has been contrived by Missy. Even so, the idea of being made to feel your own cremation is a viscerally horrifying one – and one of a different order than Moffat's usual exploitation of childhood fears to produce monsters able to give both adults and children a scary thrill. While the story is compelling, there is nothing "escapist" in the plight of the dead, nor in Clara's grief or Danny's distress. As I mentioned in my review of *Into the Dalek*, the show's audience figures took a hit after this season's finale, and while various external factors (to be discussed) were at least partly to blame, it would not surprise me at all if some found all the bleakness here to be a step too far.

12: Death in Heaven

Writer: Steven Moffat
Director: Rachel Talalay
Originally Broadcast: 8 November 2014

Cast

The Doctor: Peter Capaldi
Clara: Jenna Coleman
Danny Pink: Samuel Anderson
Missy: Michelle Gomez
Seb: Chris Addison
Osgood: Ingrid Oliver
Kate Lethbridge-Stewart: Jemma Redgrave
Colonel Ahmed: Sanjeev Bhaskar
Boy: Antonio Bourouphael
Teenage Boy: Shane Keogh-Grenade
Teenage Girl: Katie Bignell
Graham: James Pearse
Cyberman: Jeremiah Krage
Voice of the Cybermen: Nicholas Briggs
Santa Claus: Nick Frost

Picking up from where we left off after last week's cliffhanger, when Cybermen under the control of the Doctor's old adversary, the Master – now in the form of "Missy" – came stomping down the steps of St. Paul's Cathedral, Steven Moffat quickly widens the scope of the story and establishes the worldwide scale appropriate for a season finale. The forces of UNIT, led by Kate Lethbridge-Stewart and scientist Osgood (both last seen in 2013's *The Day of the Doctor*), surround the area and take Missy into custody. But they are unable to stop these new Cybermen, who now have the ability to fly, and can only watch the bizarre sight of the cathedral's dome opening up and disgorging dozens of Cybermen rocketing into the sky, rapidly dispersing over the globe and exploding into dark, roiling clouds that blanket the world's cemeteries.

The Doctor and Missy are brought aboard UNIT's flying base – just a normal jetliner this time, in contrast to the fantastical floating aircraft carrier, the *Valiant*, they had at their disposal back in the Russell T

Davies era. The Doctor is astonished to learn that protocols are now in place to install him as President of Earth in the event of alien incursion. (He later gets a good moment taunting Missy with this, mocking her for all her previous scheming to rule the world when he's just had control of it dropped into his lap.) It's a role he's not particularly happy in, which perhaps exacerbates the return of his anti-soldier prejudice from earlier in the season, UNIT's Colonel Ahmed being the latest target of his invective. It remains unclear what Moffat was trying to achieve by giving Capaldi's Doctor this character trait; there's no comment or reflection on it later, even after the world is saved by a soldier – Danny Pink – which leaves a sour taste in the mouth.

In any case, the Doctor discovers that the clouds are producing not rain but "Cyber-pollen" that can convert the bodies of the dead into Cybermen, ready to be occupied by the minds Missy has gathered in the Time Lord data storage device, the Nethersphere – which include Danny Pink. The idea of dead bodies becoming occupied by other intelligences previously occurred in 2005's *The Unquiet Dead*, when the Doctor was in favour of such "recycling" – at least until the Gelth turned out to be invaders rather than refugees. Here, the Cybermen's "rainwater" is seen moving up through drains and along streets (looking rather like the amorphous, disembodied Master in the 1996 TV movie starring Paul McGann) until it enters a funeral home and converts the bodies there, including Danny's, into Cybermen.

When I wrote about the Cybermen's previous appearance, in 2013's *Nightmare in Silver*, I predicted that the new capabilities they gained in that episode – to move at super-speed and to adapt themselves to neutralise any weapon used against them – would be toned down the next time they showed up. Sure enough, there's no sign of either ability here; justified, no doubt, by the fact that these Cybermen are Missy's creations and completely unrelated to the ones we've seen before, they are less *Star Trek*'s Borg and more a plague of zombies. Director Rachel Talalay, bringing to *Doctor Who* her extensive experience on the *Nightmare on Elm Street* film series, delivers some macabre imagery of Cybermen emerging from graves, clawing their way into the light. (She also later provides Colonel Ahmed with a death scene that cleverly replicates the shock ending of the first *Nightmare on Elm Street* film, as he is abruptly grabbed and pulled through a window of the plane by a Cyberman.) The "newborn" Cybermen, disoriented and stumbling around the graveyard, are not an

101

immediate menace but serve as a reminder of the scale of the threat: as the Doctor says, "How can you win a war against an enemy that can weaponize the dead?" The constant cloud cover casts a grey pall over all the graveyard scenes that effectively creates an ominous atmosphere for the grim drama taking place in them.

Like several previous season finales, this is an extended episode, with a running time more than ten minutes over the standard forty-five. Unfortunately, as happened with *Deep Breath* at the beginning of the season, the extra length is not particularly beneficial. Its main effect is to allow several scenes in the first half to be more meandering than necessary; UNIT's arrival, for example, under cover of Osgood pretending to take a photograph of the Doctor and Missy, or Kate's long-winded introduction of herself to the Cybermen, with some tedious back-and-forth between her and the Doctor about him being on the UNIT payroll. I don't mind in-jokes made in passing, such as showing the Doctor spooning a ridiculous amount of sugar into his coffee (referencing a similar moment in 1974's *Invasion of the Dinosaurs*), or Missy's use of the same galactic co-ordinates for Gallifrey as were employed several times in the classic series (beginning with *Pyramids of Mars* in 1975). But holding up the story so that Clara can pretend to be the Doctor and spout at some Cybermen a lengthy stream of fan-pleasing biography, as if she's memorised his Wikipedia entry, is just self-indulgent.

Clara's whole "I'm the Doctor" bluff in the teaser really only exists as a way for the episode to follow Moffat's favoured custom of starting the second half of a two-parter in the most unexpected way he can contrive. Admittedly, it does lead into a clever gag with the opening titles being altered: the names are reversed, with Jenna Coleman's coming first, and her eyes appear instead of Capaldi's. It also gives her a few moments of fast-talking comedy, to contrast with the emotional pain Clara goes through in the rest of the episode. But it's a very roundabout way to get to the payoff moment, when she finds herself unknowingly telling the Cyberman who was once Danny, "Ask anybody who knows me – I am an incredible liar." Danny can only agree as he responds with Cyber terseness: "Correct." Moffat, with his usual talent for subtle nuances in dialogue, gives Danny this simple affirmative several times, with a different effect each time depending on whether he's saying it to other Cybermen, to Clara, to the Doctor, or to Missy. We saw him earlier looking out over the Nethersphere with the boy he killed when he was a soldier still at his side, signifying that he was unable to go ahead with deleting his emotions at the end of the last episode. Now trapped in the body of a Cyberman, he takes Clara to one of the graveyards filled with the creatures and begs for her help to turn on his body's emotional inhibitor – effectively, to help him commit suicide.

When the Doctor asks how UNIT knew to move in at St. Paul's, he learns they received a tip-off from "a woman with a Scottish accent" (i.e. Missy herself). "Can't play to the gallery unless there's a gallery and here I am," he comments – but Missy's motives are deeper than simple vanity, as we will see. After hovering around the fringes of the stories for most of the season, Missy finally takes centre stage (even in *Dark Water*, she was mainly used to provide exposition and moments of humour), and Gomez gives a fantastically charismatic performance. She is psychotically unpredictable, at times even hilarious, such as when she casually disposes of her minion Seb, or when she makes her army of Cybermen pretend to be giving an airplane safety briefing. Amid the laughs, though, are moments of real nastiness, in particular the sadistic killing of the likeable Osgood. Ingrid Oliver's character became an immediate fan favourite after her first appearance, with her habit of dressing up like the Doctor's past incarnations – today she's being the Eleventh Doctor, complete with his "Bow ties are cool" catchphrase. The Doctor is impressed by her deducing Missy's identity, and holds out the prospect of her joining him as a companion, which makes even more painful Moffat's decision to sacrifice her in order to drive home just how irredeemable Missy is. Unfortunately the staging of this scene is quite unconvincing, with two armed guards standing right behind Missy who fail to react as she frees herself from her handcuffs; in fact, she somehow manages to disintegrate them before they can make the slightest move. Rather more successful is the shocking moment soon afterwards when she blows a hole in the side of the plane and Kate is sucked out to her apparent death.

The amount of extraneous padding in the first half is shown by the fact that Missy's line to the Doctor – "And now it begins" – which signals that all the preparation is done, the plot rollercoaster has crested the top and it's about to set off on its run downhill, occurs precisely at the halfway point of the episode. The line refers to Clara's call to the TARDIS phone, demanding the Doctor's help with Danny. This scene allows Moffat to neatly tie together the whole of Clara's time with the Doctor, revealing that their initial meeting (back in 2013's *The Bells of Saint John*) was set up by Missy – she was the "woman in the shop" who gave Clara the Doctor's number, pretending it was a computer help line. He also confirms (not that there was any remaining doubt) that she was the one behind the newspaper advertisement in *Deep Breath* that drew the Doctor and Clara back together. She has been running a very long-term operation, gathering up all those who have died in the vicinity of the Doctor, all the while knowing that Clara would eventually cause him to come here: "The control freak and the man who should never be controlled. You'd go to hell if she asked. And she would."

From this point, as usual in Moffat's season finales, the focus narrows down to purely the regular characters; the threat of the Cybermen and their pollinating rainclouds remains, but is pushed to the background. Until now, the Doctor has been mostly reacting, struggling to keep up with Missy's antics. Only after the explosion of the plane does he come into his own, saving himself with a *Superman*-style stunt, flying through the air until he catches up with the falling TARDIS, which takes him to Clara and Danny in the graveyard. This scene is an emotional high point for all three characters. The Doctor's anguish is obvious as he tells Danny about his childhood friend who turned out to be so different when they grew up ("Now she's trying to tear the world apart, and I can't run fast enough to hold it together") in an effort to convince him to hold on to his human identity even through the pain. But Danny once again cuts the Doctor to the quick by treating him as an officer (as in their confrontation in *The Caretaker*). He points out that he can't access the Cybermen's plans unless the emotional inhibitor is activated, ending with a bitterness ("And didn't all of those beautiful speeches just disappear in the face of a tactical advantage... *Sir*?") that leaves the Doctor in a terrible quandary. Capaldi, Coleman and Anderson are all at the top of their game here; in particular, Coleman's ability to believably show extremes of emotion comes to the fore as Clara takes over from the Doctor the task of activating the inhibitor, bidding Danny a tearful farewell as she aims the sonic screwdriver and presses the button.

But for the moment Danny manages not to be overwhelmed by the Cyber conditioning (we have seen various strong-willed individuals able to resist in previous Cybermen stories) and tells how the clouds will fall as rain and convert all still-living humans into Cybermen. Then Missy arrives (descending from above in a fashion that amusingly highlights her Mary Poppins-like costume), and staggers the Doctor by revealing her real purpose: she gives him the bracelet through which she controls the entire Cyber-army. In his first opportunity to write a Master story, Moffat has clearly put a lot of thought into the relationship between the two of them, and Gomez gives Missy an almost pitiable vulnerability as she lays bare her true motives: "I need you to know we're not so different! I need my friend back." She has set up a situation in which he will be forced to accept command of a conquering Cyber-army that can grow ever larger by recruiting the dead, and tempts him with the thought of all he could accomplish with it ("Give a good man firepower, and he'll never run out of people to kill").

This scene is Moffat's ambitious culmination for the whole season – a climax on a thematic level, rather than simply a plot resolution as was primarily the case with his previous season arcs. Flashbacks from previous episodes (in particular, the crucial "Am I a good man?" from *Into the Dalek*) remind us that the Doctor has been troubled by uncertainty about himself ever since he regenerated. It takes Missy's offer of ultimate power for him to realise the truth. His fervent "I am *not* a good man!" complete with a kiss to thank her might make us worry for a moment, but he follows up that he is not a bad man either, but "an idiot, with a box and a screwdriver... passing through, helping out, learning." Capaldi projects an almost palpable relief as, after a year of doubt, the Doctor is finally sure of himself again, and throws the control bracelet to the Cyberman that was once Danny Pink.

In past encounters, the Master's schemes always had a tendency to fall apart at the end due to some small overlooked flaw, and here she fails to notice the one Cyberman not obeying her orders. Despite being encased in heavy prosthetics, Anderson gives easily his most effective performance of the season in this episode. This ending, in which Danny's love for Clara is what allows him to hold onto his humanity to the finish, comes dangerously close to falling into sentimental nonsense. But Anderson makes it work, and his quiet confronting of Missy, followed by a parade ground speech to the army of Cybermen, is a genuinely powerful moment, ending with his final line to Clara: "The promise of a soldier... You will sleep safe tonight." I would have preferred the implied rebuke to the Doctor's earlier anti-soldier diatribes to have been more explicitly acknowledged, but Danny's victory is clear as he leads the Cybermen into the air to sacrifice themselves and burn away the clouds, leaving the Doctor, Clara and Missy standing in bright sunshine.

A lengthy wrapping-up begins with Missy quietly giving the Doctor what she says are the co-ordinates of his lost homeworld, Gallifrey. She still has ideas of travelling together with him, but Clara turns the woman's own disintegrator on her, fully prepared to kill her. The Doctor, perhaps remembering earlier occasions this season that showed sometimes one has only bad choices, takes the weapon and faces Missy himself, even as she mocks him with her catchphrase, "Say something nice." Capaldi is superb in their simple final exchange ("You win." "I know") which echoes the end of 2007's *Last of the Time Lords*, when the dying Master refused to regenerate in order to spite the Doctor. But a surprise twist lets him off the hook – a lone remaining Cyberman shoots her first (although the chances that Missy is permanently dead are, of course, zero). When Kate is found still alive, it becomes apparent that this Cyberman who saved her was her late father, the Doctor's old friend Brigadier Lethbridge-Stewart. Earlier, she had said that her father's big ambition was to get the Doctor to salute him, just once, and now the old soldier gets to see that ambition improbably realised. His death had been incorporated into a moving scene in *The Wedding of River Song* in 2011 (actor Nicholas Courtney having passed away earlier that year), and his reappearance in this form drew the ire of some fans. For myself, the sentiment of the scene worked, although it also provoked a combination of amusement at Moffat's ingenuity in finding a way to bring back the character and irritation at its weird open-endedness – although there's no doubt about the sincerity of the Doctor's heartfelt "Thank you" as the Brigadier rockets off to an unknown fate that will probably never be addressed.

Sometimes, with his big endings, Moffat is more concerned about getting to his desired emotional destination than worrying about rigorously plotting the route to it (a notable case is the loss of Amy and Rory in 2012's *The Angels Take Manhattan*), and what follows can only be described as clumsy. It's two weeks later, back in Clara's flat; she is woken from sleep, hearing Danny's voice. Moffat tries to recapture the tragedy of Rose's separation from the Doctor at the end of *Doomsday* in 2006, as Clara and Danny have one final contact before being parted forever. But in order to set up the situation, Missy's control bracelet suddenly acquires an arbitrary handicap – with the thin justification that the Nethersphere is "dying," it can now only make one more trip back to the real world, transporting one person. Danny's decision to return to life the boy he killed in his place is easy to see coming, and fails to have the desired impact. The treatment of the boy throughout has been too abstract; never even given a name, he is more a symbol – the shadow of Danny's past – than a real person. We also never had any hint earlier that Danny knew how to use the bracelet to travel between the two worlds; it emerges later that the Doctor simply expected him to work it out. The net result is that Danny's story ends much less satisfactorily than if he had been destroyed earlier in the burning of the clouds as we had thought.

One can understand why Moffat included this ending, though: it is needed in order to set up the perfect symmetry of the final scene between the Doctor and Clara. The Doctor needs to believe she has a future with Danny, and Clara needs to believe he finally has the chance to return home. But he has already discovered that Missy's information about Gallifrey was a lie – and Capaldi is devastating as the Doctor smashes at the TARDIS console in despair, his hopes cruelly dashed. As we have seen many times this season, he and Clara are both accomplished deceivers of each other, and each of them puts on a smiling face as they exchange complete untruths and agree they will be happier apart. It's a marvellously written scene, with two brilliant actors bringing out every nuance of meaning; Coleman's sigh and "Never again" as Clara looks out at the TARDIS through the window of the cafe is particularly telling. Only at one point do they allow their true feelings to show: when they share a hug, the grief that fills both of them is clear. This Doctor's dislike of hugging, a comic point earlier in the season, now provides an affecting payoff: "Never trust a hug… it's just a way to hide your face."

All the sound and fury of the season dies away in this gentle parting, as Clara watches the TARDIS leave and slowly walks off. But in a final echo of *Doomsday* – when a seemingly definitive ending was cut short by an inexplicable bride turning up in the TARDIS – the same mood whiplash occurs here in an even more jarring fashion. The end credits are interrupted by an intrusion from the next episode (the Christmas special, thankfully only a few weeks away), making it suddenly and unexpectedly clear that the Doctor and Clara still have unfinished business.

Classic Who DVD Recommendation: The interplay between the original Master (Roger Delgado) and the Doctor can be seen at its best in 1971's *The Daemons*. Starring Jon Pertwee, with Katy Manning, it also features Nicholas Courtney as Brigadier Lethbridge-Stewart, who got to play such an unexpected role in *Death in Heaven*.

Reflections: This two-parter is certainly a powerful story, but the ideas underlying it make it an uncomfortable one to watch. Death has always been a part of *Doctor Who* – in the very first episode of the revived series, *Rose* in 2005, death is described as the Doctor's "one constant companion" – but of all the hundreds of times characters' deaths have been depicted, few have had the impact of Danny's here. Then there's the way in which Missy's plot involves preying on our natural fear of death, and on depriving those buried of the dignity of resting in peace, forcibly recruiting them into her monstrous army. The one time the classic series featured death in a similar way was in 1985's *Revelation of the Daleks*, a darkly satirical story that cast Davros, creator of the Daleks, as "the Great Healer" running a galactic funeral home not unlike Missy's 3W Institute. The bodies of the dead there were supposedly being held in stasis until cures could be found for the diseases that had killed them, but actually Davros was using them to make a new race of Daleks – and selling the rejected ones after reprocessing them into food, *Soylent Green*-style, to alleviate a famine in that part of the galaxy. Despite the repugnant concepts, *Revelation* does not strike with quite the same immediacy as this story – it all happens in the far future, on another planet, and the story is mostly concerned with its own cast of rather grotesque characters; the Doctor and his companion are very peripheral and not in any way touched personally by it. Here, it is all too easy to empathise with Clara's experience, or with those traumatised by Missy's scheme.

The downbeat nature of this finale caps off a season in which the characters of the Doctor and his companion were explored and changed to a greater extent than ever before. *Doctor Who* normally sees its regular characters as more or less fixed points, around which a multifarious variety of action adventure stories take place. The modern series has always been effective at giving both the Doctor and his companions emotional complexity; his past traumas and their home and family lives have been important ever since Rose Tyler arrived in 2005. But the companion has always been an audience identification figure; we could imagine ourselves in Rose's or Donna's or Amy's place, experiencing the wonders of the universe in the company of the loveable (if sometimes acerbic) Doctor. The same was true of Clara in the 2013 stories; but this year, first the Doctor was riddled with self-doubt and dislikeable personality traits which only gradually subsided, and then the negative aspects of Clara's relationship with him were put under the spotlight. It made for good drama, but we were always on the outside, looking in.

After the success of the Matt Smith era, Moffat could easily have rested on his laurels and simply produced more of the same; he deserves applause for using the opportunity of a new Doctor to take the show in such a novel and experimental direction. But it's not surprising that some viewers were unsettled by the nature and extent of the changes, leading to a noticeable drop in audiences for the following year. In addition, scheduling considerations (mainly the logistics of the BBC's live talent show *Strictly Come Dancing*) led to the majority of Capaldi's episodes being transmitted later in the evening than usual for *Doctor Who*, which may have influenced the fact that – apart from the incongruous *In the Forest of the Night* – this season seems to have significantly less content designed to appeal to children than Moffat's previous three. Certainly, Clara's central predicament of trying to be true to both Danny and the Doctor is chiefly aimed at the adults in the audience.

Of course, Jenna Coleman's change of mind about leaving meant that Moffat had to find a way to move past the ostensibly conclusive ending of *Death in Heaven*. In the next episode Clara and the Doctor would come to recognise the mutual lying that caused their parting; then, by reconsidering the fact of Missy bringing them together and giving it a secondary purpose, Moffat would arrive at the "hybrid" arc that would underpin the 2015 season. The feeling of Clara's development taking a retrograde step, as she returned to enjoying a series of unrelated adventures with the Doctor – before eventually meeting an even more tragic fate than in this season – was an unavoidable consequence of the desire to keep Coleman on the show for another year. But it was a cost well worth paying; their second year together would give Coleman and Peter Capaldi many opportunities to show off their talents, both separately and together, in the end cementing them as one of the greatest Doctor/companion teams the show has ever seen.

13: Last Christmas

Writer: Steven Moffat
Director: Paul Wilmshurst
Originally Broadcast: 25 December 2014

Cast

The Doctor: Peter Capaldi
Clara: Jenna Coleman
Danny Pink: Samuel Anderson
Santa Claus: Nick Frost
Ian: Dan Starkey
Wolf: Nathan McMullen
Shona: Faye Marsay
Ashley: Natalie Gumede
Bellows: Maureen Beattie
Professor Albert: Michael Troughton

When writing about 2013's Christmas special, *The Time of the Doctor*, I noted the rather strained attempts Steven Moffat made to give that story a "Christmassy" feel, and wondered whether the perceived need to incorporate festive motifs into the annual yuletide episode was becoming too troublesome a tradition to be worth continuing. *Last Christmas* proves me wrong in spectacular fashion: for *Doctor Who*'s tenth consecutive Christmas special, Moffat brings *Doctor Who* and Christmas together in the most direct possible way. Almost as if cheekily daring the audience to revolt and switch off, the long (more than five minutes) pre-titles sequence plays with a completely straight face what seems like an utterly ludicrous situation. Clara, having parted from the Doctor at the end of the previous episode, encounters none other than Santa Claus himself, and a couple of snarky elves (one of them played by Dan Starkey, normally buried under heavy prosthetics as the Sontaran, Strax), when he crashes on her roof – in a sleigh drawn by flying reindeer.

Santa notes that she was a believer until the age of nine, when she stopped because "I grew out of fairy tales." "Did you really?" he says, as the TARDIS materialises behind her and the Doctor urgently tells her to get in. We had already seen him encountering Santa at the end of *Death in Heaven* (when he was roused from a snooze in the

TARDIS – in retrospect, a subtle clue – by Santa's entrance), and now his quiet seriousness as he says to Santa, "I know what's happening, and I know what's at stake," is the first hint that something more than twee sentiment is behind these events. He tells Clara there's an important question she has to ask herself: "Do you really believe in Santa Claus?" Delighted at being back in the TARDIS, she answers that right now, she does – but this misses the point; the Doctor's question is actually a key to this labyrinthine story, where the question of what is real and what is a dream will become vital.

After the opening titles, we are suddenly in a scientific base at the North Pole which is the subject of one of the show's most typical plot tropes, the "base under siege" – a small group of people, trapped in an isolated location and under monstrous attack. One of the four scientists here, Shona, nervously enters an infirmary containing four victims of crab-like creatures that wrap themselves around their prey's face like overgrown face-huggers from *Alien* (1979). In another deliberately off the wall sequence, Shona sings along and dances to Slade's *Merry Xmas Everybody* (a song used several times before in *Doctor Who*, notably in the first two Christmas specials, *The Christmas Invasion* and *The Runaway Bride*) as she makes her way past the sleepers, observed and monitored by her colleagues Bellows, Ashley and Professor Albert. But when the Doctor and Clara's arrival distracts her, the sleepers get up and shuffle towards them like the gas-masked zombies in Moffat's *The Empty Child* back in 2005. With the "dream crabs," Moffat has come up with another ingenious monster concept; the only way to remain undetected is by *not* thinking about them ("They can detect their own mental picture in any nearby mind," says the Doctor) – hence Shona's use of song and dance to keep her mind occupied. When the other three scientists burst into the infirmary to rescue them, a swarm of the creatures descends from the ceiling upon the whole group.

Suddenly, Santa and his elves arrive to rescue them – he simply orders the sleepers back to bed and they obey him, allowing them all to escape the infirmary. Despite the Doctor's earlier claim that he knows what's happening, he can clearly only have had suspicions, since he says he's only heard of the dream crabs, but never seen them before. While he is telling Clara that the presence of the creatures means she must question everything she sees and hears, Shona is methodically trying to prove that Santa can't possibly be standing in the room with them. Nick Frost (who, as Moffat happily pointed out in interviews, has the perfect name for someone portraying Santa Claus) starts out seeming merely the jolly stereotype we are all familiar with, thanks to his spot-on costume and makeup. But he soon reveals an altogether more no-nonsense character capable of taking firm control of the situation, baffling Shona with amusingly matter-of-fact statements that only highlight how ridiculous his presence is. There's the North Pole, for instance – an actual pole, complete with stripes, going through the middle of his workshop. Or how it's a scientific impossibility for reindeer to fly ("which is why I feed mine magic carrots"). Even when the Doctor himself tries a "killer question," about how all those presents fit into the sleigh, he is smugly ready with a clever answer – "bigger on the inside."

The episode strikes a better balance than some earlier Christmas specials have done between telling a satisfying individual story and simultaneously advancing the ongoing series. In Britain, a significant percentage of the audience watches *Doctor Who* only at Christmas and not at other times, and continuity-heavy stories like *The Time of the Doctor* run the risk of being quite impenetrable. (Of course, that was a case of *force majeure*: Moffat might well have preferred a lighter, stand-alone story for Christmas 2013, especially after the Fiftieth Anniversary extravaganza just a month earlier, but Matt Smith's decision to leave at that point meant there was no other opportunity to tie up all the outstanding plot threads from his era.) *Last Christmas* works as a funny, clever and creepy story in itself, while also moving the Doctor and Clara on from the mutual lying which caused their separation at the end of *Death in Heaven*. Earlier, in the infirmary, the Doctor made a crass remark about Danny Pink in order to distract Clara from the attacking sleepers, and was taken aback when she retorted that Danny was dead. Now she reveals that she kept Danny's death from him – leading to his own confession that he never found his homeworld, Gallifrey. But this quiet interlude soon turns horrific as Clara is attacked by another dream crab – only to suddenly wake up back in her bed on Christmas Day, as Danny enters dressed in a Santa Claus outfit.

Obviously this can only be a dream, and director Paul Wilmshurst makes these scenes look and feel very different, with much warmer lighting and different lenses. As Clara cheerfully banters with Danny about Christmas presents, the Doctor is trying to snap her out of it, inserting mysterious blackboards with chalked messages into her surroundings – a nice use of the motif of him scribbling on blackboards in the TARDIS which ran throughout the last season. Disorienting camera moves and discordant music show the Doctor trying to break through, but Clara finds it understandably hard to resist this beguiling fantasy of her boyfriend returned from the dead, and banishes his efforts from her mind. The Doctor is forced to enter the dream himself by allowing another dream crab to take him. However, even his gruesome description of how the creature attached to her has drilled into her brain and is slowly dissolving it fails to shake Clara, until Danny himself tells her she needs to wake up. Capaldi, Coleman and Anderson work together at this crucial turning-point of the story just as well as they did in the similar moments in *Death in Heaven*. This Danny may be merely an aspect of Clara's subconscious, but he provides some moving philosophy about how to accept and move on from the loss of a loved one, telling Clara she can miss him, but only for five minutes a day – "...the rest of the time, every single second, you just get the hell on with it." And he leaves her with a poignant reflection that shows Moffat's inspiration for the title of the episode:

Danny Pink: "Do you know why people get together at Christmas? Because every time they do, it might be the last time. Every Christmas is last Christmas. And this is ours. This was a bonus. This is extra. But now it's time to wake up."

The Doctor and Clara wake up back in the base, the dream crabs falling from their faces and disintegrating. The fact that if the crabs' feeding is interrupted they die instantly and their victims suffer no ill effects at all seems a little too convenient for the writer, meaning that no time needs to be spent on dealing with the traumatic after-effects that such an experience would logically produce. But Moffat puts the time gained to good use; in a plot development immediately reminiscent of Christopher Nolan's *Inception* (2010), the Doctor realises that they are all lost in a maze of dreams within dreams. He proves it by means of a smart piece of deduction, giving copies of the base's manual to each of the scientists; they should all be identical, but having them turn to the same randomly chosen page and read the first word on that page results in each of them saying a different word. They have all been dreaming ever since they were attacked in the infirmary and "rescued" by someone who they know can't exist. Moffat deserves particular praise for incorporating the "real" Santa Claus (i.e. not some robot or alien or some other science-fictional "explanation") into the story in a way that makes perfect sense. He is a manifestation created by the subconscious of the dream crabs' victims, trying to alert them to the unreality of what they are experiencing.

Despite the seriousness of the situation, Moffat writes the Doctor with a considerably lighter touch now that he has emerged from the severe examination of this season's stories. Peter Capaldi takes full advantage of the Doctor's many funny lines; one of my favourites occurs when Professor Albert mentions the dream crabs' aforementioned resemblance to *Alien*'s face-huggers: "There's a horror movie called *Alien*? That's really offensive – no wonder everyone keeps invading you." The Doctor's sparring with Santa gives Capaldi and Frost plenty of opportunity to show their comic talents, especially when Santa tries to paint the Doctor as just as fictional as himself, pointing out the ridiculousness of a time-travelling magician living in a phone box. (The Doctor really only has himself to blame, for saying earlier, "You know what the big problem is, in telling reality and fantasy apart? … They're both ridiculous" – a statement which is certainly true in the *Who* universe.) The funniest moment comes when Santa starts to explain about the "multi-consciousness gestalt" formed by the dream crabs, to which the Doctor splutters that "No, no, no… Santa Claus does *not* do the scientific explanation!" – to which the quick-witted Santa responds, "All right. As the Doctor might say, 'Aw, it's all a bit dreamy-weamy!'" Now that they all understand what is happening, Santa disappears, and they hold hands (to the Doctor's hilarious discomfiture) and concentrate to break out of the dream.

The Doctor, Clara, and the four scientists wake up in the infirmary, the dream crabs falling from their faces and disintegrating. After his grumbling at having to hold hands, his brusque manner from earlier in the season amusingly reasserts itself, as he simply says "Bye" and marches off, refusing to get further involved. But Clara stops him with the question which will already have occurred to the alert viewer: "If Santa was only in the dream… why was he on my roof?" What we have been taking for reality – right from the beginning of the episode – is actually another level of dreaming. In a particularly spooky touch, the crew slowly realise they can only respond "It's a long story" when the Doctor presses them about what they are doing here and what the base's mission is – and what's more, Clara can only say the same when the Doctor asks how *they* came to be here. The four sleepers are actually the four scientists – the whole setting of the polar base does not exist at all, but is simply a shared dream world, and the sleepers represent the part of themselves that has already succumbed to the attack. Moffat introduces moments of nightmarish horror as the sleepers activate and come for them, reaching straight through monitor screens to drag Professor Albert to his death. They run outside, only to be surrounded by an inexplicable horde of sleepers – "the logic of a nightmare," says the Doctor – including two that look like himself and Clara, emerging from the fake TARDIS.

The Doctor manages to find the only way to escape, with a reference back to one of Santa's earlier lines: "It's Christmas, the North Pole… who you gonna call?" The *Ghostbusters* allusion makes for an appropriately triumphant moment as Santa arrives on his sleigh to rescue them. The Doctor once again asks Clara whether she believes in Santa Claus, and this time she answers: "I've always believed in Santa Claus… but he looks a little different to me," enfolding him in a hug which it seems he has now learned to accept – or, at least, tolerate. As the sleigh careens through the skies of London, Capaldi's Doctor finally gets the chance to show pure, unconstrained joy as Santa lets him take the reins – reminiscent of the sequence in 2010's *A Christmas Carol* when Matt Smith's Doctor drove a sleigh pulled by a flying shark. After all the darkness and horror, this is a lovely warm-hearted sequence, which comes to a gentle end as the scientists realise their true identities. In fact, they have never worked together or even met before; Ashley is an account manager for perfume, while Shona works in a shop. Faye Marsay has given a lively performance throughout, and it's a sweet moment as Shona suggests they all swap phone numbers and stay in contact – but to no avail, as one by one they disappear from the sleigh.

Bellows, Ashley, and Shona wake up in their homes, the dream crabs falling from their faces and disintegrating. In a poignant touch, Bellows turns out to be a grandmother confined to a wheelchair, able to walk again in her dream. Shona evidently fell asleep after a Christmas Day DVD-watching marathon; it becomes clear she was responsible for the entire constructed dream world, as her DVD list includes the aforementioned *Alien*, plus *The Thing from Another World* (which contributed the idea of the North Pole scientific outpost) and, inevitably, *Miracle on 34th Street*. She is spending Christmas alone, and at the bottom of her list is the notation, "Forgive Dave??" – presumably her boyfriend. We'll never know who Dave is or what he did to require forgiveness, but after her experience in the dream world she places a big tick next to his name, rounding off her story with a happy ending. Meanwhile, it's time for the Doctor and Clara to wake up, too. But while the Doctor disappears from the sleigh, Clara wistfully asks to stay a little longer. Jenna Coleman was coy all through the year in interviews on the subject of whether or not she would be staying with *Doctor Who*, resulting in a genuine tension as the ending approached about just how the episode would conclude. This sequence, with Clara laying her head on Santa's shoulder as the music swells and leading to the clichéd but effective shot of the silhouetted sleigh crossing the face of the moon, has an air of finality to it, but Moffat still has some tricks left to play.

The Doctor wakes up, the dream crab falling from his face and disintegrating. He quickly travels to Clara's bedroom and removes the dream crab from her sleeping face. But she wakes up to reveal the face of an old woman, who hasn't seen the Doctor for 62 years. Under effective old-age prosthetics (although she doesn't quite manage to disguise her voice's youthfulness), Coleman shows a woman at peace with the achievements and regrets of her life. The Doctor's statement that he can't see any difference in Clara's appearance (shown from his point of view with a brief substitution of young Clara for old) is hard to take literally, but is apparently supposed to be – presumably as an explanation for all his remarks about her appearance during the season. In any case, the scene cleverly mirrors the one in *The Time of the Doctor* where Clara encounters the ancient Eleventh Doctor – right down to her lacking the strength to pull open a Christmas cracker. Noticing this, the Doctor regrets he did not come back earlier... but as Santa reappears, he realises he has still not emerged from the dream.

The Doctor wakes up, the dream crab falling from his face and disintegrating. He quickly travels to Clara's bedroom and removes the dream crab from her sleeping face. This time, a relieved Clara is back to her normal appearance. Capaldi shows a touching vulnerability in the Doctor as he asks Clara to rejoin him in the TARDIS. His offer of "all of time and all of space" recalls the Doctor's words to Amy at the end of Matt Smith's *The Eleventh Hour* (2010), and Clara's smiling acceptance and running out to the TARDIS in her nightdress also echoes the joyful ending of that episode. Although the sense of completion is somewhat undermined by a rather unnecessary homage to the ambiguous ending of *Inception* in the final shot – a tangerine (Santa's signature gift) is revealed resting on Clara's window sill while the Doctor muses that he doesn't know who to thank for his second chance with Clara – *Last Christmas* ultimately frees both of them from the baggage accumulated over the last year, and looks forward to another series of new adventures.

Classic Who DVD Recommendation: 1968's *The Web of Fear*, four of whose six episodes were returned to the BBC archives in October 2013 after being missing for decades, is a classic "base under siege" story starring Patrick Troughton (whose son Michael played Professor Albert in this episode), alongside Frazer Hines and Deborah Watling.

Reflections: The real answer to the Doctor's question of who to thank for his second chance is, of course, Jenna Coleman. Coleman's genuine changing of her mind on whether to leave in *Death in Heaven*, leave in *Last Christmas*, or (her eventual decision) stay on for another year, led to Moffat having to produce two possible endings for this episode. In the other one, this would have been one last adventure for the aged Clara, induced by the dream crab to recall her youthful travels with the Doctor and her long-ago time with Danny Pink. The Doctor would rescue her from the creature (as shown in the final version), and she would have the chance to bid him a last goodbye with all the issues between them now reconciled. Given Capaldi and Coleman's talent and rapport, there's little doubt the result would have been a heart-breaker, but the ultimate reversal achieves an ending that is just as emotional, and much more in keeping with the Christmas spirit – and it's created with an admirable economy of means. Moffat simply reveals another, previously unsuspected level of dreaming before we finally come back to reality, like a "false awakening" whereby one wakes up and goes through one's morning routine – only to wake up again and realise it was just a dream.

Moffat-era *Who* had played with dream states before, when 2010's *Amy's Choice* had the Doctor and his companions switching between two different scenarios and having to decide which of them was a dream and which was reality (a false choice, as it turned out, since both were dreams). *Last Christmas*, however, incorporates the idea of multiple, identical-looking levels of dreams, thereby adding greatly to the density of the plotting. For the most part the story hangs together sensibly; however, the additional level of dreaming revealed at the end leaves Shona and the other base crew in limbo, making it possible to imagine that they were simply dream constructs themselves, which was probably not Moffat's intention. Another anomaly is that, even in the final, real scene, Clara is living in a multi-level house which looks nothing like the flat she had earlier (and will be seen in again next season). The opening shots of the house include a stairlift which was doubtless intended to hint at the revelation of Clara as an old woman (unfortunately, the shot of the stairlift is so dark and fleeting that I never even noticed it until Paul Wilmshurst pointed it out in the DVD commentary), although later, in *Doctor Who Magazine* (issue #485), Moffat explained (albeit in his usual joking manner, meaning this could be just an after-the-fact rationalisation) that Clara was staying with her Gran for Christmas.

With this episode, we bid a final farewell to Danny Pink, a character who never worked quite as well as he really should have done. Despite being created to be with Clara, he always came most sharply into focus opposite the Doctor, responding to the Doctor's anti-soldier prejudice with intelligence and vigour, which brought out the best in actor Samuel Anderson. Elsewhere, he was mostly characterised by a lack of conflict. I certainly have no complaints over the avoidance of a "love triangle" cliché (the complete lack of romantic feeling between Clara and the Doctor being one of the most refreshing facets of the season). However, there seemed to be nothing much driving him apart from his relationship with Clara – which, due to the lukewarm chemistry between Coleman and Anderson, only rarely rose above the level of a standard rom-com. Danny's most traumatic experiences were over and done with before we ever met him, leaving him with a laid-back demeanour that, while it might make him a lovely person for Clara to be with, is not conducive to producing compelling drama. The result was a character who hardly changed over the course of the season, and Anderson himself was unable to make anything remarkable from the rather uninspiring material. Unfortunately, despite Danny supposedly being the great love of Clara's life, there is not much of a hole left by his loss; if there had been, it might not have been so easy for her to resume travelling with the Doctor for another year.

14: The Magician's Apprentice

Writer: Steven Moffat
Director: Hettie MacDonald
Originally Broadcast: 19 September 2015

Cast

The Doctor: Peter Capaldi
Clara: Jenna Coleman
Missy: Michelle Gomez
Davros: Julian Bleach
Colony Sarff: Jami Reid-Quarrell
Kate Lethbridge-Stewart: Jemma Redgrave
Jac: Jaye Griffiths
Mike: Harki Bhambra
Bors: Daniel Hoffman-Gill
Boy: Joey Price
Kanzo: Benjamin Cawley
Mr Dunlop: Aaron Neil
Ohila: Clare Higgins
Voice of the Daleks: Nicholas Briggs
Shadow Architect: Kelly Hunter
Alison: India Ria Amarteifio
Ryan: Dasharn Anderson
Newsreaders: Stefan Adegbola, Shin-Fei Chen, Lucy Newman-Williams
Daleks: Barnaby Edwards, Nicholas Pegg
Soldier: Jonathon Ojinnaka

The Magician's Apprentice begins the 2015 season of *Doctor Who* – the second for Peter Capaldi's Doctor – with a production whose swaggering confidence is quite remarkable compared with the occasionally uncertain tone and character of Capaldi's first year (particularly the first few episodes). It's like one of the bright and breezy season openers typical of the Russell T Davies era – 2008's *Partners in Crime*, say – that has been infused with Steven Moffat's penchant for non-linear narrative and many ingenious connections to moments deep in the Doctor's past. Certainly, the opening hook is one of the most impressive the series has ever produced. In a bleak, battle-scarred landscape, the Doctor encounters a young boy lost and alone, trapped in a minefield. He throws his sonic screwdriver to the boy, and is about to tell him how to use it to escape the mines. But when he learns the boy's name – Davros – he realises the child he is looking at will grow up to become the creator of his greatest enemies, the Daleks.

After that memorable teaser, ending on a close-up of Capaldi's frozen, haunted face, the Doctor is thrust offstage until the halfway point of the episode. It's an interesting move by Moffat, emphasising the fact that for the first time since 2011, the season is opening with a two-part story. As with last season's finale, the multi-episode format allows a story space to develop at its own pace, taking the scenic route and not rushing to compress a big idea into 45 minutes. In this case, Moffat can spend the first half of this episode establishing an expansive canvas, showing both friends and enemies gradually converging on the Doctor's location. While Davros, now at the end of his life, contemplates the sonic screwdriver he has kept all these years, his henchman Colony Sarff visits locations we have seen before in search of the Doctor. The Maldovarium – a wretched hive of scum and villainy, containing all manner of strange-looking aliens – was seen in the 2010 and 2011 seasons, while the Shadow Proclamation was mentioned throughout the Davies era before finally appearing in 2008's *The Stolen Earth*, the episode which reintroduced Davros into 21st-century *Who*. Sarff finally arrives at the planet Karn, home of the Sisterhood first seen in 1976's *The Brain of Morbius* and brought back in the 2013 mini-episode starring Paul McGann, *The Night of the Doctor*. Its leader, Ohila, rebuffs him, but not before he delivers his message – "Davros knows; Davros remembers" – and says the Doctor must face Davros one last time. A quick cutaway shows the Doctor watching him, silent and unseen, and after Sarff is gone Ohila's question, "Doctor, what have you done?" hangs in the air portentously.

Director Hettie MacDonald makes a long overdue return to the show after her triumph with 2007's deservedly famous *Blink*. As in that episode, she makes the most of the macabre concepts Moffat has given her to work with, which include "hand-mines" (a field of human hands emerging from the ground, with eyes embedded in their palms – a nightmarish image, in spite of some not entirely convincing CGI) and Colony Sarff, who is apparently a humanoid but actually a huge coiled snake surrounded by a writhing mass of smaller snakes. Moffat is sometimes guilty of coming up with a great creature concept and then not doing anything in particular with it (see, for example, the titular monsters in *The Snowmen*), but both of these are used well. The hand-mines are an essential part of the critical scene with the boy, and Sarff is the main enemy figure until the Doctor actually meets the dying Davros, his strange gliding motion (produced with a self-balancing scooter platform hidden under the long robe worn by the actor) peculiarly appropriate for an associate of Davros and the Daleks.

Clara, now back teaching at Coal Hill School, is drawn into the story thanks to a summons from UNIT when every airplane in the sky suddenly halts in mid-flight, frozen in time. They soon discover this is merely a ploy to get their attention by Missy, who needs their knowledge and resources to track down the Doctor. It's a welcome return for the psychopathic, scenery-chewing female version of the Master who made such an impression last year. (In keeping with long-standing tradition regarding the Master's improbable escapes from certain death, Moffat brazenly dismisses the fact that we previously saw her apparently disintegrated: "OK, cutting to the chase... Not dead, back, big surprise, never mind.") A much less welcome development in this section is the more or less complete neutering of UNIT. Kate Lethbridge-Stewart, their previously competent leader, dithers and defers to Clara from the moment she enters their HQ under the Tower of London. In the classic series UNIT started out as a fully believable military outfit, but within a few years had been softened until they were merely a backup force for the Doctor, and generally hopelessly out of their depth without him. It's rather sad to see the same degeneration taking place here, particularly since it was quite unnecessary. The dialogue could have easily been rearranged so that Clara isn't the one coming up with all the ideas – or, even better, UNIT's call to Clara could have come *after* Missy had made her appearance and demanded to speak with her.

Missy shows Clara the Doctor's "confession dial" – a golden disk apparently containing his last will and testament, delivered to her as "his closest friend" because he thinks he is about to die, and which will only open when he is dead. (It had previously been seen in a sequence cut from this episode and released online as a "Prologue" – in a continuation of the scene on Karn after Sarff has left, the Doctor gives Ohila the dial for delivery to Missy.) Once again, Michelle Gomez is so charismatic in the role that Missy has to be given a couple of hapless security guards to kill to remind us that we're not supposed to like her (and again, UNIT is made to look impotent as Kate can only order her troops not to fire on her). Clara has to struggle to regain some measure of control, and the two of them make a peculiarly fitting team as they use UNIT's historical databases to determine where the Doctor has gone to spend what he thinks will be the last night of his life. She realises they are looking not for a crisis point but for a party, and thanks to a couple of handy vortex manipulators Missy has ("cheap and nasty time travel"), the two of them arrive at a castle in Essex in the year 1138.

The Doctor's barnstorming re-entrance is an exhilarating moment of pure absurdity. Where else but in *Doctor Who* could you expect to see a sci-fi hero belting out a tune (not a million miles away from the *Who* theme) on an electric guitar to a cheering 12th-century crowd, while perched atop a tank and wearing sunglasses? Former punk rocker Capaldi is perfectly suited to portraying the Doctor as a greying headliner, playing up to the audience with some cheesy stage patter and introducing Clara and Missy as if they were his backing group ("I'd like you meet a couple of friends of mine"). The ingredient missing from last year has finally been supplied: previously, this Doctor could be funny, but rarely looked like he was enjoying it; he is now capable of actually having fun. But there's an underlying tension to this fun – when Clara points out he's being charming and playfully says "Which one of us is dying?" his response is a fierce hug, which disconcerts her even more.

When Colony Sarff turns up with the ancient sonic screwdriver, it becomes apparent that the Doctor has thrown himself this goodbye party before going to atone for an act he committed for which he feels deeply ashamed. Clara repeats Ohila's question, "Doctor, what have you done?" – and we return to the opening scene, to discover that the Doctor, shockingly, turned away from the trapped boy and left him in the minefield. We can assume that Davros then escapes on his own, embittered, goes on to create the Daleks, and many years later finally realises that the man who abandoned him was the same Doctor he has encountered many times since. Ironically, the Doctor had been intending to go to Davros anyway (and did not expect to survive, hence him sending his confession dial to Missy), but when Sarff demands he come with him, he willingly goes as a prisoner. Clara and Missy (whose indignation when the Doctor describes Davros as his arch-enemy is hilarious) decline to leave him, and surrender themselves too.

Sarff takes them to what looks at first to be some kind of hospital space station, where presumably Davros is being kept on life support.

The Doctor is led away to meet him, leaving Clara to tag along behind Missy again as they escape to the outside and realise that this "space station" is actually a building on a planet that has been rendered completely invisible. While obviously this is a contrivance for the sake of a dramatic reveal, the moment where Missy shows a tinge of fear for the first time as the planet becomes visible and she tells Clara they are on Skaro – the homeworld of the Daleks – works very well. The design work on the great city of the Daleks that Clara and Missy find themselves outside is wonderfully faithful to the work of the late Raymond Cusick on the very first Dalek story in 1963. The CGI expanse of the city exterior is extrapolated from the impressive model Cusick made for that story, and the grey interior corridors, with their distinctive sloping doorways, also closely mimic his original sets. (The doorways are a little larger, though, so that Colony Sarff can fit through them; in the original story, the doorways were deliberately sized for Daleks rather than humans, who had to stoop going through them, which made the city seem even more alien.) When the reveal comes, Capaldi even hammers on a locked door and looks around apprehensively in an intentional homage to a shot in the first episode of that story.

Whenever the Doctor encounters Davros, the confrontation scenes between them are memorable – two great intellects, with fundamentally opposing philosophical viewpoints. Davros evidently thinks so too, as when the Doctor is brought to him he reminisces about their previous conversations, and we hear excerpts from earlier stories featuring the Fourth, Fifth, Sixth, Seventh and Tenth Doctors. Then he focuses on a particular passage from 1975's *Genesis of the Daleks* (the story in which Davros was introduced), which Moffat has brilliantly used as the jumping-off point for this story. Forty years ago, Tom Baker's Doctor asked his companions: "If someone who knew the future pointed out a child to you, and told you that child would grow up to be totally evil, to be a ruthless dictator who would destroy millions of lives... Could you then kill that child?" For the Twelfth Doctor, the hypothetical conundrum became painfully real, and his attempt to evade the problem by running away has only led him back to Skaro for this reckoning. On some level, he no doubt feels this is deserved: as he mused during the journey, "Davros made the Daleks... Who made Davros?"

Clara and Missy, having been captured by a Dalek patrol, are brought to the control room of the Dalek city – and discover the TARDIS is already there, brought by the Daleks from the Earth of 1138. Again, the design work on the control room is reflective of previous Dalek stories, including the influential *TV21* comic strips of the 1960's; the huge, split-level space echoes with the distinctive "heartbeat" sound effect and is filled with a multitude of Daleks of different designs. 2012's *Asylum of the Daleks* had also made use of older Dalek props, but they were buried under a layer of grime and difficult to distinguish. Here, Daleks from all periods of the classic series are visible, all neat and shining – even including the strange Special Weapons Dalek created for 1988's *Remembrance of the Daleks* – mixed with the bronze models used throughout the modern series, along with the red Dalek Supreme from *The Stolen Earth*. The only ones missing, in fact, are the redesigned "new paradigm" Daleks introduced in 2010's *Victory of the Daleks*, which turned out to be one of the most notable failures of the Moffat era.

The Doctor, trapped in Davros's chamber, can only watch on a monitor screen as Missy offers the Daleks control of the TARDIS. This idea doesn't really stand up to scrutiny, as the Daleks are already masters of time travel, but its real purpose is to allow the Dalek Supreme to reject her offer and order her extermination. She is apparently destroyed, and the Doctor begs Davros to save Clara, with a sudden rawness of emotion which is quite disconcerting after he has been either carefree or tightly controlled in the rest of the episode. But Davros describes the Daleks as children over which he no longer has any control, taking pleasure in the sight of Clara trapped among a horde of them – until she runs for it, and they exterminate her as well. Of course, while Jenna Coleman had already confirmed before the broadcast of this episode that this season would be her last, no viewer would believe she would leave at this point or in this fashion. But as the Doctor bemoans that he ever let Davros live, Julian Bleach is brilliant as he shows Davros exultant that the Doctor might now come to share his viewpoint: "Let me hear you say it, just once. Compassion is *wrong*."

When the TARDIS itself is apparently vapourised by the Daleks, the sight propels the Doctor towards a powerful cliffhanger. We are suddenly back at the opening scene again, and he is facing the boy and carrying a Dalek gun; he levels it and says he will save his friend, "the only way I can." Does he now agree with Davros? Is he threatening to disrupt the whole timeline of the Daleks in despair over Clara? The complete lack of context means we have no way of telling right now.

The Doctor has had Davros at his mercy like this before, but always managed to avoid pulling the trigger. This time, the outcome seems wide open.

Classic Who DVD Recommendation: The abovementioned *Genesis of the Daleks* is a high point of the classic series, and stars one of *Doctor Who*'s greatest ever TARDIS teams: Tom Baker, Elisabeth Sladen and Ian Marter. The opening battlefield sequence of this episode, with its distinctive mixture of futuristic and ancient weapons, is directly inspired by the similar wasteland that forms the background to the action of *Genesis*.

Reflections: Uniquely for 21st-century *Who*, the multi-episode story format would dominate this season, although several times the line between a multi-part story and connected but distinct episodes is blurred. There may be only three "official" two-parters in the season (this episode and the next, then episodes 3 and 4, and the Zygon episodes 7 and 8), but equally there's only one episode that stands completely on its own (*Sleep No More*). Episodes 5 and 6 are obviously connected, even though they tell separate stories, while the final three, despite also being self-contained, follow directly on from each other and form an intimately linked serial story that brings the whole season to a climax. The provision of additional story material online, as in the later Matt Smith era, also returned; apart from the Prologue scene mentioned above, a six-minute mini-episode, *The Doctor's Meditation*, was released just before the season premiere. It's a mostly humorous piece, dealing with the Doctor's stay in 12th-century Essex and the lead-up to his goodbye party, although there are more sober moments as he reflects on what brought him here ("I let somebody down, when I should have been brave enough, strong enough, to do better") and what he has to do.

Among the most obvious changes in the show at the start of this season is the reinvention (for the second time) of Clara Oswald. After this episode, Coal Hill School will make no further appearances, and Clara's teaching career will barely even be alluded to. Her life on Earth apart from the Doctor, which was so important last year, simply drops away. When Missy attempts to needle her with a reference to Danny Pink's death, she simply stiffens a bit, then continues on unruffled. After being an "impossible girl" puzzle in her first year, and a much more rounded character with a dramatically convincing through-line in her second, she is now recast much more in the classic *Doctor Who* companion mould. In the mid-1970's, Sarah Jane Smith – possibly the most beloved of all the classic series companions – started out as a journalist who became an assistant to Jon Pertwee's Doctor, while still continuing to work at her day job (although, as I pointed out when discussing *The Caretaker*, we seldom saw anything of Sarah's life away from the Doctor, unlike with Clara). But when Tom Baker's Doctor arrived, Sarah quickly became purely his companion, her life revolving solely around her travels in the TARDIS. Clara in this season follows the same trajectory. The inconsistency detracts somewhat from the character's verisimilitude, but at the same time makes it easier for her to serve as an identification figure for the viewers (especially young viewers).

This move towards a more typical Doctor/companion relationship could have helped to bring back some of the viewers who found themselves out of sympathy with the unusual feel of the 2014 season. Unfortunately, some blunders were made by those responsible for promoting the new season, the most serious being a season trailer which climaxed with a line taken from the next episode: "Same old, same old... Just the Doctor, and Clara Oswald, in the TARDIS." It's a line which works perfectly well in its proper context, but as part of a trailer it could hardly have been better calculated to discourage anyone put off by the last year from expecting anything to be different. The decision that the presence of Davros in the opening episode should be completely embargoed, in case the surprise at the end of the teaser was spoiled, was also a misjudgement. It meant journalists could say almost nothing about the episode except vague fluff about lots of different types of Daleks, or the Doctor being tracked down by various friends and enemies. As a result, media coverage was unusually muted, and the normal large audience for a season premiere did not materialise – although the viewers who *did* watch, by and large, stayed for the rest of the season. Those who gave up the show after 2014 might well have been attracted again by the new season's "back to basics" approach – except that the lacklustre promotion did nothing to entice them back.

15: The Witch's Familiar

Writer: Steven Moffat
Director: Hettie MacDonald
Originally Broadcast: 26 September 2015

Cast

The Doctor: Peter Capaldi
Clara: Jenna Coleman
Missy: Michelle Gomez
Davros: Julian Bleach
Colony Sarff: Jami Reid-Quarrell
Boy: Joey Price
Voice of the Daleks: Nicholas Briggs
Daleks: Barnaby Edwards, Nicholas Pegg

The Witch's Familiar is one of those cases, rather rare in *Doctor Who*, where the second half of the story is even better than the first. Often in *Who*'s multi-part stories, the payoff struggles to match the setup, with a rushed or unconvincing resolution. Here, after the wide-ranging spectacle of *The Magician's Apprentice*, Steven Moffat changes direction and keeps the focus almost exclusively on two pairs of characters, who carry the entire second episode through a series of long but compelling dialogue scenes. The Doctor and Davros are locked in a verbal duel in the heart of the Dalek city on Skaro, while Missy and Clara start outside and gradually make their way towards them.

When on form, as he is here, Moffat is adept at constantly surprising the audience, always looking for a non-obvious way to tell the story. Absolutely nobody will be surprised that Missy and Clara are still alive after both were apparently disintegrated last week, but the pre-credits sequence still manages to find an unexpected way to reintroduce them. We find them in the desert outside the city (a location shoot in Tenerife providing a convincingly arid environment), with Clara tied up and hanging upside down, and Missy nonchalantly sharpening a stake. Clara nervously tries to work out what Missy's intentions towards her are, while the woman spins a parable of the Doctor trapped alone in a weird city, hunted by invisible android assassins. Gradually, Clara works out that the Doctor escaped his hunters by the same method Missy used to teleport herself and Clara out of the city when the Daleks fired at them. It's a nice way of getting across the explanation of how they survived without resorting to a boring info-dump, and also allows Clara to prove herself to be clever enough for Missy to keep her alive. As before, they make a strangely fitting team as they set out towards the city in search of him.

This story shows perfectly why, despite the character having always been portrayed as a dark reflection of the Doctor, we have never seen the Master with a travelling companion. Judging by Clara's experiences here, they would never survive for long. The titles of both episodes refer to Clara, but they show the very different ways she is regarded by the Doctor and by Missy. With the Doctor she is indeed an apprentice, or protégé, while Missy doesn't see her as anything more than a sort of semi-intelligent pet. Michelle Gomez again steals every scene she's in, as Missy shows an utter disregard for Clara's attempts to fill the same sort of role as she would at the Doctor's side, simply treating her as an occasionally useful tool. When they find a hole in the ground leading to the sewers underneath the city, Missy finds out how deep it is by simply giving Clara a push and seeing how long it takes her to reach the bottom. It's a funny (albeit mean) moment, but the following scene, as Clara's angry riposte is effortlessly brushed aside by Missy, shows just how out of her depth she is.

The Doctor finds a Dalek gun among the equipment in Davros's infirmary and uses it to force his way out of the chamber. Moffat provides a tremendous range of emotional material for Peter Capaldi in this episode, but also several instances of sheer fun; when the Doctor steals Davros's chair, the sight of him trundling around among a roomful of Daleks (as he tells them, "Admit it… you've all had this exact nightmare") is a laugh-out-loud moment. But there's no humour in the Doctor's ferocity towards the Daleks over what happened to Clara, as he warns of what he might do if she is really dead. In the sewers, Missy hears the Doctor's broadcast demand that Clara be returned to him, and seems simultaneously fascinated and frightened by what a Doctor without hope might be capable of. Fortunately for the Daleks, the Doctor's resolve is not tested: Davros removed from his chair makes for a grotesque sight, a helpless half-man lying on the floor of the infirmary, but soon he regains control thanks to his aide Colony Sarff, whose snakes swarm over the Doctor and immobilise him.

It is, of course, *de rigeur* in adventure stories for cities to have sewers (or ventilation ducts) that allow the heroes to get to wherever they need to under the noses of their enemies, but Moffat has actually put some thought into why the Dalek city would even have sewers, given that, as Missy tells Clara, Daleks don't generate much in the way of waste. In a nice piece of world-building, she notes that the Dalek word for sewer "is the same as their word for graveyard" – the tunnels contain a mass of dark slime, all that is left of Daleks who have aged past the ability of their mechanical bodies to keep them functioning. But the decayed Daleks are still able to sense and attack others, as Missy shows when she gleefully uses them to trap and kill a Dalek that comes to investigate the intruders. As is typical of Moffat's best plots, the Daleks in the sewers serve more than one purpose; although they may seem to be just a macabre obstacle for Missy and Clara to overcome, they will turn out to be crucial to the story's ending.

A brief glimpse of the scene we have been shown several times already, of the boy Davros trapped in the minefield, is revealed to be a dream the Doctor wakes up from to find himself back in Davros's chamber – with Davros sardonically telling him he should feel privileged to be occupying "the only other chair on Skaro." The lengthy scenes between these two are the fascinating core of the episode, as Davros attempts to establish his moral superiority over the Doctor. He explains how the machinery in this chamber sustains him by connecting him to the life force of every Dalek on the planet, and that the Daleks have no choice but to allow this because they have an inherent "design flaw" – respect and mercy towards their creator – which he could not bring himself to eliminate (another carefully planted clue to the ending). He tempts the Doctor with the possibility of interfering with the equipment and so killing all the Daleks, but the Doctor steps back from such a genocide, and when Davros taunts him with having come here because of his shame, he responds passionately:

The Doctor: "There's no such thing as the Doctor. ... And I didn't come here because I'm ashamed; a bit of shame never hurt anyone. I came because you're sick and you asked – and because sometimes, on a good day, if I try very hard, I'm not some old Time Lord who ran away... I'm the Doctor."

Davros seems strangely satisfied as the Doctor reiterates his commitment to compassion. Of course, we know that Sarff is lurking nearby, and with their earlier talk of planning to entrap a Time Lord, it's clear that Davros has carefully thought out the series of verbal grenades he lobs at the Doctor. Given a far more complex and nuanced characterisation than in the 2008 two-parter *The Stolen Earth* and *Journey's End*, where he was mostly stuck with playing a ranting megalomaniac, Julian Bleach is magnificent in conveying a full range of emotions through the heavy Davros prosthetics and makeup.

When the Doctor, perhaps unwisely, reveals that he recently succeeded at bringing his own planet and people back into existence, he is utterly thrown when Davros earnestly congratulates him. Bleach allows no hint of duplicity to show here, and indeed it's possible that Davros *is* being sincere in this – to a man whose entire existence has been focused on setting his own race against the rest of the universe, the Doctor's achievement would be deeply moving. The two of them seem to grow even closer as Davros becomes like a sage elder, giving the Doctor his blessing and telling him not to lose the Time Lords again; astonishingly, he opens his own, human eyes (and the prosthetics creators deserve particular praise for making his face totally convincing even in prolonged extreme close-ups), and quietly asks, "Did I do right, Doctor?" – leading to the following extraordinary moment:

The Doctor: "You really are dying, aren't you?"
Davros: "Look at me. Did you doubt it?"
The Doctor: (*softly*) "Yes."
Davros: "Then we have established one thing only… You are not a good doctor."

Capaldi has already shown many times that he can be compelling as the take-charge, speech-making Doctor who can dominate any situation, but here he has the equally challenging task of being the one reacting as another character makes all the big speeches in a scene. As Davros wonders "Am I a good man?" – the very question the Doctor struggled with through the last season – Capaldi superbly conveys the Doctor's scepticism about Davros's sincerity slowly melting away. And the exchange above produces a momentary stunned confusion, before the realisation that Davros actually made a *joke* leads to the incredible sight of them sharing genuine laughter. It feels like a fragile, precious moment of connection between two previously implacable opponents, and it's no wonder that when Davros seems to grow even weaker, the Doctor cannot resist helping him.

Meanwhile, Missy continues to use Clara for her own ends, convincing her to climb inside the casing of the Dalek she killed earlier. The sight of her wired into the machinery brings back memories of Jenna Coleman's first appearance in *Doctor Who*, as the doomed Oswin in 2012's *Asylum of the Daleks*. Clara has no problem controlling the Dalek, but in a very effective twist, she finds herself unable to communicate except in concepts acceptable to a Dalek. When she says her name, the Dalek's voice just says "Dalek," and the phrases "I love you" and "You are different from me" both come out as the Daleks' favourite catchphrase, "Exterminate!" It's a lovely conceit from Moffat (although it does require accepting that Clara's frantic yelling is somehow not audible from outside the Dalek – maybe the interior is just very well soundproofed?), coupled with the idea that the Dalek gun is fired by emotion – and that Daleks constantly yell "Exterminate" as effectively a means of reloading. With Clara behind her uneasily acting as a pretend Dalek, Missy uses the tried and tested prisoner-and-escort routine to return to the Dalek control room.

The pathos in the infirmary reaches a peak as the Doctor does his best to keep Davros alive long enough to witness one last sunrise – making amends for abandoning the boy on that battlefield long ago. After what has taken place between the two of them, we really want them to reach some kind of reconciliation, which makes the ultimate reveal that Davros was pretending all along all the more crushing. As the Doctor goes to provide Davros with a small amount of his own regeneration energy, he is seized by the snake-like coils of Colony Sarff, and his energy pours into the machinery feeding Davros. Instantly, Davros's frailty disappears, as he gloats at how he has used the Doctor's compassion against him, finally proving (so he thinks) his lifelong view expressed at the end of the last episode: "Compassion is *wrong*."

In fact, Davros's moment of triumph is so powerful that the subsequent reversal, when the Doctor reveals that he was ahead of Davros all the time ("I knew exactly what you were doing and I let you do it"), strikes the only false note in the script; it feels a little pat and unsatisfying, and not quite in keeping with the picture drawn by Missy earlier of the Doctor as a supreme improviser. But even as Missy grabs a Dalek gun and comes to the Doctor's rescue, bursting into the chamber and killing Sarff, some portentous hints for the future are dropped as Davros refers to a Time Lord prophecy about a mysterious "hybrid" – some kind of Dalek/Time Lord merging – with even a teasing suggestion that this might somehow be related to the Doctor's original departure from his homeworld.

All the elements of the plot neatly converge to produce the Doctor's victory. Davros has unintentionally transmitted his regeneration energy to every Dalek on Skaro – which includes all the insane, decayed Daleks in the sewers. Now, they simply surge up from the depths and tear the city apart. The Doctor and Missy escape Davros's chamber, though not before Missy humorously fulfils a promise she made last week, giving Davros a poke in his artificial eye. But once again Moffat reminds us of the true vicious nature that lurks underneath Missy's brash and exuberant surface, when the Doctor encounters the Dalek containing Clara. Unable to make him understand that she is right in front of him, Clara can only watch in horror as Missy tells him, "Clara's dead... This is the one that killed her."

Coleman is excellent at showing Clara's distress during this tense confrontation, as Missy insidiously presses her Dalek gun into the Doctor's hand and tries to induce him to kill the Clara-Dalek. Only when Clara finds a way to make the Dalek ask for mercy does the Doctor become suspicious. When the casing opens to reveal Clara, he angrily tells Missy to run. The unrepentant psychopath saunters off, with a parting shot about trying to make him see that everyone contains elements of both friend and enemy. "Everyone's a *hybrid*," she says – significantly repeating Davros's earlier usage of the term. Our last sight of her is in keeping with the way Master stories have traditionally ended: surrounded by Daleks and trapped in a collapsing city. But despite apparently being doomed to certain death, she'll undoubtedly be back at some point.

The Doctor and Clara's escape from the city is somewhat rushed, as a convenient bit of magic restores the TARDIS. The "Hostile Action Dispersal System" returns from 2013's *Cold War* as Moffat's hand-waving explanation for the TARDIS's disappearance and restoration – however, it's been slightly renamed to suit its new capability; in the earlier episode it was correctly called a *Displacement* System, as it had been when it was introduced in 1969's *The Krotons*. To activate it, the Doctor needs a substitute for the sonic screwdriver he no longer carries – and so enter the sonic sunglasses, which probably provoked groans from all those fans with suddenly superseded replica screwdrivers. It's a funny idea (and clever, to have the Doctor's replacement sonic gadget hiding in plain sight all through the story), but can't help seeming a little corny too, as he jokes about being all about "wearable technology" now.

The episode ends strongly, though, as the Doctor realises just how Clara was able to make a Dalek articulate the concept of mercy. With a typical Moffat twist, last week's cliffhanger scene has quite a different meaning when its proper context is revealed. It becomes the true ending of the story, as the Doctor journeys back to the minefield for the last time, levels the Dalek gun and tells the young Davros he will save Clara "the only way I can." He blasts the hand mines away, freeing the boy. As they walk off hand in hand – a striking image, with Davros carrying the sonic screwdriver, and the Doctor the gun of a Dalek – the Doctor has planted the small spark of mercy in the young Davros which will survive into the Daleks and eventually save Clara. It seems compassion is not wrong, after all.

Classic Who DVD Recommendation: Several years after his first appearance, Davros made the first of his many returns in 1979's *Destiny of the Daleks*, starring Tom Baker and Lalla Ward.

Reflections: The scripts for Steven Moffat's four episodes of this season (along with Sarah Dollard's *Face the Raven*) have been made publicly available on the BBC Writers Room website (http://www.bbc.co.uk/writersroom/scripts/doctor-who-series-9).

These are draft scripts rather than final versions, with a few interesting differences from the transmitted episodes. For instance, in the script for this episode, the scene in the Dalek control room at the end contains the following lines, either never filmed or cut in editing, just after the Doctor reveals his sonic sunglasses:

Clara: "Sonic glasses, an electric guitar, and a tank. You realise this is a mid-life crisis?"
The Doctor: "Mid-life? I'm only two thousand. And I am going to *love* being a teenager."

I'm glad this exchange didn't make it into the final episode; the idea of the Doctor regressing to something like a teenager doesn't truly reflect the changes in his character for this season. His grandstanding entrance in the last episode might seem like a moment of adolescent irresponsibility, but that was at least partly a response to thinking he was shortly going to die. What we see in the rest of the season is neither regression nor anything akin to a mid-life crisis, but relaxation; it was last season where the Doctor was unsure about his identity, not this one. Exactly as happened with Jon Pertwee's Doctor in his second season, Moffat has deliberately loosened up the Doctor after his spiky and severe demeanour in his first year. That loosening up includes the Doctor's costume; in this story he wears a couple of layers of casual tee shirts, along with a pair of baggy checked trousers not unlike those worn by the first two Doctors. He would remain more or less informally dressed throughout the season before getting back into his dress shirt and velvet jacket for the final few episodes.

While the tank (not surprisingly) never appeared again, the Doctor's guitar and his sonic sunglasses became fixtures for the season. However, unlike his public performance in this story, the guitar would be restricted mainly to times when the Doctor was alone, in the TARDIS. We see quite a lot of this Doctor by himself, far more than previous Doctors, and the guitar provides a useful way for him to express what he is thinking and feeling, rather than just talking to himself. As for the sonic sunglasses, despite the hilariously over-the-top reaction of some fans (going so far as to start an official petition for the return of the sonic screwdriver), the Doctor would stick with them throughout the season until a new sonic screwdriver finally appeared in the closing moments of the season finale.

The Doctor's confession dial would remain a mystery until the end of the season. It actually had no relevance to this story except for drawing Missy into the plot (which could have been accomplished in any number of other ways), but introducing it here and letting it hang over him as vaguely ominous foreshadowing was cleverly done by Moffat. Unfortunately, we never get to find out where the dial came from in the first place, leaving an annoying loose end. My own best guess is that the Doctor's had it with him ever since he originally left Gallifrey – perhaps one is given to every Time Lord at an early age – and he dug it out of some dusty drawer in the TARDIS before going off to give it to Ohila on Karn, as we saw in the last episode.

The "hybrid" arc, this season's main story thread, kicks off here in a slightly clumsy manner. In the midst of his triumph, Davros suddenly starts talking about an ancient Time Lord prophecy we have never heard of before – presumably, he thinks he is fulfilling it by taking the Doctor's regeneration energy into himself and the Daleks, but it still seems an odd non sequitur. Unlike Moffat's previous season arcs, though, this one proves to be remarkably unobtrusive. There are no weird, disconnected scenes like the ones featuring Missy last season; instead, like the Bad Wolf arc in the very first season of the modern series in 2005, there's just a word or two dropped in here and there to maintain the intrigue, before all is explained in the season finale. The mention of "the hybrid" in this episode admirably serves its function of misdirecting the audience into expecting it to be a half Dalek, half Time Lord creature. The reality, of course, would turn out to be quite different.

16: Under the Lake

Writer: Toby Whithouse
Director: Daniel O'Hara
Originally Broadcast: 3 October 2015

Cast

The Doctor: Peter Capaldi
Clara: Jenna Coleman
Moran: Colin McFarlane
Cass: Sophie Stone
Lunn: Zaqi Ismail
O'Donnell: Morven Christie
Bennett: Arsher Ali
Pritchard: Steven Robertson
Prentis: Paul Kaye

The first half of another two-part story, *Under the Lake* serves up a very satisfying slice of one of the most traditional forms of *Doctor Who* adventure: a small group of people trapped in an isolated place, coming under attack from monstrous forces, with a lot of running up and down corridors. Although the ending suggests that next week's conclusion will feature a return to the time-bending plotting more typical of Moffat-period *Who*, this episode is refreshingly reminiscent of earlier eras of the show. The setting is an underwater mining base in the year 2119, situated at the bottom of a lake in the north of Scotland that was created by a long-ago dam burst. When the crew discover a mysterious alien spaceship in the flooded valley outside and bring it aboard, what appears to be the ghost of the pilot – a Tivolian, a member of the race of cowardly aliens writer Toby Whithouse created for 2011's *The God Complex* – quickly causes the death of the base commander, Moran. Three days later, the TARDIS arrives, and the Doctor and Clara find the remaining crew in hiding from two ghosts trying to kill them – the alien pilot, and Moran. The rest of the episode consists of the Doctor joining forces with the crew to neutralise the ghosts and work out what they are and what their presence signifies.

In stories of this kind it's common for the secondary characters to be little more than stock types – cannon fodder to be picked off by the attackers – but Whithouse, returning to the show for the first time since *A Town Called Mercy* in 2012, works hard to make the base crew into real people. They are a small and efficient military group, all of them convincing and competent, with no one present simply as comic relief or to screw things up for the sake of creating plot complications. Surprisingly, even this far into the future the Doctor's UNIT credentials are recognised, which thankfully avoids the overused motif of the Doctor and his companion being treated with suspicion and having to spend time gaining the trust of the base crew; instead, they are able to start working together immediately. Lance Corporal O'Donnell is certainly happy to meet the famous Doctor, having to stop herself from gushing over him in delight. Conversely, her colleague Bennett is clearly unnerved by the ghosts but trying to hide it. He overcomes his fears enough to take part in an operation to capture the ghosts, and he and O'Donnell share a moment afterwards that clearly shows an affection between them. Arsher Ali deftly handles Bennett's insecurities; when scientific curiosity prompts him to stay with his colleagues rather than abandon the base, his wry observation, "Well, at least if I die, you know I really will come back and haunt you all," is beautifully delivered.

The only overly simplistic character is the civilian outsider Pritchard, a very thin caricature of a corporate bureaucrat type, with a single-minded focus on claiming ownership of the alien ship and its technology on behalf of his company; he is no loss at all when he is killed and joins the ranks of the ghosts. Particularly striking, on the other hand, is Cass, the second-in-command who takes over after Moran's death – and who happens to be deaf, communicating via sign language through an interpreter, Lunn. While her lip-reading ability is highlighted when she is able to understand the repeating mantra mouthed by the voiceless ghosts, the fact that otherwise the episode makes no special fuss about the incorporation of a deaf character, treating her equally with the rest of the crew, is worthy of praise. Sophie Stone, the first deaf actor to win a place at the Royal Academy of Dramatic Art, brings complete authenticity to Cass as well as wonderful expressiveness in her many close-ups. The Doctor clearly respects Cass ("Whenever I step outside, you are the smartest person in the room"), especially after she stands up to him and refuses to leave the base. The role of Lunn was Zaqi Ismail's first television acting role, but his inexperience doesn't show; his performance is very natural, presenting Lunn as a believable character in his own right even though he is mostly subordinate to Cass. She is protective towards him, preventing him from entering the alien ship (something which turns out to be important later); as with Bennett and O'Donnell, there's a hint of a closer relationship between these two, kept muted by the formality of everyone using surnames only (in fact, we never even find out the first names of anyone except Lunn and O'Donnell).

As with *The Magician's Apprentice*, the fact that this is the first half of a two-parter allows the story room to breathe and develop at its own pace. There are moments when the tension is relieved as the base switches from "night mode," when the ghosts are on the prowl, to the brighter lighting of "day mode," when they are absent. But the underlying threat is always there, since no one knows why the ghosts are not able to come out during the "day" (the base being so far underwater that the day/night distinction is purely artificial) – and the menace is heightened when the ghosts learn how to switch the base back into night mode. The Faraday cage is a special room, impervious to electromagnetic radiation, that provides a safe refuge from the ghosts, and the episode takes the time to make sure we understand what it is and how it works. At times the pacing is a little *too* deliberate; the viewers are likely to grasp the significance of the mysterious markings inscribed on the inside wall of the spaceship some time before the characters do. It turns out that the markings are the source of the ghosts' constant mantra ("The dark, the sword, the forsaken, the temple"), which the Doctor is able to decipher (somewhat implausibly, it has to be said) as a message that will direct its extraterrestrial recipients back to this place. The markings somehow cause all who see them to become signal transmitters (amusingly, the Doctor compares them to an "earworm" tune that you can't get rid of, even after death), sending the message out into space, with the signal becoming stronger as more ghosts are created. The idea of words alone having such power is certainly the biggest stretch of the episode, although a similar concept has been seen before, in 2007's *The Shakespeare Code*.

With the entire episode confined to a single location, the production design becomes critically important, and this story is a triumph for designer Michael Pickwoad – who has been creating brilliant sets for the show ever since 2010's *A Christmas Carol*. A sense of pressure being exerted by the outside environment is expressed through the curved walls and tunnel-like corridors, and moss growing on the walls and a sheen of perspiration on the crew show the ever-present humidity. *Doctor Who*'s previous attempt to create an underwater base, back in 1984's *Warriors of the Deep*, was hamstrung by the constraints of the multi-camera recording environment of the time – the stark white sets, which had to be unsubtly floodlit from above by lights bright enough to banish all shadows, never created a convincing sense of an isolated outpost constructed in hostile surroundings. Here, lighting effects contribute greatly towards the base's believability, a constant low-key shimmering in the background always reminding us that we are underwater. The sprawling geography of the base is well conveyed by first-time *Who* director Daniel O'Hara during the long action sequence where the crew execute a well-planned strategy to capture the ghosts (which, pleasingly, gives every character something important to do), the last phase of which involves the Doctor cleverly using a hologram of Clara to lure the ghosts into the Faraday cage where they can be confined. The many different corridors never seem like what they must have been in reality – a very limited number of sets, ingeniously reconfigured and reused.

O'Hara also adeptly handles the script's more horrific moments: the death of Moran in the teaser is shockingly abrupt, with the man simply engulfed in an instant by a huge plume of flame as the spaceship's rockets are activated by the ghost of the pilot. The silent ghosts themselves, with dark holes in their faces in place of eyes, are nicely macabre, and their ability to walk through walls and floors makes for a couple of good "jump" moments. Pritchard is drowned when Moran's ghost causes the airlock he is in to fill with water, and his body is later seen floating outside the base's main windows. A scene with Lunn trapped by Pritchard's ghost wielding a huge metal wrench is unusually harrowing for *Doctor Who*. The ghost peers closely at him, the wrench poised to strike – and then we hear the sound of the wrench hitting the floor as we see the ghost striding away. Only after a few moments of suspense do we find out the ghost did not kill him – obviously because he never saw the markings in the ship, just as the Doctor and Clara were not attacked until they saw them. The scene is made even more effective by Cass's reaction, watching from the control room as she is unable to help her interpreter and friend, and by her impulsive hug when they are reunited.

Unfortunately, Peter Capaldi's Doctor takes a slightly retrograde step after his nuanced and commanding performance in the previous story. Whithouse seems to have drawn most of his inspiration from the rather uncertain characterisation of the first half of last season, when the writers and Capaldi were still finding the character. There are awkward, over-mannered moments like his asking who's in command because "I need to know who to ignore." He is initially dismissive of the idea that the manifestations are ghosts, but when he is forced to admit that everything about them fits the supernatural stereotype, his excited burbling about communicating with the departed ("Calm, Doctor... You were like this when you met Shirley Bassey") seems a rather forced evocation of Matt Smith's wackier style. His exaggerated reaction to successfully working out why the ghosts are being created ("It's impossible, I hate it, it's evil, it's astonishing, I want to kiss it to death") is also pushing the eccentricity way too hard. There's a return of the mostly dropped idea of the Doctor being so inept at social interaction that he needs Clara to be his "carer" (as in last year's *Into the Dalek*); the moment where she pulls out a deck of cue cards to prompt him on the correct response when Cass points out that Moran was their friend is genuinely funny, but it's the sort of gag that would soon grow thin with repetition.

After calming himself down, the Doctor takes charge, leading the capture of the ghosts and telling UNIT to leave the base isolated when they hear that a rescue submarine (summoned by a message faked by the ghosts) is on its way. It's a clever way of removing the possibility of receiving outside help – they cannot allow any rescuers to approach lest they become victims too and strengthen the ghosts' message even more. Earlier, he had noticed that some things were missing from the ship – one of its power cells, and a suspended animation chamber that should contain the body of the pilot. They realise that the ghosts' mantra points to the church in the drowned village outside the base. Using a remote-controlled submersible, they find the chamber, and bring it back to the base.

One might expect that Clara would be affected by the presence of the ghosts, given her experiences at the end of last season. But she has definitely moved on after Danny Pink's death, and is now concentrating on enjoying her life with the Doctor. At the start, she is joking about their previous adventures and making wisecracks even as they explore the strangely deserted base (the crew are hiding in the Faraday cage at this point), and it's not until the ghosts try to kill them that she starts taking the situation seriously. With Capaldi's Doctor also being a little more superficial, the regular team feel reminiscent of the later years of Tom Baker's Doctor, when he strode through his adventures with a fellow Time Lord, Romana, at his side, giving the impression that they could easily cope with anything the universe threw at them. Nevertheless, the Doctor and Clara have an interesting moment in the TARDIS when he brings up his unease at her becoming more and more reckless – more like him, in fact. Coleman's best moment in the episode comes as she shows Clara's fondness for the Doctor mixed with a lingering pain she would prefer to keep hidden, as she simply shrugs off with a smile his suggestion that she needs another relationship.

Ironically, Clara has no choice but to remain behind at the end, when the ghosts manage to fool the base's computer into thinking its nuclear reactor is overheating, and it opens the outer doors to let in the water. Whithouse cleverly prevents the Doctor from using the TARDIS to short-circuit the story – right from the start, the time machine has been unsettled by the presence of the ghosts, and now with the Doctor and Clara separated as the central corridor of the base is flooded, he cannot use it to rescue her. He decides to continue his investigation by going back in time to when the spaceship first arrived in the valley, taking Bennett and O'Donnell with him. Clara is left to reassure Lunn and Cass that the Doctor is not abandoning them. The cliffhanger moment is a little too stretched out, so that the final shot is not quite the surprise that was probably intended, but it's still startling when Clara looks out to see the Doctor in ghost form, approaching through the murky water. Clearly whatever happened in the past has gone terribly wrong...

Classic Who DVD Recommendation: A somewhat less convincing submarine environment can be found in 1967's *The Underwater Menace* – which finally received a much-delayed DVD release in the same month as this episode was shown – starring Patrick Troughton, with Anneke Wills, Michael Craze and Frazer Hines.

Reflections: It's appropriate that Toby Whithouse, the creator of *Being Human* (2008–13), the supernatural drama series whose central characters were a vampire, a werewolf and a ghost, should be the writer of this story after previously contributing *The Vampires of Venice* in 2010. In both cases, the central conceit of the story is to establish what looks like a supernatural menace and then reveal that it has a quite different explanation. (Unfortunately, he is unlikely to get the chance to complete the trilogy with a werewolf story, Russell T Davies having got there first with *Tooth and Claw* in 2006.) As with the vampires in the earlier story, which turned out to be aliens, the "ghosts" here are deliberately designed to reflect the creatures of folklore. They are semi-transparent, they can walk through walls, and they only come out at night because that's what ghosts do, and it's up to the writer to provide rationalisations for these characteristics. Different viewers will have different opinions of how well he succeeds; Whithouse mostly hand-waves the ghosts' properties as unexplained electromagnetic phenomena, which is enough to make their ability to interact only with metal objects have a rough kind of sense (he lampshades the point by having the Doctor ask the question only to ignore it). On the other hand, their restriction to nighttime is important to the story, but is only "explained" in a throwaway line at the end of the next episode.

The DVD box set for this season provides commentaries on selected episodes, including this one and the next. DVD commentaries tend to vary from tedious to insightful, but the ones on these two episodes are worth listening to. They feature Toby Whithouse, Sophie Stone (unlike Cass, she speaks in real life) and producer Derek Ritchie. Whithouse mentions how the art department came up with the mural on the wall of the base's living area, which is inspired by the design of the Fisher King monster seen in the next episode. Stone provides many interesting details about her participation in these episodes and the effort put into the sign language used by Cass and Lunn. Ritchie noted an important aspect that hadn't occurred to me, which may have affected the pacing of some of the episode. Since the director made a point of, wherever possible, showing Lunn in the background of a scene translating for Cass when other characters were speaking, an additional constraint was imposed on the editing, with the need to always ensure that the sign language made sense before cutting away from a shot.

The scene between the Doctor and Clara in the TARDIS brings the changes in Clara's characterisation to the foreground. As I pointed out in my review of *The Magician's Apprentice*, Clara in this season is a deliberately simpler character than she was last year, much more in the generic *Doctor Who* companion mould. Her new characterisation is almost entirely in place by the end of this story – the enjoyment of adventure and the "live in the moment" philosophy, the fearlessness (verging on recklessness), and the Doctor-like willingness to take charge and push others to do whatever is necessary – and will remain more or less unchanged until her departure. The lack of need for continuing character development might explain why she is not

142

present for a surprising amount of the season. She is kept apart from the Doctor in a subplot for the whole of the next episode; then she is missing from *The Woman Who Lived* entirely (except for the final scene), and is subordinated to her Zygon duplicate in the following two-parter. Even as she models herself on the Doctor more and more, her absences mean he never relinquishes the spotlight to the same extent as in some parts of last season. The clumsiness of his social interaction in this episode would also be just a momentary aberration – the cue cards would only be seen again in *Face the Raven*, in rather more serious circumstances. And a reference to his "duty of care" towards Clara, despite being humorously brushed off here, points towards the cataclysmic events of the season finale.

17: Before the Flood

Writer: Toby Whithouse
Director: Daniel O'Hara
Originally Broadcast: 10 October 2015

Cast

The Doctor: Peter Capaldi
Clara: Jenna Coleman
Moran: Colin McFarlane
Cass: Sophie Stone
Lunn: Zaqi Ismail
O'Donnell: Morven Christie
Bennett: Arsher Ali
Pritchard: Steven Robertson
Prentis: Paul Kaye
Fisher King: Neil Fingleton
Voice of Fisher King: Peter Serafinowicz
Roar of Fisher King: Corey Taylor

It has been Steven Moffat's long-held belief that the second episode of a two-part story should not simply continue on from where the first left off, as if they were one single movie-length adventure broken into two parts for no good reason, with (on first broadcast, at least) a week-long intermission between them. Rather, the second part should immediately strike out in a different direction so that it intrigues the viewer in its own right, and only then converge to where the first part left off and continue the story. In *Before the Flood*, writer Toby Whithouse finds a particularly unusual method of accomplishing this, dispensing with the usual pre-titles teaser (apart from the standard "Previously..." montage) in favour of having the Doctor, by himself in the TARDIS, address the audience directly about a hypothetical "bootstrap paradox" involving Ludwig van Beethoven.

The type of paradox he talks about, where a time traveller comes to replace a historical figure, has been used many times in both literary and televisual science fiction; one of the most remarkable (if not subversive) is Michael Moorcock's 1969 novel *Behold the Man*, in which the subject is not Beethoven but Jesus Christ. In this case, the Doctor's fourth-wall-breaking monologue is simply designed to foreshadow the episode to come, although it feels a little unnecessary after a decade of Moffat stories (pre-eminently, 2007's *Blink*, which employs a very similar type of paradox) have made time-travel shenanigans almost too familiar to *Doctor Who* viewers. It does, however, provide an excuse for the Doctor to take up his electric guitar again, leading into a rock-based adaptation of the theme music over the opening titles that works just as well as the regular version.

The episode proper begins with the Doctor arriving in 1980 to track down the original events which would ultimately lead to Clara being trapped in a 22nd-century underwater base under attack by strange ghostly manifestations of dead crewmembers – plus a ghost of the Doctor himself. He has brought along with him Bennett and O'Donnell from the base crew, and they find themselves in the village which we had previously seen drowned at the bottom of the lake containing the base. In this time period, the dam at the end of the valley is still intact, and the claustrophobic feel of the previous episode is relieved as the story opens out to a larger canvas, with an expansive exterior location for the characters to wander about in. In a quirky touch, all the signage in the village is in Russian, even though they are, of course, still in Scotland; the Doctor explains that this is actually a Cold War-era training ground and not a real village at all – a neat device on the writer's part to remove the need for extra characters that would only be a distraction from the real story.

They immediately spot the alien spaceship that caused all the trouble, standing open in the centre of the village. But the strange symbols they found inscribed on the inside wall – which force all who see them to continue existing after death as ghostly beacons, broadcasting their message – are not present ("*yet*," says the Doctor, ominously). Other elements missing from the ship in the future – one of its power cells, and the pilot's suspended animation chamber – are still present. There's also a huge, shrouded alien body lying on a platform in the centre of the ship; the Doctor realises that the ship is actually a hearse. They have already seen the pilot of the ship as a ghost in 2119, but now they encounter him very much alive. The mole-faced alien Prentis is a creature from the planet Tivoli ("the most invaded planet in the galaxy"). As with the previous appearance of a Tivolian in Whithouse's *The God Complex* in 2011, they are basically joke aliens that would be more at home in a spoof version of *Who*. As Prentis rambles on about how his people were enslaved by the Fisher King – the creature whose body is lying in the ship – and his armies for ten years, before being liberated by the Arcateenians, who enslaved them in turn, it's hard to disagree with Bennett's disappointment ("My first proper alien, and he's an idiot"). Prentis has brought the Fisher King's body here to bury it, but he is clearly not the one who will set up the parasitic inscription.

With his investigation at a dead end, the Doctor returns to the TARDIS to talk to Clara, back in the base. The complex plotting of this episode is made possible by the existence of a means of communication between the two time periods, but that communication is fraught with danger; as soon as the Doctor becomes aware of a particular effect in the future, he is committed to taking actions in the past that will cause it. The starkest demonstration of this necessity is the first one: when Clara tells him about the ghost of him that has appeared outside the base, he calmly accepts the idea that his death is now part of the chain of events, and unavoidable. Her sudden angry reaction shows that she has not moved past Danny's death as completely as might have been thought after the last episode: "Die with whoever comes after me, you do *not* leave me!" As usual, Coleman is very convincing at showing raw emotion; Clara's protest that "You owe me, you've made yourself essential to me… and you can't do that and then die, it's not fair" may be illogical but feels very true to the character.

Whithouse plays fair with the viewer by providing plenty of clues to the ultimate resolution, with the Doctor's ghost not behaving in quite the same way as the others. Rather than chanting the same message as the other ghosts, it is repeating a list of names over and over ("Moran, Pritchard, Prentis, O'Donnell, Clara, Doctor, Bennett, Cass"). Then it moves through the glass into the room and, rather than trying to kill Clara and the others, it opens the base's Faraday cage and lets the previously captured ghosts out. Finally, its message changes to "The chamber will open tonight." While Clara, Lunn and Cass head for the Faraday cage to take refuge from the ghosts, the Doctor and the others return to the ship to discover Prentis is dead, and the Fisher King's body is gone – evidently the alien warlord wasn't dead after all. The inscription is now on the wall of the ship, put there by the Fisher King himself, and the suspended animation chamber has been dragged to the church where it would be found in 2119; as the Doctor says, "The future is still coming."

Alongside the smart plotting, Whithouse provides plenty of excellent character-based scenes for both the regulars and the base crew.

146

Functioning as substitute companions for the Doctor in 1980 are O'Donnell and Bennett. O'Donnell's obvious delight at travelling back in time with the Doctor makes it all the more painful when she is killed (like another of the Doctor's in-universe fans, Osgood, in *Death in Heaven*). Unfortunately, this is one of the few clumsy sequences in the script. The three of them hear the roars of the Fisher King and assume they need to run to get away from it – although, when we later see the creature, it's obvious that it moves too slowly to be able to chase down anyone. Entering one of the buildings, they suddenly split up for no good reason, resulting in O'Donnell getting picked off by the monster like a hapless victim in a slasher film when she emerges from hiding too soon. When Bennett and the Doctor find her, Arsher Ali is superb at conveying Bennett's pain and anger at the Doctor while staying true to a character who hardly even raises his voice even when someone he clearly knew as more than just a colleague dies in his arms. He bitterly points out that the list of names spoken by the Doctor's ghost seems to give the order in which they will see people die – and the fact that the next name on the list is Clara's means that "now you're going to do something about it, aren't you?"

Thankfully, last week's goofier excesses are absent from Capaldi's Doctor in this episode. He and Bennett return to the TARDIS and he grimly proclaims his refusal to go along with the pattern of events any more. Instead, he will return to the base to save Clara "because that's what I do, and I don't see anyone here who's going to stop me" – only to be answered immediately when the TARDIS cloister bell rings. This instantly recognisable sound, which dates all the way back to 1981's *Logopolis* and has been heard many times since, is used by the Doctor's ship as an emergency signal – either the TARDIS itself or the fabric of time is in imminent danger. In this case, the TARDIS overrides the Doctor and deposits him and Bennett back in the village – but at the same moment as their previous arrival. Whithouse creates a clever little folding of time within the larger story, as they can only watch unseen while the scenes with their previous selves and the now-dead Prentis and O'Donnell play out as before. It's a neat trick of plotting, but also an excellent character moment, as the Doctor needs to employ both persuasion and some physical force to stop Bennett from disrupting the earlier events, and both Capaldi and Ali are compelling.

Back on the base, it's a very effective "jump" moment when O'Donnell's ghost suddenly appears at the door to the Faraday cage.

Clara can only watch as the new ghost picks up her phone (which had to be left outside the Faraday cage in order to function – a pleasingly correct use of the real-life science of the device) and walks off with it. She clashes with Cass when she works out that (as the alert viewer will have figured out last week) Lunn is not in danger from the ghosts because he never saw the alien symbols in the spaceship, and so is the only one of the three of them able to retrieve the phone. Clara's willingness to send Lunn out from their safe hiding place leads Cass to bitterly wonder whether it was travelling with the Doctor that made her so comfortable with the idea of risking others' lives – explicitly highlighting a part of Clara's characterisation that first appeared momentarily in last year's *Time Heist* and has become steadily more prominent, until last week's worry by the Doctor about her becoming too much like him.

Sophie Stone and director Daniel O'Hara's expressive close-ups again combine to make Cass a compelling character. As with the previous episode, her deafness is significant – her lip-reading ability is again used, to gain information from the Doctor's "ghost" – but is not all there is to her; her feelings towards Lunn give her a dramatic arc of her own over the course of the story. Later, after she and Clara leave the Faraday cage to go in search of Lunn, there's a long sequence where one of the ghosts comes up behind her dragging a large axe. The scene effectively cuts to and from her point of view, with the sound dropping away to show that she can't hear the weapon scraping along the floor – until she kneels down to feel the vibrations. What is actually, from a structural standpoint, no more than padding becomes the most intense sequence of the episode. Eventually, she, Clara and Lunn find themselves trapped in the base's living area next to the still sealed suspended animation chamber with the ghosts closing in.

When the Doctor realises his coat now shows the same damage that Clara reported his ghost as having, he knows that his time has run out – he must now face the Fisher King. He hardly sounds confident as he sends Bennett back to the TARDIS – but then there's a quick cutaway back to the base, where we see a scared Lunn leaving the Faraday cage, then back to the Doctor saying quietly, "*Now* I'm ready." This little gap in the narrative is easily missed by the first-time viewer; only afterwards does it become apparent that during this interval, the Doctor has arranged everything he needs so that events will follow the correct path after he confronts his adversary.

Whithouse's choice of the name "Fisher King" is rather baffling, since there's no obvious connection between this alien creature and the mythical keeper of the Holy Grail in Arthurian legend. It's purely an imposing, brutish monster, lumbering around on massive hooves like the Teller from *Time Heist*. While the skull-like design of its face is very striking, it's a creature that really only works while half-concealed in the shadows of the church where the Doctor meets it. Later, when we see it striding outside in full daylight, the (lightweight fiberglass, probably) carapace behind its head wobbles at every step, unavoidably drawing attention to the fact that this is a man in a costume. A very big man, to be sure; Britain's tallest man, Neil Fingleton, is one of a trio of celebrities bringing the Fisher King to life, making the creature loom impressively over the Doctor. Peter Serafinowicz, of 2004 horror comedy *Shaun of the Dead* fame (as well as being the voice of Darth Maul in *The Phantom Menace*), provides the deep, resonant voice, while the loud, guttural roars are contributed by Corey Taylor of the heavy metal band Slipknot. The Fisher King takes a crude pleasure in confronting the Doctor with his apparently unavoidable death, but he delivers a stirring speech not unlike the one to the Boneless in last year's *Flatline*, taking a stand against the creature's robbing others of their deaths: "You bent the rules of life and death. So I am putting things straight. Here, now, this is where your story ends."

Physically the Doctor might be no match for the enemy, but he tricks it with a pleasingly simple lie, saying that he has erased the inscription from the inside of the spaceship. The monster stomps off to check, leaving it exposed and defenceless when the Doctor's previously planted explosive – the missing power cell from the spaceship – destroys the dam wall and floods the valley. The dam burst itself is a very impressive effect, the wall gradually cracking and crumbling until it gives way, resulting in an unstoppable deluge that simply sweeps away the impotently roaring Fisher King. The plot resolves itself neatly as the pre-programmed TARDIS, with Bennett inside, returns to the base, while the occupant of the sealed chamber from the spaceship is revealed to be the Doctor himself, riding out the flood and journeying back to 2119 in suspended animation. Finally, he uses a recording of the Fisher King's roars made by his sonic sunglasses to lure the ghosts back into the Faraday cage, where they can be dealt with later by UNIT. (It's amusing to note that this story was obviously developed expecting that the Doctor would still have his sonic screwdriver, which he would have inserted into a socket in the base's control panel to transmit the recorded roars. In the final version, he has to poke one of the sunglasses' arms into the console instead, which looks ridiculous.)

As the Doctor removes the implanted message from his and the others' minds, he explains that his "ghost" was actually just a hologram generated once he and his sonic sunglasses were brought into the base in the suspended animation chamber. Again, the writer played fair with the audience: we were shown that he had the ability to create such holograms in the previous episode. A sweet ending comes when, after some prompting from Bennett about not wasting time ("Tell her I wish someone had given me that advice"), Lunn and Cass finally admit their feelings for each other. Back in the TARDIS, Clara is also all smiles again now that she knows the Doctor's "ghost" was just a trick, and is suitably impressed as he points out how he programmed his hologram with the exact actions and phrases she described to him: the very bootstrap paradox he was lecturing us about in the opening. But her earlier emotional reaction to the Doctor's apparent death reminds us how completely she has now given herself over to her life with the Doctor – an ominous note for the future.

Classic Who DVD Recommendation: Another case of the Doctor having to fight to the death against a creature solely motivated by survival is in the wonderfully claustrophobic 1977 story *Horror of Fang Rock*, starring Tom Baker and Louise Jameson.

Reflections: As well as the commentaries mentioned in the last chapter, the DVD set for this season also contains some deleted scenes. One of them is a long sequence from this episode in which the Doctor and Bennett, discovering they have overlapped themselves in time, encounter Prentis and have to prepare him for his meeting with their earlier selves. It has its good points: it raises the idea of using flooding to destroy the Fisher King (although in the final version, it seems completely reasonable that the Doctor would think of causing the flood himself), and allows the Doctor to express regret at Prentis's death. But it also contains much tedious, drawn-out comedy with Prentis being baffled by the Doctor's talk of their "identical twins" that he is about to meet, and wittering on about the Tivolians and their propensity for being enslaved. On the whole it was a good cut to make, even though it left the episode significantly shorter than all the others this season.

150

This adventure is very much a stand-alone story, not connected with any ongoing plot threads of the season except as far as it illuminates Clara and the Doctor's relationship at this point in their lives. It might seem like a hint for the future is being tossed out when the Doctor tells O'Donnell that they have arrived in 1980 and she comments, "So, pre-Harold Saxon, pre-the Minister of War, pre-the moon exploding and a big bat coming out." The first of those allusions is to the plot arc of the 2007 season, while the third of course refers to last year's *Kill the Moon*. The Doctor notes the mention of the "Minister of War," but then says, "Never mind, I expect I'll find out soon enough." However, so far this tease has not amounted to anything; it's quite possible that it was included without any specific future story in mind, like the mysterious phone call to the TARDIS at the end of 2010's *The Big Bang*, which meant nothing for several years before being paid off in *Mummy on the Orient Express*.

The idea of the Doctor delivering a monologue in the TARDIS would be taken to even greater extremes in *Heaven Sent*, although there it would be framed as him speaking to his own imagined audience rather than directly to the viewers. For a previous example of the latter, there is really only the end of the 1965 episode *The Feast of Steven* (the only time the classic series ever broadcast on Christmas Day), when William Hartnell's Doctor turned to the camera and wished a happy Christmas "to all of you at home," or a couple of Tom Baker's more eccentric ad-libs in 1978's *The Invasion of Time*. The strange recklessness of this presentation of the Doctor is somehow in keeping with the recklessness Clara demands of him in this episode, telling him after he accepts his seeming death, "If you love me in any way, you'll come back." Her exhortation here to "break the rules" will find an answer in his own response to her death later. When he tries to go outside the rules here, the TARDIS stops him; in similar straits at the end of the season, he will find another way.

18: The Girl Who Died

Writers: Jamie Mathieson & Steven Moffat
Director: Ed Bazalgette
Originally Broadcast: 17 October 2015

Cast

The Doctor: Peter Capaldi
Clara: Jenna Coleman
Ashildr: Maisie Williams
Odin: David Schofield
Nollarr: Simon Lipkin
Chuckles: Ian Conningham
Lofty: Tom Stourton
Limpy: Alastair Parker
Hasten: Murray McArthur
Heidi: Barnaby Kay

For much of its length, *The Girl Who Died* seems like a deliberately jokey story, in which the Doctor and Clara are dropped into an escapade with some comedy Vikings fighting off equally silly-looking aliens. The writing credits are shared between Jamie Mathieson – whose two acclaimed episodes last year showed his talent for coming up with striking ideas and memorable images – and Steven Moffat, who ensures that this episode's stand-alone story is strongly integrated into the ongoing current of the Doctor's life in a way very characteristic of this era of *Doctor Who*. We open with the Doctor and Clara finishing up an unrelated adventure, and end with a scene that (even without the explicit "To be continued" afterwards) makes it obvious that this is merely the start of a much bigger story. Although superficially just a historical romp along the lines of last year's *Robot of Sherwood*, the episode several times pauses to contemplate important and interesting issues about the Doctor's morality, and even ties up a longstanding thread about his very appearance into the bargain.

A hectic pace is set right from the outset, with Clara floating in space as something nasty crawls up her leg inside her spacesuit, while the TARDIS comes under attack from "four and a bit battle fleets" as the Doctor labours to rescue her. After getting her back on board, he disposes of the unseen spidery creature in her spacesuit in an extremely direct fashion, producing some amusingly disgusting squelching sounds. After going outside to clean off his boot, he and Clara find themselves surrounded by Vikings. We can tell they're Vikings because some of them have the silly horned helmets that have been a cliché since the days of Wagnerian opera (and which real Vikings almost certainly never wore). The Doctor tries to intimidate them using his sonic sunglasses, but the leader simply takes them off his face and casually snaps them in two (no doubt to the cheers of those in the audience who detested the things). His comically resigned air as he says, "Clara… we're going with the Vikings," is a great way to lead in to the opening titles.

Two days later, they arrive in the Vikings' village, where the light-hearted antics continue as the Doctor tries to bluff them into thinking he is the god Odin in disguise. Unfortunately, his attempt to impress them with his yo-yo falls flat when the giant face of someone claiming to be the real Odin suddenly appears in the clouds, accompanied by thunder and a heavenly choir – like a live-action version of one of Terry Gilliam's *Monty Python* animations. "Odin" tells the awed villagers their "day of reward" has finally come, as a force of alien warriors materialises beneath him. The design of these creatures, called the Mire, fits in with the not entirely serious nature of this story. One major factor in the success of the Daleks' design is the fact that they have no visible legs; in the case of the Mire, while the top half looks impressively massive and tank-like, the pair of human legs beneath (albeit thickly armoured) can't help but make the creatures look somewhat comical when they are shot in anything other than a looming close-up.

This basic plot setup has been used before in *Who*, as long ago as 1969's *The Krotons* – an isolated, primitive settlement under the domination of an alien force who plan to harvest the best of the inhabitants (in this case, the strongest warriors). The Doctor immediately realises what is happening, as the Mire begin teleporting away the village's fighters. His first concern is that he and Clara not be noticed by the aliens, but Clara takes the risk of running over to a young Viking girl, Ashildr, who is holding one half of the Doctor's broken sonic sunglasses. Her importance has already been foreshadowed, not only by the fact that she is being played by *Game of Thrones* star Maisie Williams, but by a strange premonitory recognition felt by the Doctor when he first saw her as he entered the village. Having never seen her before, he shrugged it off as simply "remembering in the wrong direction" – an effect of too much time travel. But now, as Clara gets Ashildr to use the sonic glasses fragment to open her manacles (in a nice touch, she tells the girl to "think the word 'open'" in the same way as the Doctor got her free from the Dalek casing in *The Witch's Familiar*), the advanced technology is detected by the Mire, who take the two of them away as well. Left behind, the Doctor can only berate the remaining villagers for being taken in by the fake Odin ("What's the one thing that gods never do? Gods never actually show up!") and puts what happened in terms they can understand: "Guess what? You got raided."

Not surprisingly, Clara, Ashildr and the warriors from the village do not find themselves in the promised halls of Valhalla, but in an empty, steel-walled chamber aboard what is obviously a spaceship. All the bravado of the warriors is rendered meaningless as they are swiftly slaughtered, their essence rendered into sustenance for the aliens. Only the two women are spared, because the sonic glasses and the spacesuit Clara is still wearing indicate that she doesn't belong to this place any more than the Mire do. She demonstrates how adept she has become at handling situations like this, acting just as the Doctor would to try to convince the aliens to leave now, rather than get involved in a conflict with an adversary whose capabilities they don't know. Her question, "Ask yourself, is this a war you really want?" hangs in the air as the leader ponders, but Ashildr, with a sudden surge of Viking spirit, yells "Yes!" Having finally comprehended what has happened to the warriors, she declares war on the aliens on behalf of her village. Williams strains a little to match the enthusiastic scenery chewing of David Schofield as the pseudo-Odin, who has many bombastic lines like "Talk is for cowards" and "The joy of war!" Accepting Ashildr's challenge, he sends them back to the village.

The Doctor's relief at Clara's return is palpable; for a moment he tries to hide behind his former reserved persona ("I'm not a hugger"), but his delight soon breaks through. He is looking very Patrick Troughton-ish today, with his baggy checked trousers (reappearing from the opening story of the season) and his 2000-year diary recalling a favourite prop of the mercurial Second Doctor. But things turn serious when Clara tells how the Mire will be returning tomorrow to wipe them all out. At first, the Doctor is not unduly concerned – they have been given 24 hours' warning, plenty of time to evacuate the village and hide in the surrounding woods until the aliens leave. But the villagers intend to stay and fight, even after he points out that all their fighters have just been taken away and that none of those remaining have actually held a sword in battle. The Viking spirit rears up again ("A death in battle is a death with honour!"), but in a sudden lull afterwards the Doctor hears a baby crying in the distance and quietly says, "Do babies die with honour?"

The Doctor's ability to speak "Baby" was a piece of comic business introduced by Moffat in 2011's *A Good Man Goes to War* and used again later that year in Gareth Roberts' *Closing Time*. Here it's used for heartstring-tugging, as the Doctor gives a voice to the most helpless inhabitant of the village. It makes no rational sense, of course, but Capaldi is wonderfully poignant as he provides poetic translations of the baby's cries ("Turn your face towards me, Mother, for you... You're beautiful. And I will sing for you. I am afraid... but I will sing") and claims that babies think laughter is singing. Ashildr's plea for him to stay is rebuffed; he told them to run, and that's "all the help you needed." But he is clearly having to convince himself to override his own impulse to help; faced with Clara's sceptical gaze, he produces a stream of arguments for not interfering. It's only one village – the fate of humanity and the world is not at stake – and if somehow it did succeed in defeating the Mire, word would get around and Earth would become a bigger target; the Mire would return and the future could be changed catastrophically. But it only takes a cryptic reference from the baby to "fire in the water" to pique his interest; as the baby stops crying, Clara notes with a smile, "You just decided to stay."

The comedy returns as the Doctor tries to train the remnant of the village to fight, adopting a drill sergeant manner and giving his troops nicknames like Lofty, Heidi and Limpy – the last one after its recipient has demonstrated why they can only be trusted with wooden practice swords to start with. When he finally relents and hands out the real swords, there's a very funny immediate cut to a scene of the village in chaos and the Doctor musing, "Well, that could have gone better." Apparently, Heidi fainted at the sight of blood, knocking a torch onto some hay, which spooked a horse, which kicked open a gate, and so on. Observing this shambles, Clara wants to know what the Doctor's *real* plan is – but he protests that teaching them to fight is the only plan he's got, even if all it will achieve is giving them valorous deaths in battle. In another lovely quiet scene shared between them (and the performances of both Capaldi and Coleman are note-perfect throughout the episode), Clara brushes aside the Doctor's attempt to pre-emptively send her away before tomorrow's battle, and confidently pushes him to find a way to succeed: "Start winning, Doctor. It's what you're good at."

Clara's words prompt him into going to Ashildr, who had earlier been established as a girl preoccupied with dreams and stories; she makes puppets to help her deal with her fears when the raiding parties go out. Given the medieval, rustic nature of the episode's setting, it's difficult for Williams to avoid giving the initial impression of playing a watered down, child-friendly version of her *Game of Thrones* character, Arya Stark. But the long scene she shares with Capaldi is excellently played, dispelling such extraneous considerations; it shows Ashildr's love for her home even as she agrees with the Doctor's assessment that "by tomorrow, every single one of us will be dead." Her insistence that "This is my place" and that leaving it would be death for her is heavily ironic in view of what will eventually happen to her, as is her pitying of the Doctor for having no similar place of his own ("I will mourn for you – I know which I'd prefer," he replies). Ashildr's father Einarr (known to the Doctor as Chuckles) enters to comfort her, but movingly admits he lacks the strength to keep her safe.

Now, though, the turning point of the story is reached, as the Doctor discovers what the baby's reference to "fire in the water" means, and realises what he needs to do. The episode smoothly transitions back to comedy again as we find that the village's boathouse has several vats containing electric eels (with, naturally, no explanation of what these South American creatures are doing in Scandinavia), which the Doctor uses as the basis for a hilariously *MacGyver*-esque plan to defeat the Mire. As with Mathieson's *Mummy on the Orient Express* last season, the writers have been careful to remove the Doctor's gadgets (no sonic sunglasses, and the TARDIS is out of reach), forcing him to make do with only the resources at hand. As cheerful now as earlier he was morose ("Look happy! Winning is all about looking happier than the other guy"), he directs the villagers' frantic efforts to get everything ready in time for the next day's battle.

When the aliens finally attack, the Doctor's plan works perfectly. Some of the Mire are stunned by an electric shock, while others have their helmets removed by a magnetised anvil, revealing the strikingly hideous design of the creatures beneath, with huge mouths ringed by sharp teeth. Eventually, Ashildr is able to utilise a captured helmet to frighten them off with illusions, making them see one of her puppets as a huge, writhing dragon (as the Doctor says, "That's the trouble with viewing reality through technology – it's all too easy to feed in a new reality"). In an appropriately cheeky ending, the Mire are finally driven off when the Doctor threatens to upload a recording of their ignominious retreat to the galactic equivalent of YouTube, accompanied by the *Benny Hill* theme. As the aliens' spaceship flies away and the villagers cheer, the sense of triumph and relief is so great that the viewer might actually forget the title of the episode for a moment – until Ashildr is found dying. As the stricken Doctor realises: "I plugged her into the machine. Used her up like a battery."

The episode finally turns completely serious as Capaldi and Coleman share a pivotal moment of realisation by the Doctor. Earlier, when Clara complained that he had never told her the rules governing when and how he can interfere in events, he said, "We're time travellers. We tread softly. It's OK to make ripples, but not tidal waves." Now, with the Doctor angry with himself at losing Ashildr, there's a sudden flashback to 2008's *The Fires of Pompeii*, in which David Tennant's Doctor, at the urging of his companion Donna, defied "the rules" and saved a single family from the volcanic destruction of the city. Making a guest appearance as the head of that family was Peter Capaldi – and Moffat seizes on this totally unplanned circumstance to provide a wonderfully cunning explanation for the Twelfth Doctor's choice of face (fulfilling the clues he dropped in Capaldi's introductory episode *Deep Breath* last year: "It's as if I'm trying to tell myself something"). The Doctor now looks the way he does as a reminder: "I'm the Doctor… and I *save* people!"

However, this moment of personal triumph is not without its darker implications. Spurred on to save Ashildr, the Doctor cannibalises the leftover Mire equipment to embed a "repair kit" chip in her. But the way she revives (a sudden gasping intake of breath, exactly like the never-dying Captain Jack Harkness) suggests, even before he explicitly confirms it, that "barring accidents, she may now be functionally immortal." Interestingly, this phrase recalls the original description of the Time Lords when the Doctor's own people were first revealed in 1969's *The War Games*; it was only several years later that the twelve-regeneration limit (which Moffat had to ingeniously work around when Matt Smith departed) was introduced. Before leaving, he gives Ashildr a second chip – in case, he says, she finds someone she can't bear to be without. He makes no attempt to take one for himself, despite earlier telling Clara that he knows he will lose her someday (and, of course, the real-life knowledge of Coleman's impending departure looms large here). As he admits back in the TARDIS, his impulsive action, however admirable it may be in the short term, may turn out to be a terrible mistake. Although the season arc this year seems to be much more in the background than previously, the Doctor does pick up on a possible connection between Ashildr's new condition and the mysterious "hybrid" mentioned by Davros in *The Witch's Familiar*.

New director Ed Bazalgette has proved adept throughout the episode at keeping the light-hearted antics bubbling along, and also providing space for Capaldi, Coleman and Williams to nail the serious moments; in many of the important scenes between the Doctor and Clara or the Doctor and Ashildr, the incidental music drops away to leave only their voices on the soundtrack. He also leaves a memorable impression with the final metaphorical sequence of the camera making a complete circle around Ashildr standing still while a montage of passing days and seasons swirls around her. At the start she is smiling, but by the time the camera comes back to her face she wears a dark and troubled expression. It seems the Doctor's uneasiness may soon be proved correct.

Classic Who DVD Recommendation: Another story involving both Vikings and the possible disruption of history due to anachronistic technology is 1965's *The Time Meddler*, starring William Hartnell, with Maureen O'Brien and Peter Purves.

Reflections: Obviously, *The Girl Who Died* introduces a major new character into the story of the season. However, Ashildr's real story only properly begins at the end of the episode, when thanks to the Doctor, she becomes no longer just human (which also made her a useful red herring in the ongoing "hybrid" arc). Before that point, she is very much a girl of her particular time and place, albeit one with a mind unusually receptive to fantastic and strange phenomena. In fact, one could imagine a more conventional scenario where Ashildr, perhaps left homeless after the alien attack on her village, would end up joining the Doctor in a similar way to previous companions from historical times, like two from the Troughton era in the 1960's: Jamie (a Scottish highlander from 1745) and Victoria (an orphaned girl from 1866). However, Moffat had quite a different idea in mind, and so produced a character that would be markedly different in each of her four appearances. Here, Maisie Williams deliberately emphasises Ashildr's naive, childlike traits in both voice and movement, to better contrast with the next episode, when we see how several hundred years' worth of additional experiences have affected her.

The DVD box set for this season contains a long deleted scene from this episode. It's a good scene, and was obviously cut for time rather than quality reasons. While the Doctor is busy training what Clara points out is the Vikings' answer to *Dad's Army*, Ashildr shows her some old scrolls containing pictorial records of the Mire's previous visit. When the Doctor joins them, he expounds on his knowledge of the Mire's capabilities and the technology of their helmets – helping to explain why he put such emphasis on capturing one of their helmets later during the attack. Most importantly, though, Clara makes a wistful reference to Danny Pink, saying he would have been proud of the Doctor's efforts – to which the Doctor replies that Danny "would have laughed his head off." Clara explains to Ashildr that Danny was "a soldier who died... because, when all else fails, that's what soldiers do." It would have made for a nice foreshadowing of her next and final reference to Danny, at her own moment of reckoning in *Face the Raven*.

As in the previous story, the Doctor is worried about his "duty of care" towards Clara, but he doesn't even get to finish suggesting sending her out of danger before she firmly quashes the idea. He sees a link between his training the villagers to fight and the effect that travelling with him has had on Clara – perhaps an echo of Davros's accusation in 2008's *Journey's End* that the Doctor turns his companions into weapons. But really, Clara's greatest contribution here is to keep in mind what she told Missy in *The Witch's Familiar*: that the Doctor "always assumes he's going to win." As we will see later in *Heaven Sent*, even after Clara is lost the memory of her confidence in him ("How are you going to win?") will keep him going.

159

19: The Woman Who Lived

Writer: Catherine Tregenna
Director: Ed Bazalgette
Originally Broadcast: 24 October 2015

Cast

The Doctor: Peter Capaldi
Clara: Jenna Coleman
Me: Maisie Williams
Sam Swift: Rufus Hound
Coachman: Gareth Berliner
Lucie Fanshawe: Elisabeth Hopper
Mr Fanshawe: John Voce
Clayton: Struan Rodger
Pikeman Lloyd Llewelyn: Gruffudd Glyn
Pikeman William Stout: Reuben Johnson
Leandro: Ariyon Bakare
Crowd 1: Daniel Fearn
Crowd 2: Karen Seacombe
Hangman: John Hales
Voice of The Knightmare: Will Brown

Although the title deliberately mirrors the last episode's, giving the impression that they form the two halves of another two-part story, *The Woman Who Lived* is actually a sequel to *The Girl Who Died* rather than a straightforward continuation. Last week, the Doctor saved the life of the dying Viking girl Ashildr, by embedding in her an alien "repair kit" capable of extending her life indefinitely. Despite a few nagging worries about the implications of what he had done, he took off and left Ashildr to her own devices. Now, at a point in Earth's history over eight hundred years later, he happens to again encounter the woman he made effectively unable to die, and is forced to deal with the consequences of his impulsive act of compassion.

The story is by Catherine Tregenna, a writer new to the show – and indeed, according to an interview with Steven Moffat in *Doctor Who Magazine* before this episode's broadcast, one who took some convincing to come aboard. As was the case with Richard Curtis in 2010's *Vincent and the Doctor*, using a writer less steeped in the lore of the show than normal has both positives and negatives. There's nothing original about the idea of an Earth historical setting as the backdrop for an alien scheme that the Doctor must defeat, and this aspect of the episode is distinctly weaker than usual. However, that is only a subplot to the real story – the Doctor meeting Ashildr again, their conflict, and their subsequent reconciliation – whose drama is beautifully handled by Tregenna. Her previous involvement in the *Who* universe, several years earlier, was in writing four episodes of the spinoff series *Torchwood*, which revolved around another character who became undying after an encounter with the Doctor: Captain Jack Harkness (who actually gets name-checked late in this episode, when the Doctor wryly comments to Ashildr, "He'll get around to you eventually"). Here, she is dealing with two immortals, one free to roam the universe and jump around anywhere in time, and the other stuck on Earth, living steadily through the days and years one after another, the same way we have to do.

Their relationship is placed right at the heart of the narrative by simply omitting the Doctor's companion Clara from the episode. Travelling on his own, the Doctor arrives in the anarchic England of 1651, a land infested with highwaymen after the recent convulsions of the Civil War, searching for an alien artefact which he has somehow discovered is hidden in this time and place. Almost immediately he stumbles into a carriage being held up at gunpoint by a notorious masked robber known as "the Knightmare." Tregenna clearly took inspiration from the early episodes of last season when characterising the Doctor, particularly his casual rudeness and obliviousness towards all humans. His "curioscanner" gadget shows that the artefact he is after is in the chest of valuables belonging to the lady in the carriage, but his presence distracts the Knightmare enough to allow the victim to escape, leaving them both empty-handed. He is even more disconcerted when the robber pulls off "his" mask to reveal the girl he once saved, who greets him with a line – "What took you so long, old man?" – whose prominence in the season trailer caused feverish speculation among the fans. Evidently, the Doctor was going to be surprised at running into someone from his own past – as indeed he is, just not in a fashion that anyone expected.

Her role in the previous episode may not have been the greatest of challenges for her, but here Maisie Williams gets a far wider range of material to show what she is capable of. Ashildr has grown greatly: as she points out, ten thousand hours is all it takes to become proficient at any skill, and living more than eight centuries has allowed her to accomplish many things. On the other hand, her memory remains merely human-sized, so her past simply drains away unless she writes it down. She has a library full of the journals she has kept over the centuries, and sometimes rereads them – out of curiosity rather than nostalgia. As she describes her experiences to the Doctor, we see little vignettes of these other lives, ranging from medieval queen ("Ended up faking my own death"), to being almost drowned as a witch, to the first of several stints in male guise (not surprising, given the historical restrictions placed on women) as an archer at the Battle of Agincourt. (In a nice coincidence, this episode was first broadcast on the eve of that battle's 600th anniversary. However, Tregenna makes a gratuitous factual blunder when she has Ashildr claim she "helped end the Hundred Years War" – in fact, the war would drag on for over thirty-five more years after Agincourt.) Her shrug when the Doctor asks her how many people she has killed is an unsettling indication of how far she has grown apart from ordinary humanity. She has all but forgotten the very name "Ashildr," and has let go of her memories of the Viking village she would once rather have died than leave. Now she calls herself simply "Me" and lives by herself ("No one's mother, daughter, wife... my own companion. Singular, unattached, alone"). She is even listed in the credits as "Me," but for the sake of avoiding grammatical tangles I will continue to refer to her by her original name.

Ashildr is initially happy to see the Doctor again, thinking he has come to take her away from this existence and let her travel with him. His reluctance to do so leads to her trying every argument at her disposal to convince him, in a series of compelling scenes where Williams runs the full gamut from rebellious teenager to a cynical, detached woman, whose empathy for others has been crushed by the weight of ages. Capaldi in turn shows the Doctor horrified at how Ashildr has suffered and changed; the scene of the Doctor reading her journal entry recording how she lost her children to the Black Death, and her resolve never to have any more, is perhaps the most powerful in the episode ("From now on, it's me against the world"). Nevertheless, he stands firm on his insistence that it would not be good for them to be travelling companions, and looks for a way to reconnect with the person she once was.

It's a small-scale episode, focusing on its two central characters; there are no big vistas (in fact, the whole first half takes place at night) and only one scene that requires a crowd of extras. The plot surrounding the fundamental clash of viewpoints between Ashildr and the Doctor is serviceable but slow-paced at times, and definitely secondary. There's some amusement to be had when the Doctor falls into the role of the Knightmare's sidekick, as they creep into a manor house to retrieve the alien artefact – an amulet known as the Eyes of Hades, the very piece of jewellery that Ashildr was trying to steal. She cares nothing for the normal humans around her, engaging in robbery for the excitement. The conflict between them simmers down for the moment to comic bickering ("Humans need shared experiences." "I'm regretting sharing this one"), but when the Doctor accidentally gives away their presence he sees how immediately ready she is to kill to defend herself, and has to convince her to hide instead.

In the classic series, the Doctor's usual practice of immediately slipping away after dealing with a crisis was rarely examined, much less criticised. Each adventure was more or less self-contained and consequence-free; one of the few exceptions was when Jon Pertwee's Doctor took a brief detour away from the plot in 1973's *The Green Death*, paying a quick visit to the planet Metebelis 3 and returning to Earth with a psionic blue crystal as a souvenir. The following year, the presence of that crystal would kick off Pertwee's final story, *Planet of the Spiders*, and in some sense the act of taking it is what ended up costing the Doctor his third life. The 21st-century version of the show has a greater propensity to explore the ramifications of the Doctor's actions; in its first season in 2005, the Doctor's quick fade from the scene after disposing of the Jagrafess in *The Long Game* led to him being blindsided by the Earth becoming a Dalek-ruled dystopia a hundred years later in *Bad Wolf*. His encounter with Queen Victoria in 2006's *Tooth and Claw* led to her creation of the Torchwood Institute, which he would find opposing him at the end of that season's stories. More recently, the whole Moffat era has had fun linking the Doctor's adventures into an intricate tapestry of cause and effect. But the show has never explored the way the Doctor changes the lives of those he encounters on such a personal level before.

There was one previous occasion when it had the opportunity to do so. In 2008, the title character of *The Doctor's Daughter* was a genetically engineered creation (hence her taking the name "Jenny"), technologically extrapolated from the Doctor's DNA. The initial plan was for her to die at the end of that episode, but a comment from Moffat to then-showrunner Russell T Davies about this being what the audience would expect resulted in the conclusion being altered. She still appeared to die, but then after the Doctor had left, healed herself thanks to a regeneration-like ability (albeit without changing her appearance), took a spaceship, and headed out into the universe, never to be seen again. Rumours in succeeding years that she would be returning to the show came to nothing, until Ashildr's line in the trailer mentioned above fanned the speculation again (although in hindsight, it's obvious that Moffat would always prefer to create a new character rather than revive a thoroughly dormant, seven-year-old plot thread). The two characters are quite similar, with the crucial difference that Jenny already has the freedom that Ashildr craves, trapped as she is on one planet. As they escape the manor house, she petulantly questions the Doctor about Clara, obviously jealous of her travelling with him.

Daybreak brings more comedy as the Knightmare encounters rival highwayman Sam Swift. Last season's *Robot of Sherwood* is an obvious influence here, with the Doctor's complaints about the puns and banter between them, although he quickly gets drawn in as well when Sam taunts the Knightmare about recruiting his "dad" as a sidekick. The fight between the two of them is excellently edited, the advantage passing back and forth in comically rapid-fire fashion. As with the previous episode, director Ed Bazalgette keeps the plot rolling along while also providing space for the important moments to breathe. Williams is coldly menacing when Ashildr finally has Sam at her mercy. After the Doctor says flatly, "Kill him, and you make an enemy of me," she grudgingly lets him go. But the Doctor's reluctance to take her with him clearly stems from her failure to grasp a central point: she has previously said that the humans around her blow away "like smoke," to which the Doctor tells her here, "I know their lives are short... but those lives do matter." Her retort – "Shut up... you're not my dad" – is both a funny punchline to the scene, turning her back into a pouting teenager, and an indication of how far she still has to go.

In a sense, of course, the Doctor *is* her dad – a dad whose abandonment (as she sees it) of her has become a focus for her resentment. Their sharpest, most bitter confrontation comes when "Lady Me" finally has the opportunity to get away without his help. Her scheme involves a stranded leonine alien called Leandro (could there be a more obvious name for a lion-man?), and using the amulet's ability to open a dimensional portal and escape Earth with him. The Doctor realises almost instinctively that Leandro has an ulterior motive, once he learns that the amulet requires a death to function. Capaldi and Williams are both superb as the argument between them rises to its highest pitch ("You didn't save my life, Doctor... you trapped me inside it") as she disdains the Doctor's warnings about Leandro, not caring what happens as long as she gains her freedom. Her hardness is still partly a facade, though; she refuses to sacrifice the Doctor as part of her plan, or her aged, loyal butler Clayton. Instead, when she hears Sam Swift has been captured and sentenced to execution, she decides to use him instead. The Doctor is left guarded by a couple of comically dim soldiers, but soon outwits them and follows Ashildr and Leandro to the Tyburn gallows.

The choice to employ comedian Rufus Hound in the role of Sam prompts an amusing analogy to a stand-up routine with the highwayman's performance at the gallows, but Hound does well at showing Sam's desperation as he keeps gabbling groan-worthy jokes, knowing that once he stops making the audience laugh, he's finished (as the Doctor later says, "It gives a whole new meaning to 'dying on stage'"). The climax attempts to suddenly widen the scale of the story as "Lady Me" places the amulet on Sam, it starts draining his life away to open the portal, and a force of alien ships waiting on the other side begin firing through it upon the crowd. Unfortunately, the scene follows an entirely predictable course as Ashildr discovers her ally has deceived her about being the last of his kind, followed by her realisation that she really does care about what is happening to the people around her. It's a huge, life-changing development, which is insufficiently motivated by a confused scene of extras running in all directions to no purpose as explosions go off around them. Nevertheless, a neat resolution (albeit an easy one to see coming) is provided by the second "repair kit" chip which the Doctor left for her in the last episode precisely so that she need not be alone; when asked earlier why she had never used it, she had said, "No one's good enough." Now she makes the choice to sacrifice it to counteract the amulet, saving Sam and closing the portal – though not before the ineffectual Leandro is perfunctorily disposed of by a stray shot from his own people.

The wrap-up scene between the Doctor and Ashildr is much better, as they share a quiet moment in a tavern; in a clever touch, the background sounds drop away, leaving only the incidental music behind their two voices as they reach an understanding. Ashildr has come to accept the Doctor's argument that they both need ordinary humans, with their mayfly-like lives, around them. Having rediscovered empathy, she also has a new sense of purpose – helping others who have been affected by contact with the Doctor on his frequent trips into Earth's history. She is content to remain on Earth as "the patron saint of the Doctor's leftovers," and they part on wary but good terms. In a cute epilogue in the TARDIS, Clara rejoins the Doctor, showing him a "selfie" taken by one of her pupils – and he spots Ashildr in the background, still present on Earth more than four hundred years after he last saw her. Clearly, he and Ashildr are destined to cross paths again – but not right now; he and Clara are soon off on another adventure. As the Doctor looks at his "mayfly" companion, however, the foreshadowing is laid on thick as he says he missed her, and she tells him cheerfully that she's not going anywhere...

Classic Who DVD Recommendation: The classic series also had a case where one adventure was immediately followed by another several hundred years later which arose directly from the consequences of the first, in the two halves of 1966's *The Ark*, starring William Hartnell, with Peter Purves and Jackie Lane.

Reflections: *The Woman Who Lived* is the most satisfying of Ashildr's four appearances this season. It's certainly the one that is most centred on her, the whole plot being driven by the fundamental fact of her immortality. At the end of the episode, she is willing to answer to her old name again, although she continues to use the "Me" alias as well – which allows Moffat to engage in clever misdirection on a couple of occasions later, most notably with the final line of *Heaven Sent*. She is next seen in *Face the Raven*, but although she is an important part of the plot, the main focus of that episode is obviously on Clara. Finally, in *Hell Bent*, Williams is left struggling with a rather nebulous and ill-defined characterisation, being asked to portray a vastly changed woman who has lived through billions of years and is now the last remaining immortal at the end of the universe. The ending to Ashildr's story is somewhat unsatisfactory, pushed into the background as it is by the climax of the drama between the Doctor and Clara.

As with the two previous episodes, the DVD box set for this season contains a significant moment deleted from the final version of the story. In this case, the vignette of Ashildr's children dying from the Black Death was originally longer, showing her encountering a plague doctor outside her house (another historical error, unfortunately – the distinctive costume with its birdlike mask was not invented until the

17th century). After she leaves, the man lifts off the mask – revealing the Doctor himself. Leaving this beat in would have put quite a different spin on the scene where the Doctor reads her journals, showing us that he has been checking up on her after all. In *Face the Raven*, there is also a mention of the Doctor keeping track of Ashildr's activities, which (were it not for this deleted moment) one could imagine was prompted by his encounter with her here. As this episode stands, there is only the early mention in passing of him observing her founding a leper colony (without her knowing he was there) to suggest that he gave any thought to her after leaving her at the end of *The Girl Who Died*.

In some ways it's a pity that this second encounter with Ashildr is placed immediately after the first one. There was certainly no necessity to do so; the two episodes are quite separate, and *The Woman Who Lived* could have been placed after *The Zygon Inversion*, or even after *Sleep No More*. That would have underlined the way in which the Doctor had gone off to do other things before unexpectedly meeting her again. On the other hand, as the matching titles show, the episodes do work well in juxtaposition, foregrounding the sort of consequences the Doctor rarely faces – an aspect which is only sharpened by making one follow hard upon the other. Also on the subject of consequences, Sam Swift is never seen or referred to again, so we can suppose that the Doctor's hastily improvised opinion that he was not left immortal by Ashildr's solution is true after all. Meanwhile, the final scene contains the last vestige of the show's interest in Clara's mundane life at Coal Hill School – although even here, it's only mentioned in order to lead to the revelation that Ashildr is still around in the present day. From this point, Clara's role is wholly as the Doctor's fellow traveller – and one, as the final scene unsubtly reminds us, whose time is running out.

20: The Zygon Invasion

Writer: Peter Harness
Director: Daniel Nettheim
Originally Broadcast: 31 October 2015

Cast

The Doctor: Peter Capaldi
Clara: Jenna Coleman
Kate: Jemma Redgrave
Osgood: Ingrid Oliver
Jac: Jaye Griffiths
Claudette: Cleopatra Dickens
Jemima: Sasha Dickens
Walsh: Rebecca Front
Little Boy: Abhishek Singh
Little Boy's Mum: Samila Kularatne
Hitchley: Todd Kramer
Lisa (Drone Op): Jill Winternitz
Norlander: Gretchen Egolf
Hitchley's Mom: Karen Mann
Walsh's Son: James Bailey
Zygons: Aidan Cook, Tom Wilton
Voice of the Zygons: Nicholas Briggs

Doctor Who is largely pitched as escapist action-adventure, but *The Zygon Invasion* has an unusually hard-edged, realistic feel for an episode that pits the Doctor and his friends against the show's typical grotesque, rubber-suited monsters, thanks to a story deliberately structured to parallel some of the distressing real-world events of the last decade. Peter Harness greatly improves on last season's *Kill the Moon* by writing a script with all of that story's strengths, including excellent building up of suspense and strong characterisations, and none of its weaknesses (in particular, the egregious disregard for basic science that made it so hard to take seriously).

A race of alien shape-shifters, the Zygons appeared in just one story in the mid-1970's, but made such a memorable impression that it seemed only a matter of time before they would turn up again in the modern series. Eventually, Steven Moffat used them in a subplot of

2013's Fiftieth Anniversary special episode *The Day of the Doctor*, taking the opportunity to plant the seeds for this story well in advance. As seen here in a pre-titles flashback, the Tenth and Eleventh Doctors induced Kate Stewart to negotiate a peace treaty on behalf of UNIT with a hidden Zygon force marooned on Earth. We never saw the result of that negotiation; the plot thread was deliberately left hanging until now, when a video message from scientist Osgood and her Zygon duplicate introduces "Operation Double" – a UNIT covert operation under whose auspices twenty million Zygons have been allowed to take human form and be resettled around the world. The video also introduces the mysterious "Osgood box" left by the Doctor as a safeguard in case the agreement turns sour: "If one Zygon goes rogue... or one human... then the ceasefire will break." As the story opens, the ceasefire has most definitely broken down as Osgood is captured by a militant faction of Zygons, but not before she can send a brief message to the TARDIS, warning the Doctor his "nightmare scenario" has come to pass.

With a little rewriting of history (the claim that the Zygons are predominantly peaceful, using their shape-changing ability only as a defence mechanism, doesn't really fit with the Doctor's initial encounter with them), Harness uses this state of affairs to reflect some of the current circumstances of our world. The obvious reference is to the radicalisation of young Muslims whose parents had previously integrated into the societies they had immigrated to. Over the course of the episode, elements such as drone strikes, hostage videos, planes being attacked by shoulder-fired missiles, and the execution of captured political opponents contribute to making a splinter group of rebels within the Zygon ranks function as a substitute for real Islamist terrorists. Fortunately, the story works well enough in its own right to prevent the allegory becoming intrusive, although a final judgment will have to wait until next week, when the show will have the challenge of presenting some kind of resolution to a situation whose real-life analogue seems horribly intractable.

The Doctor makes contact with the Zygon leaders, who for no clear reason are disguised as two young schoolgirls, which makes for an oddly whimsical feel as he talks about how "pretending to be a couple of seven-year-olds is a splendid way to conceal your blobbiness" and accuses them of letting factions of their children get out of control. The staging of the scene seems to be setting up a predictable gag (where the Doctor would discover he's been addressing the wrong two girls entirely) but it avoids the punchline after all; the subversion of expectations actually underlines the seriousness of the Doctor's concern. Meanwhile at UNIT, Kate and her assistant Jac (who returns from *The Magician's Apprentice*) realise that Osgood's files about Operation Double have been hacked, giving the rebels the location of every Zygon on Earth, as a hostage video of the captured Osgood is received that amounts to a declaration of war: "There will be truth, or there will be consequences." As Kate contacts the Doctor, the Zygon leaders are abducted; the disturbing image of two children being forcibly taken from a playground and driven away in a van is most unusual for *Doctor Who*, which despite all its monsters and perilous action tends to shy away from showing violence directly affecting the young.

The Doctor has also been trying to get in touch with Clara, who we see returning to her apartment block after a presumably ordinary day at work. But before she can answer her 127 missed calls from him she finds a distressed child – one of her neighbours – whose parents seem to be missing, but then reappear acting very oddly. The little boy is screaming as they take him away, but the whole sequence apparently comes to nothing as Clara seems to accept their vague reassurances and simply walks off (its true significance, of course, will be revealed later). Harness cleverly distracts the audience at this point by having Clara finally answer the Doctor's call, and they are soon joining Kate and Jac at the Zygon leaders' compromised command centre (hidden in a junior school). Another video from the rebels arrives, showing the little girl leaders being executed (although, again in deference to its younger audience, the show is careful to have them resume their native Zygon forms before being killed) – the radicals have now taken control of the Zygons.

In the debate about what to do next, Kate favours bombing the Zygon settlement in the fictional Middle Eastern nation of Turmezistan, where the rebels are holed up and where they have taken Osgood. The Doctor, on the other hand, wants to open negotiations, since it is still uncertain how many of the Zygons are actively supporting the rebels ("If you start bombing them, you'll radicalise the lot"). Clara helpfully points out that the rebels' slogan "Truth or Consequences" actually refers to a town in New Mexico (which was indeed, as she says, renamed after a quiz show in 1950), which is one of the places the Zygons were resettled and is where Osgood was captured at the top of the episode. The story expands to an appropriately world-wide scale as

170

the Doctor decides to send Kate to investigate Truth or Consequences while he flies off to Turmezistan instead (taking advantage of the plane he was given in *Death in Heaven* for "poncing about in" as President of Earth). Last season, we saw him exhibit an antipathy towards the military that sometimes approached the cartoonish, but he's somewhat more restrained here, restricting himself to the occasional snipe like his parting shot aimed at Kate as he leaves Clara in the UK and tells her to protect her country from the scary monsters – "…and also from the Zygons."

After he leaves, Clara asks Kate about any unusual weapons they have to fight the Zygons. Kate mentions that after a previous Zygon invasion a naval surgeon on UNIT staff developed a nerve gas that can destroy them – a reference to the Doctor's companion Harry Sullivan in the original Zygon story. (The details about experimenting with captured Zygons don't actually match up with what was shown back then, though; the Zygons in that story were just a small group – the crew of one spaceship – that were all killed by the end.) However, they no longer have that gas available – it was confiscated by the Doctor. Clara makes an excuse to go back to her apartment with Jac, on the way to which they witness the same little boy she met earlier being abducted. Following the kidnappers, they discover the building's lift has a piece of Zygon technology controlling it, allowing them to descend into a large cave and tunnel system. After seeing the size of the operation they face, Clara suggests they return and fetch reinforcements. The scripting is quite deft here, since all of Clara's actions will later be revealed to have a quite different explanation behind them. It seems a highly convenient coincidence that Clara and Jac happen to arrive just as the boy is being kidnapped (complete with an ostentatious "Quick, before someone sees us!" from his father dragging him into the lift), but the whole sequence is actually a clever bit of psychology aimed at Jac, to convince her that the troops in UNIT's HQ are needed down in the caves.

In Turmezistan, the Doctor arrives at UNIT's base in full President-of-the-World mode ("I'm here to rescue people and generally establish happiness all over the place"), only to be amusingly greeted by Colonel Walsh with "Yes, we know who you are" – harking back to MP (and later Prime Minister) Harriet Jones in several stories from 2005 to 2008, who had a habit of announcing her title to everyone she met. He finds them engaged in conducting a drone strike against the Zygon "training camp" village, but the strike is aborted when the

171

drone operator sees two of the targets looking exactly like her own family. This new ability of the Zygons – to, as Osgood puts it later, "pluck loved ones from your memory and wear their faces" – is so powerful that one can understand why Walsh is so insistent on the need to bomb the village before the Zygons can disperse ("You can't track a shape-shifter"). He does at least convince her to send a force to the village so he can try and get Osgood out – and negotiate with the rebels if possible – but the planned airstrike will still go ahead. Although Walsh is presented as harsh and unsympathetic, it's notable that the Doctor doesn't have an answer for her contention that the aliens' abilities render them too dangerous to deal with peacefully: "Any living thing in this world, including my family and friends, could turn into a Zygon and kill me, any second now. It's not paranoia when it's real."

Kate, meanwhile, has arrived in New Mexico; these scenes were actually filmed at Fuerteventura in the Canary Islands, but a few clichéd tumbleweeds roll across the road to ensure that we know we're in the southwestern United States. Truth or Consequences seems deserted, but a nice sense of menace is created as we become aware of someone observing her as she sees the graffiti adorning the buildings – both Zygon symbols and "No British" slogans. In the Sheriff's office (where we earlier saw Osgood captured), she is confronted by a nervous cop named Norlander who demands she prove she is not "one of them" and wants to know where her backup is. The woman serves as a means of providing Kate (and us) with the background exposition about the unwanted arrival of the British-seeming immigrants two years ago, and the steadily growing uneasiness in the town until the accidental sight of a Zygon in its unconcealed form precipitated a mob attack, leading to a depressingly familiar cycle of violence. Finally, the Zygons became openly hostile ("They just came for us... They turned into monsters and they *came* for us"); she shows Kate dumpsters containing the remains of dozens of victims. (Oddly, it's never explained just why both humans and Zygons are apparently reduced to giant hairballs when they are killed by the Zygons' electrical bolts.)

The UNIT forces enter the Zygon training village and surround the church where the Zygons are holed up. But the troops are no match for the Zygons' ability to mimic members of their families, and end up being annihilated. Unfortunately, what should be a powerful scene is drawn out and badly overplayed, with saccharine music laid over it as well to remove any shred of believability. As happened in the opening

172

episode of the season, the supposedly highly trained forces of UNIT are shown as being hopelessly out of their depth. Here, their behaviour really does place them in the "too stupid to live" category; they stand paralysed with indecision as the disguised Zygons approach them and meekly follow them into the church to their deaths. Walsh, even more determined now to "bomb the hell out of this place," leaves the Doctor to search for Osgood on his own. He eventually finds her in a cellar and rescues her. A single Zygon menaces them, but is disabled by a providential fall of rubble as the airstrike begins. The other Zygons are already on their way back to the UK, having lured the Doctor out of the way.

A fan favourite character, with her habit of wearing clothes reminiscent of the Doctor's past outfits (this time, her shirt collar shows off the rather tasteless question marks sported by all of the 1980's Doctors), Osgood represents the opposite extreme to the Zygon rebels. Having come to terms with her own Zygon duplicate back in *The Day of the Doctor*, she and her "sister" represent the concept of peace between the two races in its most ideal form. We may never know which Osgood was killed by Missy in *Death in Heaven*, given the survivor's refusal to differentiate between her human and Zygon selves. As their captive Zygon is loaded onto the Doctor's plane, the Doctor thinks he knows which one she is; based on how the Zygons' duplication ability worked in their original appearance, a Zygon Osgood would be unable to maintain her form more than a few days after the original's death, so she must be human. However, Osgood makes it clear that those "old rules" no longer apply, and that now the original can die if the Zygons have no further need for information from it. Ingrid Oliver brings a sincerity and strength to a character previously used mainly as comic relief: "You want to know who I am, Doctor? I am the peace." (And in reply, the Doctor refers to her as a "hybrid," in what appears to be this week's teasing reference to the background arc of the season.)

A story about shape-shifters can be counted on to play the "someone is not who we thought they were" card, and this one plays it multiple times, leading up to the revelation that the Clara we have been watching is actually a Zygon. She and Jac lead the UNIT troops into a cavern holding a large group of pods containing captured humans – one of which is Clara. A quick flashback fills in the details of how the substitution was made during the gap in that odd early sequence in Clara's apartment block where she faced the little boy's parents. Of course, the problem with this sort of twist is that the scenes have to be plausible in both versions. Although all of Clara's slightly "off" behaviour is now explained (for example, her rather uncharacteristic line to Jac as they entered the cavern, "Everybody middle-aged always thinks the world's about to come to an end"), it's not really clear why the fake Clara played along with Jac for as long as she did, particularly her apparent amazement at discovering the pod containing the real Clara. But the way she is now seen to have engineered the luring of all the human UNIT personnel to the cavern is ingenious. Coleman does an impressive job with Clara's villainous duplicate (whose name is Bonnie), expunging all of her usual warmth with just a few slight changes to her bearing and voice. It's a genuinely chilling moment as a force of Zygons arrives and she orders all the UNIT troops, as well as Jac, to be eliminated.

This being the first half of a two-parter, things start out bad and get steadily worse, ending with perhaps the best cliffhanger yet of this season. The Zygons have thoroughly neutralised UNIT, and nearly all of the Doctor's allies are captured or worse. In New Mexico, Norlander turns into a Zygon and threatens Kate; when Kate appears in a subsequent scene we can't be sure whether she escaped or whether this is a Zygon posing as her. Finally, Bonnie raids the undefended UNIT armoury and launches a missile at the Doctor's plane as he hastily returns to Britain. As the captive Zygon on board tells him his plane will never land, "Clara" calls to taunt him with the statement that Clara, Kate, and the UNIT troops are all dead. Of course, the "Osgood box" shown at the top of the episode will obviously play a part in the conflict's resolution (one good possibility is that it contains the anti-Zygon nerve gas mentioned previously as having been taken by the Doctor). What's in question is not what the ultimate outcome will be, but what it will end up costing.

Classic Who DVD Recommendation: The original encounter with the shape-shifting aliens can be seen in 1975's *Terror of the Zygons*, starring Tom Baker, with Elisabeth Sladen and Ian Marter.

Reflections: Any television drama, to a greater or lesser extent, reflects the concerns of the time in which it was made. *Doctor Who* stories are seldom designed to be didactic or polemical; for one thing, they range over all of time and space, meaning that references to issues of the day can often only be made via analogy. Of course, whenever the Doctor

174

touches down in the present-day real world (or *Doctor Who*'s approximation thereof), it becomes both easier and more tempting for writers to introduce elements drawn from current affairs. It's not surprising that the periods in the show's history when it is most tied to contemporary Earth are also when political references tend to surface. For example, the first year of the modern series (2005) was anchored around Rose Tyler's housing estate in London, allowing Russell T Davies the opportunity to include jabs at the Blair government's involvement in the Gulf War in *World War Three* and *The Christmas Invasion*. With references like these, their very specificity can make them seem dated even after just a few years; the best (or rather, worst) example from Davies is the worshipful treatment accorded to Obama in 2009's *The End of Time*, written at the height of the media genuflection towards him, and which now looks completely ridiculous.

Similar allusions in the classic series naturally tend to be even more dated; the anti-Thatcher satire in 1988's *The Happiness Patrol* was gratingly unsubtle at the time, but will probably be entirely missed by any young viewer watching it now. The advent of politically-minded script editor Andrew Cartmel saw the last three years of the classic series (with Sylvester McCoy as the Doctor) making statements on multiple contemporary issues, from racism to urban blight to nuclear disarmament. The most politically influenced period of the show, however, was possibly the Jon Pertwee era of the early 1970's, when the Doctor spent much of his time stuck on present-day Earth. The producer, Barry Letts, sanctioned stories which addressed topics ranging from colonialism and feminism to apartheid in South Africa, and his interest in the growing environmentalism of the time led directly to 1973's *The Green Death*. Each of his five seasons contained a story written by Malcolm Hulke, a (literally) card-carrying communist (his membership of the Communist Party of Great Britain led to him being placed under secret surveillance by MI5, the files of which have only recently been declassified) with a gift for creating well-rounded characters and dialogue that makes his stories some of the most interesting of that time.

The Zygon Invasion and its follow-up episode would probably have been very much to Hulke's taste. This story's treatment of the Zygons not as a monolithic mass of identical "monsters" but as a varied population containing factions with conflicting goals and ideals echoes his depiction of the eponymous creatures in 1970's *Doctor Who and the Silurians*. The Doctor and UNIT being at loggerheads over the approach to take to the Zygons also parallels that story; in this case, the Doctor successfully manages to restore the peace at the end, unlike the conclusion of *The Silurians*, when the military pragmatism of Kate Stewart's father prevailed (to the Doctor's disgust). It's notable, though, that although the Doctor resolves the immediate crisis here, the state of affairs it sprang from remains in existence, with no guarantee that the "nightmare scenario" won't recur in the future. This is to the writer's credit; even a simplified rendering of a complex problem (as this story undeniably is) should be able to prompt the audience to think about the real-world issues that inspired it, rather than pretend they can be solved at one stroke. Or as J. Michael Straczynski, the creator of *Babylon 5*, puts it: "A good story should provoke discussion, debate, argument... and the occasional bar fight."

21: The Zygon Inversion

Writers: Peter Harness & Steven Moffat
Director: Daniel Nettheim
Originally Broadcast: 7 November 2015

Cast

The Doctor: Peter Capaldi
Clara: Jenna Coleman
Kate: Jemma Redgrave
Osgood: Ingrid Oliver
Etoine: Nicholas Asbury
Zygons: Aidan Cook, Tom Wilton, Jack Parker
Voice of the Zygons: Nicholas Briggs

The Zygon Inversion, possibly the best episode yet this year, is a powerful conclusion to the story started last week. Writer Peter Harness places the Doctor and Clara – or rather Bonnie, Clara's Zygon duplicate – on opposite sides of a confrontation that has even more blazing intensity than he provided at the climax of last season's *Kill the Moon*. Showrunner Steven Moffat has a co-writer credit, and his handiwork is visible in the way the episode conforms to his usual practice with the second half of a two-parter: after a sprawling first episode, the story's focus is now confined almost exclusively to the regulars. There are practically no other on-screen characters (and only one other speaking part) besides the Doctor, Clara and Bonnie, UNIT leader Kate Stewart (the representative of humanity in this conflict with the shape-shifting aliens), and scientist Osgood, who gets to be the Doctor's companion while Clara is held captive.

Apart from a couple of scenes where Jenna Coleman is playing against herself, the real Clara has only a minor role in the episode. At the start, she suddenly wakes up in her own bed, back in her apartment – a deliberately disorienting change of setting which is another technique Moffat has previously employed to begin the second half of a two-part story (see, for example, 2008's *Forest of the Dead*). The situation rapidly becomes surreal as her bedside clock face is momentarily reversed, her toothpaste is the wrong colour, and she discovers her door and windows open onto blank walls. Recalling the method the Doctor used to reveal the multiple levels of dreaming in

Last Christmas, she finds the text in the newspaper on her table is gibberish – making it clear that she is trapped in this dream replica of her home while her real body is still in a Zygon pod. But as her TV begins showing her scenes from Bonnie's point of view, she cleverly works out that the mental link between them allows her to influence her duplicate's actions. Last week's cliffhanger is resolved when Clara's efforts cause the first missile fired at the Doctor's plane by Bonnie to miss, giving the Doctor and Osgood time to parachute from the plane before a second missile destroys it.

As in the last episode, Ingrid Oliver is excellent as she shows Osgood enjoying her adventure at the Doctor's side. The banter between them as they walk off the beach where they landed is not only funny, as she notes that the first item of business for any alien invader of Earth should be to shoot the Doctor – multiple times if necessary ("You've really thought this through, haven't you?" "I'm a big fan"), but also shows her analysing the situation intelligently as she wonders why Bonnie didn't kill them immediately. When they receive a text message from Bonnie ("I'm awake"), Osgood is able to work out that it means Clara is still alive, and actually sent the message without Bonnie's knowledge. There's more sharply written dialogue as the Doctor talks with Bonnie and pretends to be confused by her winking at him – actually more signals from Clara – and amusingly tells her she's sending out "some very mixed messages" ("I'm old enough to be your messiah!"). He playfully refers to Bonnie as Zygella (a pun on the name of famous British TV chef Nigella Lawson), and deliberately brings up the fact that Clara knows how to get to the "Osgood box" – the mysterious object he left with UNIT when he originally set up the whole human/Zygon agreement.

With Bonnie taking centre stage, Coleman is again outstanding at playing a character who is much more than just an "evil twin" version of Clara. As the leader of the Zygon revolution, Bonnie displays all the self-righteous certainty of the true fundamentalist, convinced that all twenty million Zygons around the world will automatically side with her against the humans when they are forcibly unmasked, even though (as is the case in all such conflicts) the vast majority simply want to live their own lives in peace. ("Then it's time we stopped giving them a choice," she will later tell Clara – arrogating to herself the right to make their decisions for them.) These "moderate" Zygons are symbolised here by one man, Etoine (his name is not actually used in the episode, though, appearing only in the credits). Bonnie somehow disrupts his human disguise, rendering him a monstrous amalgam of human and Zygon that she intends to use to create a climate of fear. In the course of tracking Bonnie down, the Doctor finds Etoine and tries to help, but cannot prevent the man from suiciding in despair at the way he has been used. It's a powerful moment, although not quite as compelling as it could have been had we actually seen the reactions of ordinary humans to his change. The impassive bystanders, like the weirdly expressionless police officers the Doctor and Osgood encountered earlier, are all Zygons who must either be sympathetic to Bonnie's cause, or desperately trying to keep out of her way.

Having already found out that the Osgood box is not at UNIT HQ, Bonnie returns to the underground chamber holding the pod where Clara is imprisoned to interrogate her directly. In her dream apartment, Clara is able to talk with Bonnie through her television, and Coleman's timing is impeccable as she shows the advantage passing back and forth between the two of them over the course of the conversation. Realising that Bonnie can't force the information she wants out of her, Clara smugly sits back to await her questions ("I am a brilliant liar," she says – something we have seen proven in previous episodes), only to be taken aback when Bonnie points out that the mental link between them makes it impossible for either to lie to the other. When she threatens to destroy the pod, Clara can have no doubt that she is sincere; therefore, Clara admits that the Osgood box is held in the Black Archive – UNIT's top-secret repository of captured alien technology – and Bonnie sets off, taking the pod with her.

Shortly afterwards, the Doctor arrives in search of Clara, guided by Kate, who has returned from New Mexico. The suggestion that this is a duplicate of Kate is made even stronger when the two soldiers with her are revealed to be Zygons, only for a neat reversal to occur as she catches them off guard and shoots them. She tells how she dealt with her Zygon assailant last episode in the most straightforward way with a fan-pleasing reference to one of her father's most famous lines: in 1971's *The Daemons*, Brigadier Lethbridge-Stewart issued an order for "five rounds rapid" as an equally forthright way of responding to a hostile alien. Jemma Redgrave is careful to show Kate somewhat apologetic at using a gun to solve her problems, although equally she is firm in her insistence to the Doctor that his peace deal has now irretrievably broken down, and they need access to the anti-Zygon nerve gas developed by his former companion Harry Sullivan (and which it was mentioned last episode that he had confiscated from

UNIT). It's definitely a good thing to see Kate back to being a strong character after the dithering, watered down version of her seen in *The Magician's Apprentice*; however, with both sides now uninterested in peace, the Doctor's only option is to ensure that they all come together in the Black Archive for a showdown.

It's hardly a surprise that the Osgood box proves to be crucially important, but in an excellent twist (which, as the Doctor points out, should have been obvious given there were two Osgoods, human and Zygon), it turns out there are two boxes, not one, and Kate and Bonnie each take up a position next to one of them. Inside each, the phrase used as a glib slogan by the revolutionaries – "Truth or Consequences" – assumes a terrible significance; Kate and Bonnie are each faced with two buttons, either of which will end their war but only one of them in a way that they would wish. For Kate, one button will release "the imbecile's gas" (another reference to the Doctor's former companion – in 1975's *Revenge of the Cybermen*, the Doctor memorably yelled "Harry Sullivan is an imbecile!" after he nearly set off an explosive booby trap), and the other will destroy the Black Archive and everyone in it. Bonnie's two alternatives are to unmask every Zygon in the world as she desires, or to cancel their shape-shifting abilities, leaving them human forever. As the Doctor says, there are multiple levels of safeguards built in to the agreement ("I did this on a very important day for me"), and he sets about trying to convince them both to refrain from selecting any of the dreadful alternatives.

Peter Capaldi is absolutely mesmerising in this showpiece confrontation. It's a scene that continues unbroken for over ten minutes. For a long stretch of it there's only his voice on the soundtrack, no incidental music at all, but he controls the tempo masterfully as the Doctor tries to persuade Bonnie to break the cycle of violence. Her first response is to blame him for engineering this situation, as though what she has done is his fault. But having recently been faced with similar accusations (with considerably more justification) from Ashildr in *The Woman Who Lived*, he simply shrugs off Bonnie's attempt to pin responsibility for her actions onto him. As he accurately points out, "You're not superior to people who were cruel to you, you're just a whole bunch of new cruel people." He compares her behaviour to a child's tantrum: no thought for the future, no plan to actually accomplish anything, simply a desire for revenge against an innocent population for mainly imaginary slights. After showing that she has no idea what her "brave new world" of a human-

180

free homeland will be like, he calls to mind another quote from Aldous Huxley (from *Time Must Have a Stop* in 1944: "Only one more indispensable massacre of Capitalists or Communists or Fascists or Christians or Heretics, and there we are – there we are in the Golden Future") as he tries to make her see that troublemakers like her cannot have any future in such a world ("How are you going to protect your glorious revolution from the next one?").

But Bonnie deliberately closes herself off from thinking about the future; as she had earlier told Clara, if they all die in this war, she doesn't care. Her commitment to that view is now tested, as she prepares to take the fifty percent chance of getting what she wants even as Kate moves to make her own choice. Mutually assured destruction seems imminent, but then the writers brilliantly throw a curveball as the Doctor suddenly adopts the persona of a game show host ("And we're off! Fingers on buzzers! Are you feeling lucky?") – his *faux*-American accent and catchphrase "I mean that most sincerely" are a direct parody of Hughie Green hosting the talent show *Opportunity Knocks* in the 1960's and 70's. Rather than being dissipated, the tension is raised even higher as both Bonnie and Kate are thrown off balance – and then the Doctor drops the act and fervently expounds on his "scale model" of war, making the point as forcefully as he can that once launched, the course of a war is not predictable, leading to who knows how many casualties before "everybody does what they were always going to have to do from the very beginning – sit down and talk!" Capaldi's performance is wonderful here – he is yelling as loudly as the Doctor ever has, but there is no sense of histrionics; rather, he seems to be bringing to the surface something fundamental to the character.

Coleman rises to the occasion as well, showing Bonnie's certainty melting away under the Doctor's onslaught. She still maintains a hard exterior, but there is a brittleness there now as she says she's gone too far to turn back. In response, the Doctor employs the same weapon that the Master found unanswerable in 2007's *Last of the Time Lords*: "Well, here's the unforeseeable... I forgive you." At last she is reduced to griping, like a petulant teenager, that nobody understands her. The music steals back in, and Capaldi soars to the climax of the scene as the Doctor recounts how his experiences in the Time War – a vastly greater conflict than she will ever know – not only mean he understands her perfectly, but have instilled in him an absolute determination to preserve this peace. He wants her to think about both truth *and* consequences (as he said earlier, "Thinking's just a fancy word for changing your mind"). In the face of such passion (the way his voice catches as he talks about the screams he hears when he closes his eyes is a fabulous piece of acting), Kate finally makes the decision to close her box; her quiet "I'm sorry" as she comes back to her senses and the Doctor's heartfelt "Thank you" is a moving moment, enabling him to now devote his attention fully to Bonnie.

Almost half a minute goes by without a word, just close-ups on the two characters, but Capaldi's expressive face charts the growing realisation on Bonnie's part – the two boxes are actually empty. Their whole point was to bring her to the realisation that the war she so desired was futile. The scene reaches a satisfying, even amusing, conclusion as Kate points out that now everyone knows the boxes are empty, only for the Doctor to use the Black Archive's memory-wiping technology on her and the Zygons ("You've said that the last fifteen times"). His lure for warmongers is once more reset, but Bonnie's memories are left intact; she proves that he has finally broken through her self-centeredness by asking him what happened in the Time War. It's a very clever touch that the design of the Osgood boxes echoes that of the Moment, the super-weapon from *The Day of the Doctor* which he nearly used to destroy his own people, and the turning point of that episode is evoked as he tells Bonnie that the same thing happened to both of them: "I let Clara Oswald get inside my head." The whole sequence is the finest yet of the Capaldi era, and a defining moment for his Doctor.

While the previous episode had many obvious references to real-world events, such allusions are considerably toned down here. Even though Bonnie is now working for peace, to the extent that she represented a true aspiration among the Zygons (to live in their natural form), that issue remains to be addressed. But the lack of specific applicability to a current, ongoing conflict makes it easier for the story to reach a definitive (and happy) ending. As the Doctor and Clara return to the TARDIS, he offers Osgood the chance to travel with him. But despite her desire to do so, she declines the opportunity – she still has a planet to protect. And she will have help; in a neat final twist, Bonnie takes on Osgood's appearance to replace the Osgood twin who was previously killed. From fiercely insisting on keeping her own Zygon identity apart from humans, she is now willing to consider such distinctions meaningless. Gaining a place in the group protecting the planet is a fitting reward for her ultimately realising that there was no route to a quick victory, just the prospect of a war that would cost millions of lives. Only with that understanding did her desire for war wither; as the Doctor always knew, the key to peace is all in the mind.

Classic Who DVD Recommendation: The 1967/68 story *The Enemy of the World* was *Doctor Who*'s first attempt at the near-future (it's set in 2018) global conspiracy thriller. It also plays games with identity, thanks to its villain being a physical double of the Doctor (a kind of mirror image of this story, where every character *except* the Doctor is or could be a duplicate). Coincidentally, one of its guest actors is David Nettheim, whose nephew Daniel was the director of this Zygon two-parter. Missing for many years from the BBC archives (it was only finally returned in 2013), *The Enemy of the World* stars Patrick Troughton, with Frazer Hines and Deborah Watling.

Reflections: According to a later interview, it was while working on Peter Capaldi's big set-piece speeches here that Moffat conceived the idea of giving him a whole episode to carry by himself. The fact that it prompted the creation of the masterpiece that is *Heaven Sent* is just another reason to savour the great confrontation scene here. Although the Doctor often gets to show bombastic defiance (see, for example, Matt Smith's oration in 2010's *The Pandorica Opens*), it's rare that he is allowed room to set out his moral philosophy with such force and clarity. One unexpected example comes in 1978's *The Pirate Planet*, the first story written for the show by Douglas Adams. While it mostly shares the hilarious absurdity of *The Hitch-Hiker's Guide to the Galaxy* which Adams was working on at the same time, at one point Tom Baker's Doctor drops the comedy and delivers a blistering riposte excoriating the villain who expects him to appreciate the cleverness of his scheme. 1986's *The Trial of a Time Lord* is not generally considered a high point for *Doctor Who*, but towards the end of its long course, when the machinations of his fellow Time Lords that led to the trial are revealed, Colin Baker gets to let loose with a speech that is possibly the finest moment of his sadly truncated era. Perhaps the closest analogue to Capaldi's speech here comes at the end of *Battlefield* in 1989, when Sylvester McCoy's Doctor delivers a sermon about the horrors of nuclear war in order to convince his adversary to abort the launch of a captured nuclear missile.

The way this story ties in with the events of *The Day of the Doctor* – and not just the Zygon thread which is its direct prequel, but the other parts of the episode as well – is extremely ingenious, and done in such a way that *The Zygon Inversion* still retains its force even if the viewer has not seen the Fiftieth Anniversary special. The terrible memories of the Time War are still very much present for the Doctor; even though he was granted the opportunity to reverse his ultimate fatal decision in *The Day of the Doctor*, that reversal did not undo all the other things he did in the course of the war. Perhaps the confrontation with Bonnie provided a much-needed catharsis for both of them; certainly, the idea of turning his traumatic memories of wartime deeds into a positive determination that "No one should have to think like that… not on our watch" is a wonderfully inspiring message for the episode to promote. The comment about Clara getting inside both his and Bonnie's heads (in different ways) is a clever way of showing the importance of Clara to both stories, in spite of the fact that she gets so little to do here – and, of course, his comment "Trust me, she doesn't leave" is horribly ironic foreshadowing for the end of the season.

As I noted in the previous chapter, it's to the story's credit that it leaves the underlying situation in being at the end, with the possibility that the same crisis could occur again in the future. In real life, we don't have the Doctor to neatly cut through Gordian knots for us, but the Earth of the show doesn't either – the Osgood boxes were really just a clever bluff, and the story only reaches a satisfying conclusion thanks to the Doctor's ability to convince Bonnie to change her course. There's another, rather more unfortunate aspect that echoes our world: remarkably, Kate Stewart is the sole actual human being to appear in this episode (setting aside Clara, being the Doctor's companion, and Osgood, who deliberately considers herself a human/Zygon hybrid); the extras populating the exterior shots are all Zygon duplicates. The human population of the UK (and, indeed, the world) is given no voice at all in the momentous decisions that affect them – either the original choice to allow the Zygons to settle among humanity, or the actions to be taken against the rebels – and no one ever seems to consider the possibility that they should be. It may be an unavoidable consequence of the simplification necessary to distil a complex real-world situation into a manageable adventure story; nevertheless, for ordinary people in the 21st century, with our lives increasingly encroached upon by unelected, unaccountable bureaucrats and transnational organisations, the effect is to ensure that this tale of shape-shifting alien doppelgangers feels uncomfortably close to reality after all.

22: Sleep No More

Writer: Mark Gatiss
Director: Justin Molotnikov
Originally Broadcast: 14 November 2015

Cast

The Doctor: Peter Capaldi
Clara: Jenna Coleman
Rassmussen: Reece Shearsmith
Nagata: Elaine Tan
Chopra: Neet Mohan
474: Bethany Black
Deep-Ando: Paul Courtenay Hyu
King Sandman: Paul Davis
Sandmen: Tom Wilton, Matthew Doman
Morpheus Presenter: Zina Badran
Hologram Singers: Natasha Patel, Elizabeth Chong, Nikkita Chadha, Gracie Lai

It takes a certain amount of chutzpah for the opening line of an episode to be an emphatic "You must *not* watch this," addressed directly to the audience. *Sleep No More* is a very odd and experimental episode from the pen of Mark Gatiss, who last season contributed the light and frothy *Robot of Sherwood*, as great a contrast to this as could be imagined. He is aiming here for the sort of effect more associated with the episodes of Steven Moffat – turning an aspect of our mundane, everyday experience into a nightmarish threat. It obtains some suspense and kinetic vigour from a couple of novel scripting and/or directing choices; however, as the first truly stand-alone episode this year, it can't help but feel rather insubstantial after the previous weightier tales, even before a surprise ending reveals the whole thing to be one big shaggy dog story.

The speaker of the aforementioned opening line is Professor Gagan Rasmussen (played by Gatiss's *League of Gentlemen* collaborator Reece Shearsmith, who also made an appearance as the second Doctor, Patrick Troughton, in the 2013 Gatiss-written docudrama about the origins of *Doctor Who*, *An Adventure in Space and Time*). Throughout the story he takes us into his confidence, providing explanatory narration over a collection of "found footage" showing the events on Le Verrier Station, his laboratory in orbit around Neptune. *Doctor Who* rarely visits the outer solar system, and this is the first time it has made use of Neptune; there are some lovely shots of the station floating above the giant blue planet (the station itself is named after Urbain Le Verrier, the French mathematician whose calculations led to the discovery of Neptune in 1846). Rasmussen is apparently the only survivor after everyone else on the station has been killed in some disaster; the story opens as a rescue ship from a human colony on Neptune's moon Triton docks, and its crew are surprised to encounter the Doctor and Clara wandering around the darkened, deserted facility.

A familiar *Doctor Who* scenario – an isolated outpost, a small group of humans trapped in it, and monsters picking them off one by one – is given a very off-kilter feel thanks to several tricks of presentation. Most startlingly, for the first time in the show's history the opening titles and theme music are omitted. As Rasmussen finishes his introductory spiel with "This is what happened..." the screen fills with a mass of alphanumeric characters, among which the words DOCTOR WHO are slightly highlighted; then the episode simply continues on. Even the story's name, along with the usual writer, producer and director credits (the latter two of which are normally superimposed on the action immediately after the opening titles) are not seen until the end. (If it had been allowed, perhaps Gatiss would have preferred to omit the ending credit sequence as well, which would have given the story even more the appearance of a "real" piece of recovered footage.) Another possible place for the pre-credits sting to burst in comes when the gun-toting rescue crew surround the Doctor and Clara as they are bantering about the sci-fi cliché of putting "space" in front of common words to make them seem "all sort of high-tech and future-y." Again, though, the episode just keeps going, as the Doctor pulls out his psychic paper and passes himself and Clara off as "engineering stress assessors."

The characters of the rescue crew are fleshed out more than is usual in this type of story; as the ship is docking, Rasmussen's voiceover gives us a capsule introduction to each of them, even as he ominously warns us, "Don't get too attached." There's the commander, Nagata ("Quite a baptism of fire, I'm afraid"); the cheerful Deep-Ando ("the joker of this little group"); the young, nervous Chopra ("Bit of an attitude, in my opinion"); and finally the "grunt" – an artificially grown, low-intelligence trooper – designated merely as "474." We are also introduced to the Morpheus machine, a piece of sleep-enhancement technology being used by Deep-Ando, which will play a central part in what follows. Chopra, by contrast, distrusts the Morpheus process and refuses to use it, leading Nagata to order him to keep his politics to himself. Gatiss gets a surprising amount of unobtrusive world-building into the script, with the Doctor's references to an unspecified "Great Catastrophe," after which India and Japan were tectonically merged and became a dominant world power, providing intriguing hints to this 38th-century milieu. Rather like the Indian Space Agency in 2012's *Dinosaurs on a Spaceship* (which was set in the 24th century), this "Indo-Japanese" crew, with elements such as their standard communicator greeting "May the gods look favourably upon you," provide a distinctive feel to this futuristic setting.

The grunt, 474, clearly has something of a crush on Chopra, and in her clumsy way expresses protectiveness towards him. We learn more about her programming when he irritably brushes her off; she switches immediately to aggression and has to be calmed down by her commander. Interestingly, Clara's disgust at the idea of a genetically engineered soldier is simply dismissed by the Doctor ("Well, that's how they roll in the 38th century"), in stark contrast to how he will react when he finds out about the Morpheus process later. But there's no time for ethical debates, as they have their first encounter with the monsters that have ravaged the station. For classic series fans, these lumpish, vaguely humanoid brutes bear an unfortunate resemblance to the embarrassingly poor Plasmatons in 1982's *Time-Flight*, although here the creatures can at least move well enough to believably chase people. Their design also improves on the Plasmatons by giving them huge, open mouths – dark, yawning vertical chasms in their otherwise featureless faces – which allows them to generate a certain amount of menace as they loom over their victims.

For no very good reason, Deep-Ando becomes separated from the others, running off in a different direction while they take refuge in a laboratory. Thanks to 474's strength, the arm of one of the creatures is trapped in the door, and then simply crumbles to dust as the door is pushed closed. While the Doctor investigates the composition of the dust, Clara pokes around the rest of the lab, which includes an array of Morpheus pods. After being a central part of the previous two episodes, Jenna Coleman is very much in a secondary, generic companion role this week, with Clara's only contribution of note being falling victim to the Morpheus process, as one of the pods grabs her and draws her in. She is quickly freed, with no apparent ill effects – although not before a cute touch of whimsy, as the activated pod displays a hologram of four women singing "Mr. Sandman" in imitation of the 1954 version of the song by The Chordettes.

In another of the pods, they find Rasmussen hiding from the monsters ("Ah, this is where I come in," his narration comments). The full details of the Morpheus process are finally laid out; an invention of Rasmussen, it's a means of sending coded electrical signals to the brain that can effectively compress a night's worth of sleep into just five minutes. A holographic advertisement for the process extols its virtues ("Now you can go a whole month without sleep!"), which are apparently revolutionising the society on Triton. The new generation of "Wide-Awakes" is contrasted with "Rip Van Winkles" like Chopra – which retrospectively explains Nagata's line to him in their first scene ("Spoken like a true Rip") as he complained about Morpheus. There's a witty touch as the holographic presenter disappears, only to pop back with a final "Terms and conditions apply," before the Doctor voices his disgust at the idea of interfering with the natural function of sleep, and Clara aligns herself with Chopra's opposition to the process.

As I mentioned above, the Doctor's attitude to Morpheus here is somewhat inconsistent with his *laissez faire* stance towards this society's engineering of grunts like 474. It will later turn out, of course, that they do have good cause to be suspicious of Morpheus, but that is because of its side-effects which Rasmussen is carefully concealing, not because of some inherent wrongness in the basic idea – the Doctor's automatic hostility right from the start leaves him looking oddly like a he-tampered-in-God's-domain moralist from an old Frankenstein movie. As they set out in search of the missing Deep-Ando, the Doctor presents his theory to explain how the new, upgraded version of Morpheus which Rasmussen has been working on here has given rise to the monsters. The culprit is the "sleep dust" we wipe from our eyes every morning when we wake up – somehow the Morpheus process has incubated it and accelerated its development into these creatures. Meanwhile, there's a lengthy sequence as Deep-Ando tries to take refuge from the monsters, but the station computer won't let him past the door to his chosen hiding place without singing "the Morpheus song" (a.k.a. "Mr. Sandman"). It's intended to build up suspense, but (partly because a very similar idea was previously used in the 2007 episode *42*) instead comes across as tedious padding.

Fortunately, there's a good "jump" moment as he finally enters the room, only to be surprised by one of the creatures. As Rasmussen's narration sombrely informs us, "He was the first of them to die. We heard the scream, but... we had our own problems."

We suddenly cut to an action sequence, as the station's gravity shields fail and one of the monsters attacks again and absorbs Rasmussen – although it's actually quite difficult to see this due to the extent to which the picture is shaking to simulate the various points of view of the people looking on. Neptune's gravity takes hold and the monster is pulled apart, but then the crisis abates as the Doctor successfully gets the gravity shields running again. As happened before, the group are split for no clear reason, with Chopra and 474 being separated from the others as the Doctor, Clara and Nagata take refuge in the station's cold store, an inhospitable place full of hanging carcasses, knives and saws. After some banter about Clara rather than the Doctor coming up with a name for the creatures (the "Sandmen") and the Doctor moodily quoting the passage from *Macbeth* that gives the episode its title, a crucial realisation occurs when the Doctor discovers that the station is storing helmet cam footage from the crew, and Nagata simply says, "We don't have helmet cams." As the Sandmen attack again, they escape to the station's engine room, making use of the creatures' blindness. Rasmussen, surprisingly, continues his addresses to camera, complimenting the Doctor's ingenuity and telling us, "I'm not dead... You've probably guessed that by now."

Presenting the whole story as found footage (interspersed with Rasmussen's close-ups in the role of narrator) presents several unusual challenges for both Gatiss and first-time director Justin Molotnikov. Every time the camera angle changes, the new point of view needs to be justified. This is managed fairly seamlessly thanks to the fact that the Sandmen have visual receptors scattered all over the station as minute particles of dust. The desaturated, security-camera-like views from these receptors are intercut with shots directly representing various crew members' points of view – which have been acquired by the station through a side-effect of the Morpheus process; in the engine room, the Doctor demonstrates that all the crew except Chopra (who refuses to use Morpheus), as well as Clara, have suffered the same "infection." These point of view shots can be disconcerting, as they feature a lot of staring straight into the camera by the other actors, combined with much erratic panning and tilting to simulate characters walking or looking around. At times the shakiness of the camera work is so pronounced that, together with the darkness of the environment and the very subdued incidental music (although that also makes sense, from the standpoint of verisimilitude), it makes for a distinctly uncomfortable viewing experience.

In the engine room, the Doctor finds disconnected power cables where something had been maintained, using the warmth of the engines to keep it alive. Thanks to Rasmussen helpfully including various cutaway shots in his presentation, we are ahead of the Doctor at this point, knowing that a mysterious levitating Morpheus pod is floating through the station, heading for the rescue ship. Chopra and 474 are making for the ship, too, with Chopra realising that he may have to destroy the station to ensure that the creatures are eradicated. Under attack from the Sandmen, 474 sacrifices herself so that Chopra can make it to the ship, but the pod has arrived ahead of him; all his efforts are ultimately futile as he dies at the hands of the Sandman inside.

When the Doctor, Clara and Nagata arrive, Rasmussen emerges from hiding and admits he is behind everything. He tells them the pod contains the very first Morpheus client ("Patient Zero"), now full of spores ready to infect the humans on Triton and beyond, and sets the creature free to attack them. Then the story seems to peter out in a strange anticlimax; the Doctor distracts the creature with a recording of the Morpheus song so they can escape, and Nagata simply shoots Rasmussen. But the Doctor has picked up on the inconsistencies and puzzling features of the events, such as the contradiction between the presence of "a man who hasn't slept in five years" and the fact that the Sandmen consume their hosts, or the way the gravity shields were sabotaged earlier for no obvious reason. Gatiss needs the Doctor to ultimately miss the real point, so he doesn't manage to penetrate to the truth; in the end, he destroys (or so he thinks) the threat by causing the station to self-destruct, as they evade the Sandmen and make it to the TARDIS, and finally exits the story with a plaintive cry that "None of this makes any sense!"

Only after the TARDIS has dematerialised is the real climax reached, as the supposedly dead Rasmussen pops up yet again. As the station starts falling apart around him, he tells us that all that stuff about the spores was a lie; the whole point of the story, with its action, suspense and scary monsters, was to keep the audience watching. The unexplained bursts of static we've been seeing throughout during shot transitions are actually the Morpheus control signal, and now we watchers have been infected! (As he smugly says, "I did tell you not to watch.") The most memorable moment of the episode is the final one, as "Rasmussen" is revealed to be a Sandman himself and disintegrates while laughing crazily at the audience, just before his infectious recording is transmitted to the whole solar system. It's a clever "meta" conclusion, in a similar vein to the tag at the end of 2007's *Blink*, which put forward the idea that every statue in the world might be a Weeping Angel. However, that was simply a bonus, coming at the end of a tale that had already been properly wrapped up in its own right. Here, the effect of the surprise twist is to undermine the rest of the episode. In the end, as a technical exercise and an expansion of *Doctor Who*'s boundaries, *Sleep No More* is moderately engaging; but as a satisfying adventure in its own right it can only be described as a snoozer.

Classic Who DVD Recommendation: The dark and foreboding space station environment here is somewhat reminiscent of 1983's *Terminus*, starring Peter Davison, with Janet Fielding, Sarah Sutton and Mark Strickson.

Reflections: *Sleep No More* was, by some margin, the most poorly received story of Peter Capaldi's second year. Not only was the audience size down by comparison with the other episodes of the season, but those who did watch were notably unimpressed with what they saw. The appreciation index (a score generated for each BBC programme by surveying the reactions of a representative panel of viewers) dipped significantly below the season average, to an extent not seen since the equally experimental *Love & Monsters* in 2006. Non-standard episodes like these have tended to find it tough to impress the general audience; in this case, viewers tuning in expecting another adventure with the Doctor and Clara found themselves faced with a deliberately disjointed narrative in which Clara barely appears and the Doctor is ultimately totally fooled and achieves nothing. As if that wasn't enough, the dark, "shaky-cam" nature of much of the episode may well have been too off-putting for some viewers.

Nevertheless, the ingenuity with which Gatiss (on Rasmussen's behalf) has constructed his account is worth noting. His previous episode, *Robot of Sherwood*, had contained a wink to the audience at its end acknowledging its artificial nature, featuring as it did a

Hollywood caricature of Robin Hood while steadfastly maintaining him to be the real deal. In this episode, Rasmussen cheerfully admits how his presentation was deliberately put together to entice us to keep watching: "I did try to make it exciting. All those scary bits. All those death-defying scrapes, monsters, and a proper climax with a really big one at the end! Compulsive viewing." It's the same concerns that inform the writing of every episode of *Doctor Who* – Steven Moffat, in particular, has noted in past interviews how he bears in mind the necessity to keep the audience continually intrigued throughout his episodes – here made explicit in the story itself.

Equally ingenious is Gatiss's answer to the issue that faces all stories that use the found footage device: to explain how it is that footage is being generated even in the most chaotic, threatening, or action-packed situations (also known as the "why don't they stop filming?" problem). Here the question is sidestepped by the fact that images are being involuntarily gathered from the point of view of everyone affected by the Morpheus process, as well as anywhere on the station the Sandmen's visual receptors can plausibly reach. The resulting multiplicity of viewpoints gives a welcome variety to the shots, leading to a visual style for the episode that is halfway between a "pure" found footage approach, with only a few points of view (or even just one) used to tell the story, and the normal omniscient-camera style, in which the director can compose every shot for the best effect. It also, amusingly, contrives to produce a found footage story that has no actual cameras in it at all.

According to the commentary by Gatiss (with Reece Shearsmith) for this episode in the DVD box set, the story was originally conceived as a two-parter. It works quite well as a stand-alone tale (certainly, the found footage idea would not stretch to being used for two episodes), but there is undoubtedly scope for a sequel to exploit Gatiss's world-building, showing us the 38th-century civilisation that we have so far only heard about. This would presumably follow up the results of Rasmussen's transmission and its unleashing of the Sandmen on humanity, allowing the Doctor to realise what he had missed the first time around and rectify his mistake. Given the mixed reception of *Sleep No More*, it's uncertain whether such a continuation will ultimately materialise, but I hope that it does; it would turn into a strength the main weakness of the episode as it currently stands – the "So what?" ending that leaves it feeling pointless.

23: Face the Raven

Writer: Sarah Dollard
Director: Justin Molotnikov
Originally Broadcast: 21 November 2015

Cast

The Doctor: Peter Capaldi
Clara: Jenna Coleman
Rigsy: Joivan Wade
Ashildr: Maisie Williams
Jen: Naomi Ackie
Kabel: Simon Manyonda
Rump: Simon Paisley Day
Anahson: Letitia Wright
Chronolock Guy: Robin Soans
Alien Woman: Angela Clerkin
Habrian Woman: Caroline Boulton
Elderly Woman: Jenny Lee

Face the Raven is an episode that will obviously be most remembered for its climax, which brings a tragic end to the adventures of Clara Oswald with the Doctor. But along the way, new writer Sarah Dollard proves to be a real find for the show, much as Jamie Mathieson was last season. Steven Moffat has related how immediately intrigued he was by Dollard's initial pitch: what if trap streets – the fake streets inserted by some map-makers into their products so that they can prove theft if their work is plagiarised – were actually real places? Following the implications triggered by that thought does indeed produce an excellent idea for a novel place to set a *Doctor Who* story: a secret world in the heart of London which acts as a refuge for a host of different aliens, hiding from the humans all around them. (There are some vague parallels with the current European refugee crisis, but unlike *The Zygon Invasion*, contemporary political references are very much in the background here.) Nevertheless, the most praiseworthy aspect of the episode isn't the setting or the mechanics of the plot, but the handling of the characters, in particular the Doctor and Clara.

Dollard has the good fortune to be able to bring back and further develop a couple of memorable characters from previous episodes, the first of whom appears almost immediately in the teaser. Rigsy, the affable graffiti artist who functioned almost as a companion to Clara while she was playing at being the Doctor in last year's *Flatline*, kicks off the story by phoning the TARDIS to ask Clara and the Doctor to investigate a tattoo on the back of his neck that he doesn't remember getting. The Doctor is not pleased at his number being given out to someone who wants them to deal with what seems a trivial problem. But his opinion quickly changes when he sees the tattoo in question: it's just a number, but it keeps changing, counting down minute by minute to zero. The cue cards that were employed for a gag about the Doctor's social skills in *Under the Lake* reappear, but they can't help him now: as he says, "There is no nice way to say you're about to die." The tattoo provides a literal ticking clock to drive the plot, and having someone who we already know is a good guy in danger (and to increase the stakes further, he now has a fiancée and a young baby) ensures that we are invested in the story right from the beginning.

They discover that Rigsy has had recent contact with alien life and then been dosed with retcon (the amnesia drug introduced in the spinoff series *Torchwood*), which has resulted in him losing his memory of the entire previous day's events. The Doctor takes them to the map room of the Great British Library, where old maps of London might show streets that are now hidden from general view where aliens could be living. When Clara brings up the aforementioned concept of trap streets, the Doctor's incredulous reaction is amusing: "A whole London street just up and disappeared and you lot assume it's a copyright infringement." But in the end, they try a more direct search technique: assuming that their target has some kind of technological camouflage, the Doctor flies the TARDIS over the city as Clara lies on the floor in the doorway scanning the streets below with his sonic sunglasses, looking for areas where her gaze is involuntarily deflected. She is enjoying herself hugely, even when the TARDIS lurches slightly and she nearly falls out. As we saw at the very start of the episode when she and the Doctor rushed into the TARDIS laughing and celebrating an improbable escape concluding another unseen adventure, she has now given herself over fully to her life with the Doctor. Rigsy is astonished at her completely unfazed reaction to dangling recklessly high above the ground, but the Doctor can only comment, "Tell me about it… it's an ongoing problem."

Back on the ground, and after some searching, they stumble across a place where Rigsy experiences brief flashbacks to some act of violence, breaking through his amnesia. As they enter the hidden street, the feeling is very much one of walking out of normal, everyday London and into some *Harry Potter*-like world – Diagon Alley with aliens. Director Justin Molotnikov, having been saddled last week with a stark, futuristic space station setting (which could not be shown to its best advantage anyway thanks to having to be shrouded in darkness and shot with lots of shaky camera movement), seizes the opportunity to show off a richly detailed environment. The narrow, cobbled street is lined with a mish-mash of pseudo-medieval architecture on either side and illuminated with a golden light emanating from creatures called "Lurkworms" which conveniently also generate a telepathic field that allows all the alien residents to appear as ordinary humans (although the disguise can be seen through under certain conditions, revealing brief glimpses of many familiar creatures – Ood, Judoon, Sontarans, and even a Cyberman).

One of them, a man with wolfish features who traps the Doctor, Clara and Rigsy when they first enter, has the wonderfully Dickensian name of Mr. Rump; he is played by Simon Paisley Day, previously seen (credited simply as Simon Day) as the blue-skinned Steward who was almost the first alien to appear in the modern series, in 2005's *The End of the World*. Then the mayor of this community arrives and orders their release – and is revealed to be none other than Ashildr, last seen in *The Woman Who Lived*. Several hundred years after the events of that episode, she seems a lot less angry now. Maisie Williams portrays her with a calm maturity; she has found a place and a purpose, taking care of this refuge. Even so, the Doctor's wariness towards her is not helped when he learns that she is the one responsible for Rigsy's peril. It seems Rigsy is believed to be responsible for the death of Anah, one of the street's residents – a member of a species called the Janus, which like the Roman god they are named for, have two faces which can psychically look into both the past and the future. He was found yesterday at the entrance to the street, over her body.

Given the animosity to Rigsy, the Doctor makes Ashildr personally guarantee Clara's safety (to her slight irritation – "Shut up, I can handle myself"), before they enter and attempt to find out what really happened. Rigsy worries that he may have "freaked" on seeing Anah's alien appearance and hurt her without meaning to, but Clara had earlier discovered that his phone records show he received a call yesterday morning that drew him to the street. But despite this evidence of Rigsy being used by someone else, Ashildr is unmoved about carrying

195

through the death sentence on him. She controls the raven of the title – the instrument by which she keeps order on the street among all the potentially hostile aliens. It looks like an ordinary bird in a cage, but when she places the countdown tattoo on a person and it reaches zero, the raven transforms into a writhing black cloud which inescapably pursues, enters and painfully kills the victim. Although given a sci-fi gloss (the tattoo is called a "chronolock," and the raven is a "quantum shade"), the use of the macabre bird as a harbinger of death is more akin to a dark fairytale, in keeping with the design of the whole production. Unfortunately, it's a little too obvious that the extended sequence with one of the aliens being punished for theft is there solely as exposition, to make sure we understand the raven's nature and power. The victim is not even given a name, being credited only as "Chronolock Guy" (a second appearance, incidentally, in *Doctor Who* for Robin Soans, previously seen back in 1981's *The Keeper of Traken*), so the attempts to evoke pathos at his demise fall rather flat.

However, the plotting of the investigation itself is well done, with the intrigue rising as the Doctor realises that Ashildr must have known of Rigsy's connection with him, and was only pretending to be surprised when he turned up in her street. The crucial clue comes when Anah's child (who shares her psychic gifts) reveals that whatever Ashildr is planning is centred on the Doctor, not Rigsy. It becomes clear that Ashildr injured Anah herself and called Rigsy to entice him to the street, counting on him to bring the Doctor to her ("She needed a mystery. You can never resist a mystery"). Anah is not dead after all, but held in stasis by a mechanism that can only be opened with the TARDIS key. The Doctor releases her, but in return gets a teleport bracelet fixed onto his arm by the machine. Ashildr confirms that she has made a deal with some unknown group to deliver the Doctor to them, in exchange for protection for her community, after which she will happily remove the chronolock from Rigsy. Although she has only a secondary part in the story, Williams still manages to take Ashildr on a journey from a strong leader, confidently in control and standing up to the Doctor, to guilt and dismay as she realises that her neat plan to trap him without causing permanent harm to anyone has gone awry, thanks to a single impulsive act by Clara.

The story aims to be a tragedy in the literal sense, which means that Clara's end must come about as a direct consequence of a flaw in her character: the overconfidence and recklessness that has been growing during her time with the Doctor. Her proposal to take the chronolock from Rigsy is very easy to see coming from the moment she questions Rump about the man she saw being killed by the raven, and he tells her that the death sentence can be transferred: "It has to be taken willingly. The death's already locked in. You can pass it on, but… you can't cheat it." She overrides Rigsy's protestations about putting herself in danger by arguing that his young family need him to survive, and trusts that Ashildr's promise of protection will save her from that "locked in" part since the mayor has control of the raven. She is very much acting unselfishly as the Doctor would ("This is us talking the opposition into their own trap. This is Doctor 101. We're buying time"), showing how her travels have changed and enriched her. Unfortunately, she could not foresee all the ramifications of her act, just as Ashildr could not foresee that Clara would take the chronolock and so doom herself.

Or at least, that's the theory; in practice, the hand of the author is (again) a little too obvious in the way the story contrives to ensure that Clara has no way out. For reasons that seem rather arbitrary, she can't now pass the death-mark to someone else even if they volunteer, and neither can Ashildr remove it now that its original victim no longer has it, since the change in the raven's contract has somehow "cut [her] out of the deal." As seen in previous companion departure stories (in particular, *The Angels Take Manhattan* in 2012), the Doctor is such a powerful and capable character that the show sometimes strains to find a believable way to permanently separate a companion from him. But if we go along with the story's premise that there is no other possible outcome, then once Clara realises that she will have to match Danny Pink's heroic end in *Death in Heaven*, Capaldi and Coleman shine in a climactic scene of remarkable power.

The Doctor starts going through the stages of grief in advance. There's blank denial ("No, this isn't happening… this can't be happening") mixed with furious threats to destroy Ashildr's work by exposing the street to the outside world, even though she is obviously being honest when she says there is nothing she can do. But his menacing promise to "rain hell on you for the rest of time" is negated by Clara pointing out that he could never do that ("Your reign of terror will end with the sight of the first crying child and you know it"). She stops him from going down a literally self-destructive path ("The Doctor is no longer here – you are stuck with *me!*") by taking full responsibility for this outcome to herself, owning the choices that have brought her to this point ("Maybe this is what I wanted… why I kept running... why I kept taking all those stupid risks") and rejecting the Doctor's anguished – but patronising – statement, "I let you get reckless... I should have taken better care of you." He's right to say that he's less breakable than she is, meaning her attempt to become like him always had the possibility of ending in disaster, but she is not a child and never asked him to take care of her; the fundamental truth is, as she says: "This is my choice."

Clara becomes truly heroic as she takes full control of her last moments, looking beyond her imminent demise to do what she can to ensure the Doctor will stay true to his proper nature, whatever he is feeling right now: "There will be no revenge. I will die, and no one else, here or anywhere, will suffer." Capaldi is extraordinary as the Doctor replies simply "What about me?" showing a vulnerability almost never seen before. These two, such accomplished deceivers of each other in the past, end with complete honesty. They both now accept that nothing can be done; their final "bargaining" exchange ("Stay with me." "Nah") even draws a wry smile from each of them. It's possible to feel that the remainder of the scene is slightly overstretched in an attempt to squeeze out every possible drop of emotion; the performances are so good, though, that the temptation to linger is understandable. But eventually, after a simple goodbye, Clara walks bravely out to meet her fate.

The final ingredient is provided by Murray Gold's music, which lifts this compelling scene onto an even higher plane. The wistful melody of Clara's theme, heard many times before, makes a couple of telling appearances in a quiet rendition for piano. Her final moments, as she goes to face the raven, are accompanied by an inexorable slow march which soars to a climax as the bird strikes her, mercifully covering her agonised dying scream. This theme had been introduced earlier in the scene (at the point where she is ordering the Doctor not to take revenge) in a subdued, half-speed version, cleverly giving the whole long sequence a musical progression alongside the dramatic one. With a poignant harmonic change, the music resolves to a moment of quiet peace over the last shot looking down at her body lying on the ground.

This is not the last we'll see of Clara; she will be back (in some form, at least) for the season finale. But Jenna Coleman's tenure as the Doctor's travelling companion effectively ends here, after a performance that ranks highly among the many great performances she has given over the last three years. In the final moments, the season arc plot comes to the forefront, as Ashildr takes the Doctor's confession dial (last seen in the opening two-parter) on behalf of her mysterious associates and prepares to teleport him away to who knows where. After what has happened, she can only nod silently when he warns her that, while he will try to live up to what he promised Clara, it would be a very good idea for her to stay out of his way from now on ("You'll find that it's a very small universe when I'm angry with you"). It seems likely that this anger will drive him through the next two episodes, as the season reaches its climax.

Classic Who DVD Recommendation: The Doctor has lost one of his companions in similar circumstances before, in the memorable 1982 story *Earthshock*, starring Peter Davison, with Janet Fielding, Sarah Sutton and Matthew Waterhouse. It might be no more than a strange coincidence, but in the course of his efforts to find the secret street in this episode, the Doctor is given the line, "Remember: eighty-two" – just possibly a sneaky allusion to the year of *Earthshock*'s broadcast.

Reflections: It's pleasing to see that the quality of Sarah Dollard's first script for the show has gained her a swift return to *Doctor Who*, being commissioned to write one of the early episodes of the next season (to be broadcast in 2017). *Face the Raven* showed her ability to produce a story that works up to a powerful emotional climax, although obviously that climax's effect when it was first seen was different to how it appears looking back on it after the strange, open ending of the season finale. As I noted above, it was already known that Clara would be seen again; *Doctor Who Magazine* had featured an image of her in the waitress outfit from *Hell Bent* on the cover of its most recent issue (#493). (The magazine evidently had an interesting timing problem here; the issue was published a couple of days before *Sleep No More* was broadcast, at a time when viewers would have been expecting Clara to be in the finale anyway. It was only after *Face the Raven* was shown that the cover image could be considered a possible spoiler.) But it seemed likely that her involvement would be in some kind of dream or flashback sequence (as, in fact, would occur in the next episode), rather than the Doctor actually going back and interfering with the very moment of her death. Although Clara's death is still nominally a fixed point in time that cannot be changed, a necessary part of the history of the universe which she fully intends to return to, the fact that the ending of *Hell Bent* moves that point indefinitely far into her personal future can't help but attenuate its impact.

There are some deleted scenes from this episode to be found on the DVD box set for the season. Some not especially funny banter between Clara and Rigsy about the illusionist Derren Brown (previously name-checked in *The Day of the Doctor*, as well as making an appearance as himself in a 2014 episode of Moffat and Gatiss's *Sherlock*) while they are searching for the hidden street is no great loss, but there is also an ending scene in which Rigsy's fiancée Jen holds him as he returns home and breaks into tears. Naomi Ackie is still credited as Jen even though the removal of this scene means that she doesn't actually appear in the episode (except for a couple of off-screen lines when Rigsy makes a brief phone call home, thinking he may never see her again). It's a nicely played scene, showing the impact of Clara's sacrifice on Rigsy, which is somewhat glossed over in the final edit. The scene may well have been cut simply for timing reasons – excluding the final two episodes, which are specially extended, *Face the Raven* is longer than any other instalment of the season apart from *The Witch's Familiar*.

As I mentioned in my review for that episode, a draft script for *Face the Raven* can be found on the BBC Writers Room website. Interestingly, that draft (in which the episode is still called by its working title, "Trap Street") omits the moment of Jen comforting Rigsy, but she (and the baby) do appear in an extended final scene, watching Rigsy paint his memorial to Clara on the TARDIS (which in the final episode becomes a brief post-credits tag). That painting will, of course, be seen again at the end of *Hell Bent*, where its dissolution will signify the true ending of Clara's involvement in the Doctor's life. The scene immediately after Clara's death was also originally longer, making it clear that the Doctor moves her body from the street to another room of the infirmary. He asks Rigsy to take care of her, and notify her family and school, and extracts a promise from Ashildr that she will let Rigsy depart with his memories intact. In the final episode, these details are skipped over in order not to dilute the intensity of the Doctor's last exchanges with Ashildr. Again, *Hell Bent* makes this ending read differently by making it clear that the Doctor had already realised the Time Lords were behind events at this point. As the episode was originally shown, it seemed the Doctor was being sent off into the complete unknown. Now we can see that, especially with Ashildr having just taken his confession dial from him, he already had a hint of the fate that awaited him.

24: Heaven Sent

Writer: Steven Moffat
Director: Rachel Talalay
Originally Broadcast: 28 November 2015

Cast

The Doctor: Peter Capaldi
Clara: Jenna Coleman
Veil: Jami Reid-Quarrell

In an interview published before this season began, Steven Moffat described *Heaven Sent* as the most difficult script of his entire career – a story unlike anything he had ever written before. In the light of that statement, perhaps the greatest achievement of this amazing episode is how effortless the unfolding of its narrative seems. Almost from its very opening, it feels completely natural that we're watching only the Doctor, with no one else around him – stuck in a place designed to be his own personal hell, and working his painful way out entirely by himself. Everyone involved in making it seems to have realised that this was something very special. All aspects of the production – writing, acting, direction, design, music, and editing – come together in a *tour de force* of storytelling.

> *As you come into this world, something else is also born.*
> *You begin your life, and it begins a journey... towards you.*

Except for a couple of lines from Jenna Coleman in one scene, literally every word in *Heaven Sent* is spoken by Peter Capaldi (a feat made even more impressive by the fact that the episode is ten minutes longer than usual) – and it's difficult to imagine any other actor doing a better job. He compels attention right from the first moments, with the Doctor's sombre voiceover accompanying a montage of intriguing images which hint at the experiences we are about to see him undergo. One of the challenges Moffat faced in constructing this episode was to justify every utterance of the Doctor; with no possibility of dialogue and interaction with other characters, there has to be a reason for every occasion when we hear his voice. 1976's *The Deadly Assassin* – the only time in the classic series when he was without a companion – also begins with a scene-setting voiceover from the Doctor. In that case, however, it was an unmotivated piece of omniscient narration, simply using Tom Baker's rich tones to establish a portentous atmosphere right from the start. Here, the Doctor's speech is integrated into the plot when the text is (briefly) seen inscribed on a wall in front of him. As with the images, the speech is actually a clever encapsulation of the story to come.

Having been teleported away from Earth at the end of the last episode on the orders of persons unknown, the Doctor arrives in a weird, empty castle – which, as we will discover, is standing isolated in the middle of an endless ocean. The labyrinthine interior of this edifice is a triumph of production design, seamlessly integrating parts of various real Welsh castles with constructed sets to produce a building unlike any other. The central tower (at the top of which is the teleporter chamber) is linked on several levels by narrow, straight bridging corridors to the ring-shaped main body of the castle, making the structure look from above like a stack of spoked wheels. The surrealism of the environment is enhanced by the use of deliberately non-naturalistic lighting, with hard-edged shadows and a willingness to have the sunlight apparently coming from multiple directions at once (when the Doctor is moving down the long radial corridors, he casts shadows on both sides even though there are no artificial light sources in view). The cinematography throughout emphasises the aesthetic beauty of each part of the castle – this episode is one of the most visually sumptuous that the show has ever produced.

It moves slowly, but it never stops. Wherever you go, whatever path you take, it will follow. Never faster, never slower, always coming.

When writer Robert Holmes was interviewed about *The Deadly Assassin*, he remarked that the first episode, when the Doctor was completely alone and had not yet become involved with the other characters, was notably difficult to structure. A certain amount of talking to himself was unavoidable, combined with observing other characters via scanner screens and commenting aloud on their words and actions. Moffat's task here is even more difficult, since there is no option to cut away to another part of the story; apart from a few wide shots to establish geography, we stay at the Doctor's side throughout. When he first arrives, the memory of Clara's death at the end of the previous episode is still fresh, and he angrily challenges his unseen captors, yelling at them to show themselves. He gets no response, but does become aware of the only other occupant of the castle: a silent, hooded figure surrounded by buzzing flies, which moves with a constant lurching gait through the building, pursuing him slowly but inexorably. It's named only in the credits as "Veil"; he recognises it as a nightmarish twisting of a disturbing memory from his childhood.

The Veil follows him into one of the long, straight corridors leading to the outer ring – which becomes a trap when he manages to unlock the door at the end only to discover nothing but a blank wall behind it. With no way to avoid the creature shambling towards him ("Finally run out of corridor... There's a life summed up"), he admits out loud that he is scared of dying – a confession which momentarily freezes the Veil (and even its attendant flies) in place and causes the castle to reconfigure itself. An impressive CGI shot shows the various stacked levels rotating at different speeds; eventually the wall behind him moves aside to allow access to a small bedroom. Here he finds his first clue about what is really going on – a portrait of Clara so old that the paint is flaking away. Before he can investigate further, the Veil corners him again. But the previous narrow escape seems to have invigorated him; before the creature can touch him, he smashes the window and dives out, plummeting towards the water far below.

Rule one of dying – don't. Rule two – slow down. You've got the rest of your life. The faster you think, the slower it will pass.

With a beautifully unexpected cut, he is suddenly striding into the TARDIS, talking animatedly about how he deliberately jumped out ("If they're going to threaten you with death, show them who's boss – die faster!"), and how he's going to survive his seemingly certain doom. This is an imaginary TARDIS, of course – the real one was left behind on Earth, last seen serving as Clara's memorial shrine – which the Doctor uses in the same way as Sherlock Holmes employs his "mind palace" in Moffat's *Sherlock*, as a mental construct which lets him work through a problem at super-speed. The connection with events in the castle is firmly maintained thanks to the TARDIS scanner screens, which remind us that he is still falling, and transitions between the two worlds are stylishly made with matching eye-blinks, as the Doctor's eyes close in one world and open in the other.

As he rapidly explains how he worked out that the castle is standing in the sea and how far he will fall before hitting the water ("Am I spoiling the magic? I work at this stuff, you know"), he is addressing a silent image of Clara, frozen with her back to him, as he last saw her at the end of *Face the Raven*. An easier way to emphasise the special nature of these TARDIS sequences would have been to have the Doctor talking directly to the viewers (as with his lecture at the start of *Before the Flood*), but Moffat eschews such fourth-wall breaking here, except for one cheeky moment: the Doctor quips to Clara that "I'm nothing without an audience," with the briefest of glances down the camera lens in passing.

Can't I just sleep? ... Do I have to know everything?

The imaginary TARDIS is a wonderfully ingenious device that gives Moffat the control over the tempo of the storytelling essential to making this episode work. It provides a natural way to insert exposition during an action sequence, or to take a breath after one. The lighting here also serves to indicate the Doctor's current state; when he hits the water the room goes dark, and then the lights slowly come back on as he recovers consciousness. In the outside world, his awakening underwater and swimming back to the surface takes only seconds, but Moffat is able to stretch the moment out as the Doctor in the TARDIS imagines Clara (her face still unseen) chalking questions for him on his blackboards – the questions he needs answers to in order to understand the situation. Back in *The Witch's Familiar*, Clara told Missy that the Doctor survives because "he always assumes he's going to win," and now we get a glimpse into that mental process: her imagined avatar's last question, "How are you going to <u>win</u>?" – the final word emphatically underlined – is enough to get him going again.

Equally, Moffat is not afraid to have no speech at all for long stretches. The sequence where the Doctor climbs out of the water, changes his clothes, and explores more of the castle proceeds for nearly three minutes without a single word. Instead, the music assumes an unaccustomed prominence, with Murray Gold providing a stately, dignified orchestral melody that maintains the scene's continuity even as the Doctor's actions are being effectively punctuated with multiple small jump cuts. Meanwhile, director Rachel Talalay is filling the screen with eye-catching images. After the Doctor realises that the sea bottom below him is covered with skulls, a wide shot shows uncountable thousands of them, stretching as far as the eye can see. The chamber where he finds a set of clothes identical to his own left to dry in front of a fire (the first real clue that some kind of repeating cycle of events is occurring – something which the Doctor evidently thinks, too, as he deliberately places his own wet clothes on the drying stand in the same arrangement) is richly lit with a warm glow from the fire, contrasting with the austere corridors and rooms elsewhere.

It's a killer puzzle box, designed to scare me to death, and I'm trapped inside it.

Earlier he had absentmindedly addressed Clara as he unlocked the wooden door, momentarily forgetting that she was gone. Now, he proceeds as if he still has Clara at his side, asking her questions and imagining her answers chalked on his blackboards. He considers the monitor screens mounted on the walls throughout the castle that show the Veil's point of view, always reminding him where it is and warning of its coming. As in *Sleep No More*, he recognises the artificial nature of the events he is caught up in ("This is theatre! It's all about fear"), but it seems far more pertinent here than in the earlier episode; this whole scenario has been designed specifically to get at him. Looking for further clues, he discovers a kitchen with a slab missing from its stone floor and then a creepy, overgrown walled garden with what looks like a freshly filled grave at its centre.

After consulting with his imaginary Clara, he decides to find out what is in the grave. (When he asks what she would do, her reply is simply "Same as you" – the very attitude, as he poignantly observes, which ended up killing her.) He digs down while the tension rises as the Veil approaches ever closer. Talalay utilises her background in horror films, giving the creature two very effective "jump" moments. The first comes when it is suddenly revealed standing behind the door to the garden and reaches out for the Doctor; he only just manages to get the door closed again, and the Veil seems to wander away, discouraged. Then, after he discovers what was buried – the missing slab from the kitchen, which has been inscribed with a cryptic message ("I AM IN 12") – the creature reveals that it is capable of more than just mindless pursuit. It erupts from the bottom of the grave and looms over him.

It's not just truth it wants... It's confession. I have to tell truths I've never told before.

Back in his mental TARDIS, he realises that the Veil can only be stopped by giving up his secrets. When he confesses that he ran away from Gallifrey not because he was bored, but because he was scared (suggesting that Davros was right when he insinuated in *The Witch's Familiar* that the Doctor ran from the coming of the mysterious "Hybrid" creature), the castle again reconfigures itself and the Veil freezes so he can escape. But now he has a goal to work towards, thanks to the message on the slab; in another long montage, he explains to "Clara" how he manages his life in the castle around the Veil, keeping out of its way while he eats, sleeps, and seeks room 12 among all the jumbled, numbered rooms. Capaldi is again compelling as Moffat gives the Doctor a philosophical soliloquy in contrast to the more immediate concerns that have preoccupied him until this point. He wonders if perhaps he is in Hell ("I'm not scared of Hell… it's just Heaven for bad people"). Another striking image, of him eating alone at a large dining table, has been said by Talalay to be inspired by the breakfast-table scene in *Citizen Kane* (although I was immediately reminded of the surreal final section of *2001: A Space Odyssey*). Back in the teleport chamber, he finds something he hadn't noticed when he arrived: the word BIRD written in the dust on the floor, next to a skull attached to the machinery. "Nobody remembers being born, and nobody remembers dying," he muses, while looking at the teleport equipment and the skull – which, we will discover, embody both of those moments for him. As with all of Moffat's best scripts, later twists are constantly providing new context for what has gone before.

Eventually he finds his target, hidden away at the base of the castle, but its entrance is blocked by another blank wall; to move it, he will need to speak another confession. An arresting dissolve from the Doctor's face to the skull, now resting on the battlements of the tower, might seem just a directorial flourish – but it's actually another cleverly planted clue to the final revelation. There's another hint as the Doctor waits for his adversary, noting that the stars in the night sky are out of position, even though he knows he hasn't time-travelled to get here: "If I didn't know better, I'd say I've travelled seven thousand years into the future." Having worked out that his unknown tormentors are after information about the Hybrid, when the Veil arrives, he confesses that "I know where it is, and what it is." The castle shakes and changes again, causing the skull to fall into the water to join all the others, as the Doctor runs downstairs and enters room 12.

Why is it always me? Why is it never anybody else's turn?
Can't I just lose? Just this once?

I have already noted the work of composer Murray Gold, whose contribution to this episode goes well beyond the normal remit of "incidental" music (although that is up to his usual high standard too, with effective horror-movie atmospherics and discordant screeches for the Veil). At this point, while the Doctor slowly advances along a darkened, narrow corridor, the music actually becomes the centre of attention, and Gold provides a piece worth listening to on its own account, with a touch of Beethoven about it – in particular, the well-known second movement of the Seventh Symphony. A steady rhythmic line in the lower strings is joined by a plaintive melody in the violins; more and more instruments are added, until at last the full orchestra is playing as the Doctor emerges from the corridor and finds himself facing his final obstacle – an adamantine wall twenty feet thick, beyond which lies the way out.

Suddenly, everything falls into place for the Doctor; in some manner not yet apparent, the BIRD message makes him intuitively leap to the full, horrifying realisation of what is going on and what he will have to do. The intensity of Capaldi's performance reaches a peak as, in the mental TARDIS, he rails against his fate, tempted to give in and reveal what he knows about the Hybrid. A chalked "NO!" from the avatar of Clara stops him – but in the castle he is still slumped despondently against the base of the wall as the Veil enters the narrow corridor. As at the end of the last episode, Capaldi lets us see a moment of extraordinary vulnerability in the Doctor as he reaches the nadir of despair: "Whatever I do… you still won't be there."

Do you want me to tell you a story? ... There's this emperor, and he asks this shepherd's boy, "How many seconds in eternity?" And the shepherd's boy says...

The emotional turning point is signalled by the only non-Capaldi lines of the episode. Imaginary Clara speaks up, gently reminding him that he's "not the only person who ever lost someone." In *The Girl Who Died*, we saw Clara prodding him to keep going and win; now his memory of her performs the same service. Even with just a brief cameo appearance, Jenna Coleman makes an impact, as she repeats her last gesture to him from *Face the Raven*, reaching up to touch his face.

207

"Get up, off your arse, and win," she tells him – the drolly unexpected mild profanity injecting the energy needed to pull him to his feet.

Knowing what has to happen now, the Doctor faces the approaching Veil which has him trapped in this chamber: "No more confessions, sorry. But I *will* tell you the truth." Refusing to give any more information about the Hybrid, he simply turns and punches the diamond-hard wall with all his strength – Capaldi's acting here being so convincing that it's hard to watch without involuntarily flinching. He begins telling the Brothers Grimm tale of the shepherd's boy, and the triumphant music tells us that he is on the right track to victory even as his situation seems hopeless. He keeps punching at the wall, heedless of the pain, until the creature finally catches him. At its touch (the point-of-view shot of its hands closing over his eyes being another memorable image), he collapses painfully to the floor. The Veil then simply vanishes, its job done; whatever the Doctor's plan was, it seems to have failed.

How long can I keep doing this, Clara? Burning the old me, to make a new one?

But now a magnificent peroration begins, over an even more splendid version of the same music from the earlier montages. The Doctor is still talking to his imaginary Clara, telling her how Time Lords "take forever to die" as, in reality, he makes his agonised way back to the top of the tower. His terrible condition is conveyed with a level of blood and burning makeup very unusual for *Doctor Who*, especially in one particularly disturbing close-up of his bloodied hands as he drags himself along the stone floor. Moffat's invention of the mental TARDIS pays off beautifully, providing a way for the mortally wounded Doctor to deliver what becomes a four-minute explanatory monologue. He slowly describes his realisation that the castle is a torture chamber specially crafted just for him, and that he was right earlier about not having time-travelled – "I've just been here a very, very long time." Yet again, Capaldi's delivery of this speech is remarkable, with the Doctor's broken, disjointed phrases a perfect counterpoint to his crawling, stumbling progress through the castle.

He finally makes it back to the teleport chamber, where the last piece of the puzzle falls into place. Earlier, we were shown how each room of the castle, if he leaves it for long enough, resets itself to its state upon his arrival. It seemed like just a neat idea in keeping with the strangeness of the whole setting ("It tidies up after itself – automated room service"), but now Moffat reveals the crucial point. The teleport chamber has also reset – meaning a copy of the Doctor at the moment he arrived is still contained within the teleporter. He attaches himself to the machinery, immolating himself to provide the energy to activate it, completing the cycle and explaining the images we saw at the top of the episode, of a burned hand pulling the lever before dissolving into dust. As he scrawls the BIRD message and the light of the imaginary TARDIS goes completely out, we finally understand that he has been doing this over and over again.

I am the Doctor. I'm coming to find you. And I will never, ever stop.

A new Doctor materialises in the teleporter, exactly as we saw him at the start of the episode, ready to find and punish those responsible for Clara's death. As the cycle begins again, the Doctor's threat to his captors acquires a terrible irony. It seems he will indeed never, ever stop – he is trapped in the same way as the previous one and all the others, for seven thousand years, that are now no more than skulls in the sea. We begin to see a series of abridged and speeded up repetitions of the whole story we have just witnessed playing out, and Moffat's ingenuity in incorporating an external indication of time passing into the cycle of events is highlighted when the Doctor's line on the tower roof changes to: "If I didn't know better, I'd say I've travelled twelve thousand years into the future." The intervals get larger and larger as he endures the same experiences an unimaginable number of times – a torment apparently set to continue forever.

And yet, Moffat has hidden the solution in plain sight from the moment of the Doctor's final confrontation with the Veil. It's a brilliant moment of narrative legerdemain when the repeated cycles slowly reveal that his apparently futile punches at the wall are having a cumulative effect; over aeons, the wall is – ever so slowly – being worn away. It takes literally billions of repetitions, but gradually an indentation in the wall becomes a tunnel leading to freedom. Each new Doctor gets a tiny bit further before the Veil catches him – and little by little, the tale of the shepherd's boy gets completed:

"There's this mountain of pure diamond. It takes an hour to climb it, and an hour to go around it... Every hundred years, a little bird comes and sharpens its beak on the diamond mountain...

And when the entire mountain is chiselled away, the first second of
eternity will have passed!"

This is not a temporal loop of cause and effect of the sort Moffat has used several times in his stories; instead, it's more akin to the 1993 movie *Groundhog Day*. But the point of the repeating cycle in that movie was to change Bill Murray's protagonist, to make him a better person. Here, the Doctor can only make progress towards his eventual escape by remaining true to himself. Appropriately, the music underscoring this sequence is derived from the culmination of the Fiftieth Anniversary special, *The Day of the Doctor*, when the Doctor finds a way to avoid destroying his own people in the Time War. The music drives towards a triumphant peak as the significance of the BIRD message is revealed and a montage of visuals changes faster and faster – a masterpiece of editing, with dozens and dozens of cuts – as thousands, then millions, then billions of years pass, creating a truly transcendent climax. At last, one final blow shatters the wall before the Veil can catch him, and the creature collapses, falling apart into a mass of cogs like those making up the mechanisms of the castle, leaving the Doctor free to go.

Tell them, I'm back. Tell them, I know what they did...
and I'm on my way.

He emerges into a desert wasteland – and in a last dizzying shift of perspective, the castle is revealed to have been inside his confession dial all along; like all Time Lord technology, it's bigger on the inside. Approached by a curious local (a shepherd's boy, perhaps?), he sends the lad running off towards a very familiar-looking domed citadel in the distance. In a totally unexpected way (unless you had read the BBC's promotional synopsis of the episode, which annoyingly gave away this surprise), the Doctor has fulfilled his promise in *The Day of the Doctor* to journey "the long way round" to his homeworld of Gallifrey. The episode comes to a perfect cliffhanger ending with a bolt from the blue to the Time Lords who have put him through this hellish experience in their determination to possess his knowledge of the Hybrid, prophesied to conquer Gallifrey: "The Hybrid... is me." But then, the sight of Ashildr (alias "Me") in the preview of the next episode leaves a wonderful ambiguity hanging as all the threads of the season begin drawing together for the grand finale.

Classic Who DVD Recommendation: As mentioned above, the only classic series story where the Doctor is on his own is *The Deadly Assassin* – which, at the time, was just as envelope-pushing as this episode. The first story to be set entirely on Gallifrey, it also features a long sequence of the Doctor being pursued through a nightmarish dream world, along with a depiction of the Time Lords that became the bedrock of all future stories dealing with the Doctor's people.

Reflections: As is no doubt obvious from the foregoing, I consider *Heaven Sent* to be one of the best things *Doctor Who* has ever done. The script takes a stunningly original idea and works through its implications rigorously, and the production really can't be overpraised. The plotting proceeds with a clockwork elegance, apart from some minor fudging here and there regarding exactly how comprehensive the castle's automatic-reset mechanism is. After the episode's broadcast, Moffat addressed this and some other points raised by readers of *Doctor Who Magazine* (in issue #495). His intention was that things moved into or out of rooms (like the slab from the kitchen, which was buried in the garden by the Doctor in a previous cycle) can survive the reset. The diamond wall doesn't reset because it's not part of the castle – it's the outer wall of the confession dial. The Doctor's skull is the only part of him that survives each time because it is directly fused to the teleport mechanism. And no, the first time he left his clothes to dry did not result in a naked Doctor running around the castle. The castle provided him with clothes (different from his own) which he used while his were drying, just as it provides him with food and a bed. Then, one time, the Veil caught him before he managed to change back into his own clothes, and the situation we see in the episode was formed and became self-perpetuating.

Indeed, although the final montage gives the impression of a tightly constrained repeating cycle of virtually identical events – because that gives the maximum impact to the final revelation – this does not, in fact, preclude there being many cycles along the way that went quite differently. To me, it seems that the plot loop Moffat has constructed is impressively robust. The only invariants are: the Doctor arrives; he is pursued by the Veil; it eventually catches him and inflicts injuries that are fatal but not immediately so; and he must finally realise that his only remaining option is to return to the teleporter and restart the cycle. This last is the only element under his control, and the story spells out in the most forceful way that it's inherent in his nature to always find the way to win (where winning, in this case, means getting a chance to start over). Among the billions of Doctors there might be many that get caught prematurely by the Veil, perhaps failing to leave the BIRD message for their successors and leading to a number of cycles where no progress is made at punching through the wall. But sooner or later, like a spinning gyroscope, the sequence of events will right itself, leading ineluctably to the Doctor's victory.

In the DVD box set for the season there is a deleted scene that properly shows the text of the Doctor's opening voiceover inscribed on the tower corridor wall. This should have been left in; without it, freeze-framing is required to understand the significance of that speech. A few moments like this seem a little over-obscure; the buried stone the Doctor digs up in the garden is never fully shown, so the fact that it's actually the missing octagonal slab from the kitchen floor is easily missed. And, as Rachel Talalay pointed out in a blog entry afterwards, it should have been made clearer that room 12 is at the base of the castle – that's why he waits for the Veil on the tower roof before confessing about the Hybrid, to give him as much time as possible to deal with whatever is in the room once he opens it. But these are trivial nitpicks; the only real directorial lapse involves the boy right at the end. Despite the dubbed-on running footsteps, it was amusingly obvious even on first viewing that this hapless young extra had been standing rather woodenly next to Peter Capaldi from the start of the shot, simply waiting for the camera to tilt down and reveal him.

Ultimately, though, *Heaven Sent* sits at the zenith of the first two Capaldi seasons – which is perhaps all the more remarkable given that, from a structural point of view, it's merely a wonderfully elaborate detour between *Face the Raven* and *Hell Bent*. The story could have moved directly from the former to the latter; all that would be required is a more explicit indication at the end of *Face the Raven* that the Time Lords were responsible for the events leading to Clara's death due to their need for information about the Hybrid, and for their teleporter to then take the Doctor straight to Gallifrey. But the extremity of his experience here serves perfectly to place him in the frame of mind appropriate for the next episode, in which his need to save Clara will drive him to unprecedented lengths. It's a supreme example of the maxim "Show, don't tell," making us viscerally understand exactly what Clara means to him – which in turn will explain how far he is willing to go in order to get her back.

25: Hell Bent

Writer: Steven Moffat
Director: Rachel Talalay
Originally Broadcast: 5 December 2015

Cast

The Doctor: Peter Capaldi
Clara: Jenna Coleman
Ashildr: Maisie Williams
The President: Donald Sumpter
The General: Ken Bones
Female General: T'Nia Miller
Gastron: Malachi Kirby
Ohila: Clare Higgins
The Woman: Linda Broughton
Man: Martin T. Sherman
Wraiths: Jami Reid-Quarrell, Nick Ash, Ross Mullen
Voice of the Dalek: Nicholas Briggs

It's an interesting question whether the last three episodes of this season are best considered as individual, stand-alone stories, or whether they comprise a prologue (*Face the Raven*) followed by a two-parter dealing with its consequences, or whether they form one big three-part epic. The episodes are each totally distinct in setting and tone, and they were produced quite separately from each other. On the other hand, they are intimately linked in a way that recalls the three-part finale of the 2007 series, and the "Previously" montage at the top of *Hell Bent* draws on both prior episodes, before following Steven Moffat's usual practice with multi-part stories and finding a way to open with a moment of maximum disorientation for the viewer. The Doctor appears as a lonely drifter, hitching a ride through Nevada and stopping at a roadside diner whose interior was filmed in the same American-themed Cardiff eatery used for 2011's *The Impossible Astronaut* (a point lampshaded at the end when he suddenly recalls his adventure with Amy and Rory). Behind the counter is Clara, dressed in a waitress uniform – but neither of them apparently recognises the other. A poignant mood is created from the outset in this framing sequence, as he picks out Murray Gold's "Clara" theme on his guitar

("Is it a sad song?" "Nothing's sad till it's over... Then everything is") and begins telling her the story of how he came to be here.

Only now do we return to where we left off, with the Doctor having endured a torment that lasted billions of years as he refused to provide information about the mysterious "Hybrid" prophesied to threaten all of time and space, breaking through at last to arrive on his homeworld, Gallifrey. In the dry wastelands outside the Time Lords' globed citadel, he retreats to the old barn that we first saw in 2013's *The Day of the Doctor* (the first shot of it here echoes its first appearance in that episode), and which we know from last season's *Listen* figured importantly in his childhood. Director Rachel Talalay, following up her triumph in *Heaven Sent*, constructs a hugely enjoyable sequence in which the Doctor's confrontation with the Time Lords is played as a pastiche Spaghetti Western. He exchanges his velvet coat for a simpler black one (the same one he is wearing in the diner sequences) more appropriate for a Clint Eastwood-style protagonist. It's a significant act; he will later tell Clara he put aside his "very Doctor-y" coat because "I can't be the Doctor all the time." But however much he adopts the persona of the laconic mysterious stranger, taken in and fed by the peasants living outside the opulent city, it's actually his identity and reputation as the man who won the Time War that intimidates all those sent to fetch him.

He sees off a floating gunship sent to bring him to the citadel without needing to speak a single word – he simply draws a line in the sand, daring the pilot to cross it, then turns his back and walks away. He ignores a squad of soldiers, then the assembled High Council in their elaborate robes and collars, until finally the President himself comes to see him. Face to face at last with the man who ordered his imprisonment in the confession dial, the Doctor tosses the disk at his feet and utters his first line of the episode: "Get off my planet." The President orders him executed by firing squad, in a sequence which recalls the end of an episode of 1984's *The Caves of Androzani*, when Peter Davison's Doctor faced a similar seemingly certain death. In a clever touch, after the shots we momentarily cut back to the diner where the Doctor is telling Clara the story ("Oh, you like a cliffhanger, don't you?"), before the reveal that the soldiers all deliberately missed. Forced to choose between their war hero and their President, all the soldiers, and then the general commanding them, discard their weapons and move to the Doctor's side (while the incidental music throws in a Western-style variant of the theme Murray Gold created

214

for the war-damaged Ninth Doctor back in 2005). Through sheer force of personality, he deposes the man responsible for his torture and takes control of Gallifrey.

The Gallifrey sequences benefit from Moffat's recycling of elements previously established in episodes from *The Day of the Doctor* (in which Ken Bones' general was first seen), to *The End of Time* in 2009 (where Timothy Dalton played a megalomaniacal President Rassilon, reinvented here by Donald Sumpter in a more brittle form, his facade collapsing as he is abandoned by his soldiers). Indeed, Moffat references all the way back to the seminal Gallifrey story, *The Deadly Assassin* in 1976, which established such features as the dark, labyrinthine Cloisters and the Matrix, the predictor of the future and repository of all Time Lord knowledge, into which their minds are uploaded when they die. That story's sequel, 1978's *The Invasion of Time*, also began with the Doctor high-handedly taking over the presidency as he seemingly betrayed his homeworld to a race of invading aliens. His apparently self-centered motives at that time were a ruse; here, they are definitely not. Although he pretends to be interested in the general's concerns about the Hybrid ("All Matrix prophecies concur that this creature will one day stand in the ruins of Gallifrey") and says he can help them by talking to "an old friend," he soon reveals the true purpose that has been driving him ever since he saw Clara die at the end of *Face the Raven*: to circumvent that fate and restore her to a normal life.

We return to the climactic moment of Clara's death, but now time stops just before the raven strikes her; with his past self frozen and oblivious in the background, the Doctor leads her away from Earth through a portal into the Time Lords' "extraction chamber." Clara's shock and disorientation are only increased when she discovers that she now has no heartbeat – her death is still a fixed fact of history, and she is only walking and talking thanks to the Time Lords' super-advanced technology. If the ugly splintering sound of time being fractured as her death is interrupted was not enough to convince us that this is a bad idea, the Doctor's behaviour certainly does. Capaldi is magnificent throughout as he shows a Doctor driven to dark extremes – a being of almost limitless power, with his moral compass disconnected. His shooting of the general when the man tries to stop him shows how completely his usual principles have been replaced by a ruthless single-mindedness. (As the Doctor and Clara run off into the Cloisters, the general regenerates, in the first on-screen instance of a

Time Lord changing gender after a regeneration. Kudos to Moffat for slipping in this important stepping stone towards an eventual female Doctor in a completely matter-of-fact way.)

The impression of the entire season being brought to bear on this episode is enhanced by the return of Ohila, leader of the Sisterhood of Karn, from *The Magician's Apprentice*. Right from their introduction in 1976's *The Brain of Morbius*, the Sisterhood have been shown as peers of the Time Lords, and Ohila certainly defers neither to Rassilon nor to the Doctor. She and the general lead the search for the Doctor and Clara into the Cloisters. A new element created for this story is the macabre Cloister Wraiths: spectral avatars of dead Time Lords that glide silently around the shadowy corridors, serving as guards for the Matrix; fear of them stops the soldiers from simply walking into the Cloisters and capturing the Doctor and Clara. There are also various aliens here – a Dalek, a Cyberman and some Weeping Angels – that have tried to break into the Matrix over the years and been neutralised. Strictly speaking, the sequence where Clara encounters these creatures is padding, but the brief interruption by the parade of famous monsters provides some useful immediate excitement in an episode that is surprisingly slow-burning for the climax of a season-long story. Apart from a few CGI vistas of the Time Lord citadel, there are no flashy visuals at all; as usual with Moffat finales, the focus quickly narrows down to just the central characters. Before leaving the extraction chamber the Doctor took a human-compatible "neural block" – which he intends to use to wipe Clara's memory of him in order to keep her safe. A brief cut back to the diner, where waitress Clara is listening to the Doctor telling his story, induces us to believe we're seeing the result of that process – a masterful piece of misdirection by Moffat, since it will eventually emerge that the truth is quite different.

The inward nature of the episode puts the spotlight onto Capaldi and Coleman, who are compelling as always in their scenes together. Clara, still trying to come to terms with her situation, wants to know what the Hybrid is and why it is so important that the Doctor would endure such torture rather than reveal it. But the surprise comes when the Doctor admits he doesn't actually have knowledge of the Hybrid at all; no one does. The prophecies of the Hybrid are just stories he heard from the Cloister Wraiths when he broke in here as a young student, which scared him so much he ran away from Gallifrey. He only pretended to have knowledge of it to have something to bargain with for Clara's life, after realising the Time Lords were responsible for her death. "I just had to hang on in there for a bit," he says, with devastating understatement. When Ohila confirms that the Doctor was trapped in the confession dial for four and a half billion years, Coleman is superb at showing Clara's horror at what he has suffered, almost unable to speak as he reiterates the idea he has expressed before in this season of having a "duty of care" towards her. As she regathers herself, their conversation continues in a moment of intimacy that we don't get to see, the picture discreetly zooming out and dissolving away to a panorama of the citadel.

The Doctor echoes his original departure from his homeworld by stealing another TARDIS (whose interior is a beautiful evocation of the original TARDIS control room from the 1960's) and fleeing with Clara – though not before receiving a tongue-lashing from Ohila about the folly of hoping to change Clara's fate. In another parallel with *The End of Time*, Ohila's role here is reminiscent of the mysterious woman in the earlier episode who writer Russell T Davies implied (though never stated outright) was the Doctor's mother. There are definitely maternal overtones to Ohila's "Come out of that TARDIS and face me, boy!" – although even she cannot dissuade him from his purpose. But the Doctor's initial elation at travelling again with Clara at his side turns increasingly desperate as her heartbeat remains stopped. At the very beginning of his relationship with Clara, when he was faced with the death of the Victorian version of her in 2012's *The Snowmen*, he tried to coax her back to life, despite his friend Madame Vastra telling him he was trying to bargain with an uncaring universe. Now, as he and Clara journey forwards to the end of everything, he is no longer interested in bargaining.

When Clara suggests that the universe might *need* her to die, the Doctor angrily retorts that it doesn't have a say any more. "As of this moment, I am answerable to no one!" he says, in a return to the "Time Lord Victorious" attitude displayed by the Tenth Doctor in 2009's *The Waters of Mars* – the last time the Doctor went off the rails like this. He is unexpectedly answered by four knocks on the door of the TARDIS – a rather unnecessary, crowbarred-in homage to the moment in *The End of Time* that heralded the Tenth Doctor's final fall. The end of the universe has become an oddly crowded place in the last couple of years; one might wonder if the knocking will herald an appearance by the mysterious creatures from *Listen*, but in fact the Doctor exits the TARDIS to find the immortal Ashildr waiting for him – the last living being in the universe. Unfortunately, although this fourth

217

appearance for her provides the opportunity to round off Ashildr's story, it is much less successful than the previous three. Maisie Williams is left high and dry by being asked to embody a character whose wisdom of ages is simply out of her range (as it would be out of the range of any eighteen-year-old actor). Only once does she manage to project the completely unruffled control and serenity Ashildr should now have, when the Doctor asks her how she is sustaining the reality bubble she is dwelling in, and she simply replies, "Brilliantly."

What's more, the story provides nothing for Ashildr to do beyond some conversational sparring with the Doctor, as the nature of the Hybrid is finally revealed. We already know the general belief that it is half Dalek, half Time Lord is wrong, and the Doctor accuses Ashildr of being the Hybrid – a mixture of human and the Mire. She rejects this, suggesting instead that the creature could be half Time Lord, half human – Moffat teasing for a moment that he might be going with the idea of the Doctor being half human (a ridiculous concept advanced in the 1996 telemovie starring Paul McGann, and resolutely ignored ever since by both fans and writers). The Doctor laughs this off, but in a way she is right. The true answer is that the Hybrid is not one creature but two – the Doctor and Clara – who, as the Doctor has come to realise, will be disastrous for the universe if they remain together, and who were brought together (as was confirmed last year in *Death in Heaven*) by Missy ("The lover of chaos, who wants you to love it too"). It's an ingenious idea in itself, but has the effect of reducing the overarching plot of the whole season to a mere semantic quibble. The answer wasn't even needed in order to convince the Doctor to stop travelling with Clara, since he'd already decided to do that. As he says, "I know I went too far"; his intention, after using the neural block on Clara, is to leave her on Earth at some time and place where she can live out a normal life without him.

There's an obvious similarity here with the fate of Donna in 2008's *Journey's End*, when the Doctor had no way to save her life except to wipe her memory of her time with him. It was a heartbreaking ending, made even more traumatic by Donna's frantic protests at being forced back into her old life. Here, Moffat makes an important improvement on the earlier episode by ensuring Clara retains control over her own destiny; after eavesdropping on the Doctor and Ashildr's talk from inside the TARDIS, she uses his sonic sunglasses to make a modification to the neural block. When they enter, she stands up to him with a powerful line: "Tomorrow is promised to no one, Doctor, but I insist upon my past. I am entitled to that. It's mine." Only when the Doctor discovers that her fiddling with the neural block has ensured it will affect one of them randomly does she acquiesce to his decision ("This has to stop. One of us has to go"). They activate the device together and wait to see which of them will succumb. (Showing just how superfluous she is at this point, Ashildr can only look on as the drama plays out in front of her. Amusingly, the wide shots do their best to keep her hidden behind the console's central column; perhaps the director is hoping we will forget her presence.)

Coleman's tear-streaked face as Clara realises that the Doctor is the one chosen, and is gently bidding her goodbye, shows one last time her ability to give a hugely emotional performance in the most thoroughly believable way, which she has displayed all through her time with the show. The Doctor tells her, "Never be cruel and never be cowardly. And if you ever are, always make amends." Earlier, Ohila had accurately needled him for being either or both of those things with his banishment of Rassilon. This restatement of his core beliefs, harking back to the climax of *The Day of the Doctor* (which in turn, was based on an influential description of the Doctor's character by classic series script editor Terrance Dicks), indicates clearly that he has chosen the right course in giving up the relationship that caused him to fulfil the legends of the Hybrid (which, like most fictional prophecies, turned out to be completely accurate, but not in any useful way). The music and staging of the whole climactic scene parallels the end of *Face the Raven*, even down to a last wistful, light-hearted exchange in defiance of fate. But this time, the huge orchestral crescendo does not lead to the slow march of Clara walking to meet the raven; it is cut off, replaced by a quiet, bell-like tolling as the Doctor's memory of her is burned away.

As we return for the last time to the Nevada diner, we now understand that the Doctor has no idea the woman he is talking to is the Clara he once knew. Coleman is again excellent as she shows Clara nearly lose her composure when he says, "There's one thing I know about her... If I met her again, I would absolutely know." Moffat's grand design completes itself with the reveal (unseen by the Doctor) that the diner itself is the camouflaged exterior of the second TARDIS. It fades away, leaving the Doctor alone in front of his own TARDIS, still bearing Rigsy's memorial painting of Clara. The development of her character over the past two seasons reaches a conclusion as she effectively becomes another Doctor, with Ashildr as her companion. Unfortunately, the very neatness of this happy ending for her obscures the idea that she is supposedly still one heartbeat from death. It's true that she promises Ashildr she will eventually go back to Gallifrey to be returned to her fixed death (and after all, she has been left with the knowledge of the Doctor in her head which he said would enable the Time Lords to track her down), but her final grin as she talks of going "the long way round" leaves the impression of the fine ending of *Face the Raven* being arbitrarily negated.

Moffat here falls into a trap similar to the one Russell T Davies encountered with Rose Tyler in *Journey's End*. Rose's first departure (in 2006's *Doomsday*) was powerfully tragic, as she was left in a parallel universe, separated from the Doctor forever. Bringing her back, in circumstances where she had to go away again at the end of the story, left Davies with the dilemma of either repeating the earlier tragedy or undermining it – in either case, leaving Rose's story with a less effective ending. As documented in the wonderful behind-the-scenes book, *The Writer's Tale*, he struggled mightily to come up with a satisfactory conclusion, eventually having Rose choose to remain in her parallel universe with a half-human clone of the Doctor accompanying her. In the same way, to show Clara's true ending here – actually having her resume her interrupted death – could never match the impact of the original scene, not least because the Doctor could not now be part of it. And so, as they fly away, the last scene for her and Ashildr feels more like a trailer for a cheery spinoff series – which, judging from the dialogue, appears to be named *Wiggle Room* – the story of two gal pals who knock around the universe in their own time machine. Fun though that might be to watch, the scene does both characters a disservice by leaving them on such a superficial note, and jars badly with the rest of the episode's conclusion.

It's a great pity that the season stumbles in this way just as it approaches the finishing line, since the parts of *Hell Bent* that do work – the parts that concentrate on the Doctor and the resolution of his relationship with Clara – are very fine. The serious flaw in Clara's story, however, makes it an imperfect finale to what has otherwise been an excellent season, possibly Moffat's best as showrunner. There was only one serious misfire, the stand-alone episode *Sleep No More*, and the predominance of multi-episode stories meant that each adventure had a greater than normal significance. It has been a tremendous season for Peter Capaldi, too, who now completely owns the role of the Doctor. As with the opening scenes on Gallifrey, he requires no words at the end to convey the Doctor almost reassembling himself before our eyes. Murray Gold's "Clara" theme fades out for the last time as he finally re-enters his TARDIS, and the darkened interior returns to life just like its imaginary equivalent in *Heaven Sent*. On his blackboard he finds a last message left by Clara, harking back to her "Impossible Girl" days, but with a twist – "Run, you clever boy... and be a Doctor." As if in answer, he puts his velvet coat back on, closes the door with a click of his fingers, and is even presented by the TARDIS with a new sonic screwdriver. Outside, the painting of Clara flakes away as the police box vanishes; an era is ended, as the Doctor heads off confidently towards new adventures.

Classic Who DVD Recommendation: 1969's *The War Games*, starring Patrick Troughton, with Frazer Hines and Wendy Padbury, is the story that introduced the Time Lords into *Doctor Who*. A ten-episode epic that was the last story for all three regular cast members – with the Doctor's companions eventually being mind-wiped into forgetting him, just as he tried to do to Clara here – it provided a momentous conclusion to Troughton's tenure as the Second Doctor.

Reflections: After the tightly integrated marvel that was *Heaven Sent*, it was inevitable that this rather sprawling and untidy follow-up would suffer by comparison. One source of negative reaction was from fans who were hoping the story would focus more on Gallifrey itself, perhaps incorporating some of the extensive mythos developed by the ancillary novel and audio play ranges (particularly during the years before the revival of the TV series, with stories aimed purely at hard-core fans). It's not a view I share; I tend to agree with the Doctor's opinion (as expressed in *The Witch's Familiar*) that "It's a boring place, Gallifrey," noting his immediate desire to get away from it every time he has found himself back there. Nevertheless, given that *The Day of the Doctor* supposedly started him off on a quest to find the resurrected Gallifrey, which was reinforced in last season's *Death in Heaven*, it's understandable that some felt a little short-changed when he finally got there, only to brush off Clara's question about how the Time Lords managed to return to this universe with, "I didn't ask – it would make them feel clever." Similar grumbling ensued when the Hybrid, whose identity was the subject of fevered online speculation (with suggestions including not only Ashildr, but also Jenny from 2008's *The Doctor's Daughter*, and even the half human Doctor from

Journey's End), turned out to be just a "Bad Wolf" style MacGuffin.

Not helping matters is the fact that, after the first twenty minutes or so, this is an undeniably subdued and unshowy episode for a season finale. The second half is virtually nothing but conversation involving just three characters confined to three sets, one of which is reused from earlier (the Cloister set does double duty as Ashildr's bubble at the end of the universe). Behind the scenes information does indeed suggest that a budget squeeze occurred. *Heaven Sent* was meant to be the season's cheap episode, but ended up needing some unanticipated extra spending (which we can hardly begrudge, given how it turned out), leaving *Hell Bent* in a situation uncomfortably akin to some of the end of season "Oops, the money's run out" efforts of the classic series. It's not quite at the level of 1979's *The Armageddon Factor*, which tries to tell an epic interplanetary space opera while only being able to afford a handful of small, dull rooms and a bunch of corridors, but the lack of visual spectacle is still notable. Fortunately, the episode is able to generate powerful drama entirely through dialogue, when that dialogue is being handled by one of the best Doctor/companion teams in the show's history.

Jenna Coleman's contribution over the past three seasons, first with Matt Smith and then with Peter Capaldi, has been immense. Never once giving a sub-par performance, she smoothly handled the sometimes bumpy path of Clara's journey with the Doctor. The intellectual puzzle of the "Impossible Girl" developed into a warm relationship with the Eleventh Doctor; the following year, she was at the heart of a more nuanced, character-based drama as she clashed with the new Doctor and loved and lost Danny Pink. This year, with Clara drawing closer to the Doctor again, she rose to the emotional challenges of episodes like *The Zygon Inversion* and *Face the Raven* with impressive ease. It's no surprise that Coleman went from *Doctor Who* straight into the lead role in a miniseries about the young Queen Victoria – just the first in what should be a long line of post-*Who* triumphs for this talented actor. Even in the slightly disjointed ending of Clara's story, she manages to leave on a touching final note – the suggestion that some memories could become songs when they're forgotten, implying that the melody of Clara's theme we have been hearing for years is the Doctor's unconscious recall of that moment they shared in the Cloisters, which no one else will ever know. As he says with a sad smile in his last line of the episode, "That'd be nice."

26: The Husbands of River Song

Writer: Steven Moffat
Director: Douglas Mackinnon
Originally Broadcast: 25 December 2015

Cast

The Doctor: Peter Capaldi
River Song: Alex Kingston
Nardole: Matt Lucas
King Hydroflax: Greg Davies
Ramone: Phillip Rhys
Flemming: Rowan Polonski
Scratch: Robert Curtis
Concierge: Anthony Cozens
Alphonse: Chris Lew Kum Hoi
Receptionist: Nicolle Smartt
King Hydroflax's Body: Liam Cook
Voice of Hydroflax: Nonso Anozie

The fact that 2015's Christmas special appeared less than three weeks after the ending of the regular season makes it seem more closely integrated into the season, a coda or appendix that reflects some of its themes, than several of the previous totally separate holiday specials. Nevertheless, there's a definite air of relaxation after the intensity of the second half of the season, as Steven Moffat serves up a frothy combination of romantic comedy and a farcical caper plot, which gradually transforms into a poignant tying off of a long-running thread introduced as far back as 2008, even before he took over the running of the show.

In contrast to *Last Christmas*, the actual festive content of *The Husbands of River Song* is minimal. There are a few shoehorned-in references to Christmas in the final scenes, and the story begins on Christmas Day in a far-future human colony – which, from its appearance, could just as well be present-day Earth, were it not for the rather conspicuous flying saucer straight out of a 1950's sci-fi movie parked at the edge of town. On board the ship is the Doctor's occasional wife, River Song, and a simple case of mistaken identity leads to him being drawn into her current scheme. He is more than a little disconcerted to find that, not only does she not recognise him, but her plan involves killing her husband, the notorious galactic marauder King Hydroflax – with the help of yet another husband, a debonair spaceship pilot named Ramone.

After delivering powerfully dramatic performances in several of this year's episodes, Peter Capaldi seizes the opportunity to loosen up here. The light-hearted mood is set right from the outset, when the Doctor answers a knock on the TARDIS door wearing a pair of comedy antlers – his sentient time machine having apparently generated the hologrammatic headwear in an effort to cheer him up after the loss of Clara. When he meets River and she doesn't know him, it's like a strange mirror image of the situation we have just seen in the framing sequence of *Hell Bent*, employing the sort of comic misunderstandings ("I'm the Doctor." "You'd better be, you've got an operation to perform") which that episode – preoccupied as it was with more serious matters – steered away from.

Most of River's previous appearances have been at crucial turning points of her complicated timeline; here both we and the Doctor get to see what she is like in her normal adventuring life, away from his influence. Thinking he is the surgeon she has hired to remove a priceless diamond lodged inside Hydroflax's head, she tells him she wants him to remove the whole head instead. ("Wouldn't that kill him?" "You're the medical expert, but I'd say so, yes.") Alex Kingston has a lot of fun as the story emphasises the character's rather amoral nature (when the Doctor accuses her of being a thief and murderer as well as an archaeologist, she cheerfully replies, "An archaeologist *is* just a thief – with patience"), not batting an eyelid as she double-crosses Hydroflax. It seems she has been hired by the diamond's owners to retrieve it, and married the King as a means to that end ("I basically married the diamond"). Moffat makes sure that she doesn't entirely lose our sympathies by giving her a moment of defiance as Hydroflax discovers her betrayal and confronts her. She says that his murder "wouldn't weigh heavily on my conscience, even if I had one." But when she speaks of his butcheries and passionately declares that after he has stolen so much from so many, "I'm the woman who's going to steal it all back," we can see the River we know from previous episodes – the woman who started out as a programmed assassin before becoming something much more after her encounters with the Doctor.

Apart from that moment, the first half of the episode is almost entirely comedic in nature, and the performances are appropriately unsubtle. Matt Lucas (of *Little Britain* fame) provides some amusement as Nardole, River's rather dim assistant whose bungling gets the Doctor involved in the first place. As the grotesque Hydroflax, with only his head visible perched atop an enormous robotic body, Greg Davies has little to do besides shout a lot, exchanging deliberately overinflated dialogue with River while he still thinks she is his loyal queen. Hydroflax's self-centred stupidity is so great that it's even used to advance the plot, as he voluntarily detaches his head, thereby solving River's problem for her, to her own surprise ("You married a cyborg and you didn't even know it?" the Doctor acidly comments). The Doctor and River fight off his warrior monks and his headless body (which is equipped with its own separate intelligence that seems rather more capable than Hydroflax's own) and are teleported away with the head by Ramone.

Outside in the snow, the Doctor can only laugh at Hydroflax's impotent threats of retribution now that he has been reduced to a head being carried around in a bag. "I can't approve of any of this, but I haven't laughed in a long time," he says, reminding us of what he has recently been through. The comedy continues as River still doesn't realise who he is no matter how many hints he drops, and Ramone arrives to report that he still hasn't found "Damsel" – their code name for the Doctor ("Damsel in Distress – apparently he needs a lot of rescuing"). It becomes apparent that River deliberately brought Hydroflax's ship here expecting to find the Doctor, but she doesn't know about the new cycle of regenerations that he received at the end of 2013's *The Time of the Doctor.* When the Doctor suggests that this "Damsel" could have more than the twelve faces she knows about, she simply replies, "He has limits."

Her real goal, in fact, is not the Doctor but the TARDIS; she intends to temporarily steal it to help her carry out her scheme. When she calmly assures him that because it's a time machine, she can use it and put it back without its owner ever knowing, his spluttering indignation that "He'll just *know*" is met with a superbly droll (and intriguing) punchline: "Well, he's never noticed before." Perhaps the funniest moment of the episode, however, comes when she sends Ramone off and invites the Doctor into the TARDIS, warning him that "you'd better prepare yourself for a shock." Capaldi indulges in some exultant scenery chewing as the Doctor revels in the opportunity to try out the companion's role, hilariously pretending to boggle at the inside of his own ship ("I've always wanted to see that done properly," he smugly concludes, with almost a wink to the audience).

River finds that the TARDIS refuses to take off while part of Hydroflax (i.e. his head) is inside and the remainder is outside. However, that problem is solved when the cyborg body, having captured Nardole and Ramone along the way and taken their heads to use in place of Hydroflax's, barges its way into the TARDIS. By Moffat's standards, this is a very simple and linear narrative, basically comprising a string of set pieces with quite straightforward links between each one and the next. And so the Doctor and River run around the console a few times, keeping out of the way of the robot while the TARDIS takes them to River's chosen destination – a space cruise ship reserved for the galaxy's super-criminals, where she has arranged a meeting with a buyer for the diamond (which she has no intention of returning to the people who hired her). She is known and welcomed by Flemming, the *maitre d'* of the ship, who shows her and the Doctor into an opulent dining room.

Only now, as the heist plot recedes into the background while River waits for her contact to appear, does the episode start to become something deeper as the focus moves to the relationship between her and the Doctor. He is still unsettled by her cynical pragmatism towards Hydroflax, but spots an underlying sadness as she brings out the diary we have seen her carrying ever since her first appearance. It's now nearly full, and she worries because, "The man who gave me this was the sort of man who'd know exactly how long a diary you were going to need." The hard exterior returns as she responds to the Doctor's probing "Not somebody special, then?" with a rather wounding agreement ("But terribly useful now and then"), but Kingston makes it clear that the hardness is purely a self-protective cover. Before the Doctor can make another attempt to convince her of who he is, however, her buyer – a man named Scratch – interrupts them, and he reverts to playing along as River's sidekick.

Director Douglas Mackinnon keeps the action bubbling along, aided by some clever creature design, including the insect-inspired heads for Flemming and his fellow cruise ship staff, and the striking appearance of Scratch. Living up to his name, he has a scar running diagonally right across his face, which is revealed as a seam along which his whole head can be opened. It's a rather gratuitous (though impressive) effect, prompting the Doctor's dry observation, "Just a thought, you probably shouldn't do that in a restaurant." But it provides an easy way to quickly raise the level of tension as all the other patrons in the dining room turn around to reveal the same diagonal scar on their faces. River successfully carries through her negotiation to sell the diamond, but as she is about to hand over the bag containing Hydroflax's head, the comic reversal strikes: Scratch and his people are revealed to be fanatical followers of the King.

The weakest part of the episode follows, with Moffat resorting to some stretched-out comedy antics as the Doctor tries to delay Scratch's realisation of what is in the bag. Then, when he is forced to reveal the head, the padding continues as he fulsomely declaims Shakespearean phrases at it before holding a mock auction to find out who is "the most truly devout" of Hydroflax's followers. The whole sequence amounts to nothing in the end, when the Doctor and River's escape is blocked by the arrival of the cyborg body. Hydroflax cements his status as one of the most ineffectual villains the show has ever had as the body scans the detached head and determines that it will unavoidably deteriorate and die soon anyway. The robot destroys the head, leaving the diamond sitting in the remains. Flemming suggests that it could obtain a new head by using River as bait to get to the Doctor; naturally, many of the criminals on this ship "would be happy to see his career cut off, as it were, at the neck." To her fury, he takes her diary and reads out some of its entries, reminding us of several of her past adventures and revealing she has just come from 2012's *The Angels Take Manhattan* (where she witnessed the loss of her parents, the Doctor's companions Amy and Rory).

Moffat gives Alex Kingston a bravura scene as River dismisses the idea that she could be used to lure the Doctor; her earlier brittleness is explained as she declares that the Doctor "does not, and has never loved me." Kingston shows the conflicting hurt and passion swirling within River as she suddenly lets slip emotions she has perhaps kept hidden for a long time ("When you love the Doctor, it's like loving the stars themselves. You don't expect a sunset to admire you back"). Of course, it's an obvious comedy trope to have her blurting out her true feelings about the Doctor while being unaware that he is standing at her side, but the revelation that she has no expectation of him loving her as she loves him ("And I'm just fine with that!" she shouts, unconvincingly) is genuinely affecting. Meanwhile, Capaldi is in the background, giving a master class in how to react without stealing the focus of the scene, until the realisation strikes her as the Doctor says simply, "Hello, Sweetie" – the same line she entered his life with back

227

in 2008's *Silence in the Library*.

Once they start working together, Kingston's chemistry with Capaldi is just as good as the rapport she had with Matt Smith, while also being very different. In keeping with the less touchy-feely nature of Capaldi's Doctor, the relationship is less flirty and romantic and more that of a couple of old friends completely at ease with each other. She happily accepts his non-explanation of how he managed to unexpectedly get a new body ("A thing happened." "I bet it probably did"). As usual, she is one step ahead of her opponents, having taken the precaution of conducting her negotiations on the day she knows the ship will be crippled by a meteor strike. Her parting shot at Flemming as the chaos hits ("I'm an archaeologist from the future – I dug you up!") is delightful. The Doctor quickly disables the robot while River takes the diamond and goes to try and save the ship. As it falls towards the planet below they each, amusingly, take turns trying to sacrifice themselves to save the other, with the Doctor replying directly to River's contention in the earlier scene: "River, not one person on this ship, not one living thing, is worth you." Finally, they have no choice but to take refuge in the TARDIS as the ship is destroyed. (The fact that all the occupants of the ship, even the staff, are explicitly said to be hardened criminals is a rather obvious plot contrivance to keep the viewer from feeling too many moral pangs when they all get wiped out in the crash.)

With her history with the Doctor already being so complex that (as he puts it) most people need a flow chart to follow it, River's story could have been left where we last saw her, in 2013's *The Name of the Doctor*. Instead, the episode's emotional climax begins with her recognising the planet they are heading towards; it's Darillium – as in the Singing Towers of Darillium, which were mentioned in her very first appearance as the place where she met the Doctor for the last time before journeying to the Library where we saw her meet her end. The DVD box set for the 2011 season included two short bonus scenes (titled *First Night* and *Last Night*) featuring the Doctor and River and which Moffat intended to show the tying up of River's story with the trip to Darillium. However, he now has River describe that earlier occasion as one of many where "You always say you're going to take me there for dinner and then you always cancel at the last minute." With River still unconscious on the floor of the TARDIS after the crash, the Doctor emerges to find himself in a wasteland with two huge rock pillars in the distance – the Singing Towers. The diamond, having served as a MacGuffin throughout the story, is finally put to good use as he gives it to a friendly passer-by looking for survivors, with the suggestion that the man should use the reward money to build a restaurant with a view of the Towers. Then, with a quick hop forwards in the TARDIS, he sets in motion the last night of River's life.

As she comes to their table overlooking the Singing Towers, she discovers that Hydroflax's body – still bearing the heads of Ramone and Nardole – was salvaged from the crash and is now working at the restaurant ("Don't worry, the nasty part's all gone," Ramone assures her). Then the Doctor shows up with a gift for her – a sonic screwdriver, to replace the rather amusing "sonic trowel" she had wielded against Hydroflax earlier. Unusually, Moffat provides no real help (with flashbacks, for example) for viewers who don't remember plot points from years ago, instead relying on Capaldi and Kingston's acting to convey the importance of the moment. The reason for this is probably that the details don't quite match up – in *Forest of the Dead*, River says the Doctor gave *his* screwdriver to her, not a different one he had made. Of course, when Moffat wrote that passage in 2008, he had no plans to revisit it; it's not surprising that seven years later, he might feel the need to slightly adjust events in retrospect. Nevertheless, as the screwdriver is revealed to a reprise of the music from the end of that long-ago episode, the sense of destiny working itself out is inescapable.

The gorgeous music continues with a beautiful slow vocal piece as they look out at the Singing Towers themselves, followed by the unexpected return of one of Murray Gold's most moving pieces – used for the Doctor's farewell to Amy from 2010's *The Big Bang* – as he has a similar conversation with her daughter. River, suspecting that this night is the end of their time together, all but begs him to change her future. But after his experience with the loss of Clara, he now understands what Clara herself learned in the previous Christmas episode: "Every night is the last night for something, every Christmas is last Christmas." This is an exceptionally well written and performed scene as the two actors tease out every nuance of Moffat's dialogue. When River says she is ignoring the Towers because "They're ignoring me... but then, you can't expect a monolith to love you back," he agrees, going off into a mini-lecture about the Towers and where their sound comes from, before circling back to indirectly express his true feelings about her:

The Doctor: "All anyone will ever tell you is that when the wind stands fair and the night is perfect... when you least expect it... but always when you need it the most... there is a Song."

A sudden shaft of humour lightens this bittersweet ending, as the Doctor reveals that a night on Darillium actually lasts for twenty-four years. As they lean in for a kiss, the episode ends with the caption "And they both lived happily ever after..." – except that "ever after" soon dissolves, followed by the first four words, leaving just "happily" as a fitting epitaph for the finally completed story of River Song and her husband.

Classic Who DVD Recommendation: In 1985 *The Two Doctors*, starring Colin Baker and Nicola Bryant, with guest appearances from Patrick Troughton and Frazer Hines, provided a similar mix of a returning face (or two) from the past thrown together with the current Doctor in a rather gaudy story strewn with sardonic humour.

Reflections: My initial reaction to *The Husbands of River Song* was not especially positive. Coming so soon after the powerful climax of the 2015 season, this jokey, very undemanding romp made it seem like the show was heading into an extended hiatus with a rather weak episode (as had happened with the 2011 Christmas special, *The Doctor, the Widow and the Wardrobe*). However, when watched again, considerable wit and charm become apparent – particularly in the less comically exaggerated second half, when the Doctor and River's relationship moves to centre stage, leading to the emotional ending. Moffat has mentioned being particularly proud of his work on the two crucial scenes between River and the Doctor (her realisation of his identity, and the final scene at the Singing Towers) and he is right to be. As I have noted above, Capaldi and Kingston seize on the opportunities those scenes provide to show a wonderfully complex interplay of emotions between the two characters.

With the final tying up of River's story here, there are practically no ongoing story threads left to be carried forward to the next season, unlike any previous point in the Moffat era. This tidying up of loose ends was deliberate on Moffat's part; there was a strong possibility while he was writing it that *The Husbands of River Song* would be his last episode before moving on after five seasons at the helm.

Interviewed recently in *Doctor Who Magazine*, he revealed that his original intention was to do only three seasons, but that the production headaches of his third season (a period of turmoil behind the scenes which was complicated further by the Fiftieth Anniversary celebrations and Matt Smith's departure) led to him staying on, not wanting to leave on a "miserable" note. The two seasons covered in this book certainly took the show in a whole new direction with a very different Doctor, and continually found novel ways to put the relationship between the Doctor and his companion under the spotlight. With some very strong scripts by both Moffat and others, the 2014 and 2015 seasons represent a creative renaissance for the show that would have seen Moffat leaving on a high, had Christmas 2015 indeed been the end of the line for him.

Not long after *The Husbands of River Song* was shown, it was announced that Chris Chibnall will be *Doctor Who*'s next showrunner – but also that, because he is currently occupied running the hit detective drama *Broadchurch*, his first season will not be shown until 2018. And so, Moffat has agreed to stay and oversee one more season before Chibnall takes over. After 2016's Christmas special, this season – the tenth since *Who* was revived in 2005 – is expected to appear in early 2017, and will again feature Peter Capaldi as the Doctor, with the relatively unknown Pearl Mackie joining as his companion. Somewhat surprisingly, it has also been announced that Matt Lucas as Nardole will have a recurring role in the 2017 series; presumably, his situation at the end of this episode, in which he was reduced to one of the heads attached to Hydroflax's robotic body, will have to be reversed or otherwise gotten around in some fashion. Although details are, as usual, being kept firmly under wraps, Moffat has already said that his aim is for the next season to have the feel of a whole new show. It's a trick he has already pulled off twice, with the introductions of first Matt Smith and then Capaldi. I'm very much looking forward to watching him reinvent *Doctor Who* for a third time.

Steven Cooper is also the co-author of:

Steven Moffat's Doctor Who 2010

Steven Moffat's Doctor Who 2011

&

Steven Moffat's Doctor Who 2012-2013

http://www.slantmagazine.com/house/

http://www.slantmagazine.com